American Sportsmen
and the Origins of Conservation

AMERICAN
SPORTSMEN

AND THE ORIGINS OF

CONSERVATION

John F. Reiger

Winchester Press

Library of Congress Catalog Card Number: 75-9254
ISBN: 0-87691-173-4

Library of Congress Cataloging in Publication Data

Reiger, John F
    American sportsmen and the origins of conservation.

    Bibliography: p.
    Includes index.
    1. Wildlife   conservation—United   States—History   2.
Nature conservation—United States—History.
I. Title.
QL84.2.R43   333.9'5'0973   75-9254
ISBN 0-87691-173-4

Published by Winchester Press
205 E. 42nd St., New York 10017

Printed in the United States of America

To Andrea

"He was always to be seen in serene afternoons haunting the river, and almost rustling with the sedge. . . . His fishing was not a sport, nor solely a means of subsistence, but a sort of solemn sacrament and withdrawal from the world, just as the aged read their Bibles."

Henry David Thoreau describing a local angler. From his *Week on the Concord and Merrimack Rivers* (1849).

"Some of our newspapers reported that the President intended to hunt in the Park. A woman in Vermont wrote me, to protest against the hunting, and hoped I would teach the President to love the animals as much as I did,— as if he did not love them much more, because his love is founded upon knowledge, and because they had been a part of his life."

John Burroughs commenting on his trip through Yellowstone National Park in 1903 with Theodore Roosevelt. From Burroughs, *Camping and Tramping with Roosevelt* (1907).

CONTENTS

INTRODUCTION

I

There is in America today a fascinating phenomenon called the "hunting controversy." Almost any outdoor-oriented individual who reads popular magazines, watches television, or goes to cocktail parties is aware that an acrimonious struggle is going on between two determined opponents. On the one side is a large group of self-styled "animal lovers" who claim that the killing of wildlife is wrong and must be stopped. Against them is pitted the so-called "sportsman" (and "sportswoman"), whose ranks include many of the twenty-one million hunters[1] and their allies: biologists, wildlife-management experts, and conservation-department personnel at both state and federal levels. Despite the great economic and political power of the second group, they seem to be barely holding their own.

The sportsman should not really be surprised that he is under siege, for he is a victim of fashion, that juggernaut that determines everything from the width of ties to the vote on the floor of the United States Senate. Even though a number of recent studies on the subject have been published, one does not have to resort to statistics to know that it is becoming increasingly fashionable to be against all hunting. In recent years the writer, for example, has suddenly found himself being attacked—particularly in academic circles—more times than he would care to remember. Many other sportsmen in various urban centers around the nation have reported to me similar experiences. It seems that the very mention of a liking for hunting at a social gathering immediately elicits an outpouring of righteous condemnation. The reason why this deep and apparently growing feeling is significant is that it has already permeated and distorted the writing on the history of American conservation.

One of the truisms of the historian's craft is that the judgments of scholars are always influenced by the social and intellectual milieu in which they live and think. If this is so, then one can only wonder what future historians will write of sportsmen and their role in conservation. As urbanization and industrialization proceed apace, more and more scholars will be removed from contact with the natural world. Believing that water comes from the tap and sirloin from the supermarket—instead of the land[2]—these writers may well be incapable of understanding why earlier Americans found it pleasurable to hunt their own food; nor will they comprehend how hunting nurtures a love for the quarry and its environment.

Perhaps, though, it is not too late for one historian to speak out. One hundred and forty years ago, the French observer Alexis de Tocqueville warned Americans of the tendency in democracy to exert what he called the "tyranny of the majority."[3] This nation has had a long history of such despotisms against racial, ethnic, and political minorities. In the intellectual sphere the concepts of "majority rule" and "supremacy of the people" mean that any minority that has a view different from the prevailing one is in real danger of being overwhelmed by the tide of public opinion; after all, "the people" are always right. The sportsmen minority, therefore, is quite correct in seeing its position as precarious.

Many historians have added measurably to the weakened status of the sportsmen. The eminent scholar, C. Vann Woodward, has pointed out that "history has had to serve Americans as a source of the folk-lore, myth, and legend that seems essential to the spiritual comfort of a people in time of stress."[4] Unlike other nations that have had "a long and misty prehistoric past,"[5] the United States has *only* its short history to sustain and guide it. Thus, it is particularly important for the student of America's past to prove Voltaire wrong when he defined history as " 'a pack of tricks we play upon the dead.' "[6]

By judging the past with the assumptions of the present, many historians have done their best to fulfill the truth of the old saying that " 'who controls the present controls the past.' "[7] In fact, they have gone one step further. Because the past is continually used as a guide for the future and because "history" is only what historians say it is, "who controls the past controls the future"[8] as well. As "keeper of the public memory,"[9] the historian who attacks as immoral the sportsman of the past aids those who would see his extinction in the future.

Examples of the intellectual community's prejudice against sport hunters are so numerous it is difficult to choose which ones to cite. The following, however, should suffice for now. An historian of the West, Robert V. Hine, suggests that sportsman George Bird Grinnell was a hypocrite because in the 1870s he attacked commercial gunners who were killing Western big game solely for their hides, while he failed to shoot a bighorn ram (for its head *and* meat) only because the beauty of the animal momentarily stopped him and allowed its escape.[10] The obvious implication is that sport hunting was no different than the market hunting that nearly exterminated the bison, elk, and other large mammals.

A second historian, Holway R. Jones, writing about wilderness proponent John Muir and his Sierra Club, sarcastically comments on the alleged need of the Boone and Crockett Club, the eminent sportsmen's organization, to rationalize its interest in "big game destruction [hunting]" with its professed concern for conservation.[11] The implication here seems to be that anyone who shoots an animal cannot be a conservationist, no matter what his accomplishments. Parenthetically, the reader should be reminded that President Theodore Roosevelt and his Chief Forester, Gifford Pinchot, were just two of the club's famous "killers"!

A third, and last, example of this prejudice can be found in Robert Shankland's biography of Steven T. Mather, first director of the National Park Service. The author sneeringly uses the term "sportsman" and then makes the incredible statement that one can always tell a real conservationist if he, too, employs the word in a sarcastic way.[12] Shankland's effusion is all the more remarkable because, only two pages before, he describes how Mather, a man with little knowledge of animals, relied on "three private organizations of wildlife lovers" whenever he needed advice on how to settle some wildlife problem in the parks. The three associations Shankland alludes to are the Boone and Crockett Club, the Camp Fire Club of America, and the American Game Protective and Propagation Association, all of which were founded by sport hunters.[13]

Of course, what really disturbs these historians and all the others of their ilk is the "idea" of killing. The main reason many of them have not bothered to separate sport and commercial hunting is the simple fact that any killing, except perhaps for alleged "necessity," is wrong. Because it is a moral question, there is no need to make any "subtle" distinctions. Committing one of the worst of all historians' sins, these scholars prejudge their subjects according to their own value system, instead of trying to understand them within the context of their times.

Against all that is known of the dynamics of wildlife populations, these historians seem to believe that the killing of an animal means a permanent reduction in the number of that species. Despite the wishful thinking of the tenderhearted, the destiny of virtually all wild creatures is death by starvation, disease, or predation.[14] This is precisely the reason why the science of wildlife management has proven so successful in the twentieth century. In order to perpetuate itself in the face of wholesale "premature" losses, every species produces in an average year a harvestable surplus that can be tapped by the hunter or fisherman—acting in the role of predator—without any danger whatever to the species as a whole. How the surplus dies, whether by so-called "natural" causes or by "unnatural" ones (i.e., human predation), is unimportant, for nature reverses the sacred tenet of American culture: The species is everything and the individual nothing.

Strangely, historians' sympathy for wildlife rarely extends to fish; hunters are condemned explicitly and implicitly all the time—anglers hardly ever. But unlike game fish, most game animals and birds either get away after a missed shot or are killed fairly quickly. Even the minority that are hit and escape to die suffer no worse a fate than their fellows. Neither are they "wasted" as is so often claimed, for their bodies return to the land, providing sustenance for everything from bobcats to bacteria.

In terms of the anguish a sporting animal allegedly suffers, game fish are much worse off than game birds and mammals. With a hook tearing its mouth or stomach, a fish struggles to escape the inexorable pressure of line and rod, and this misery may go on for more than an hour in big-game angling. To bring a large fish like a king mackerel or striped bass aboard, one usually impales it with a gaff, a huge barb-less hook mounted on a pole. Then, with blood streaming down its sides, the fish is hoisted in and hit on the head, often repeatedly, with a mallet, club, or hammer ironically termed a "persuader" or "priest." Surely this "heartlessness" ranks with that of duck shooting or deer hunting.[15] Yet where are the critics?

Anthropomorphism is the reason the king mackerel and striped bass are of little concern while the "innocent" deer, "comical" bear, and "noble" Canada goose get all the attention. People seem to find it easy to identify with mammals and birds, but "ugly" fish, reptiles, and amphibians fail to make the grade. Yet, if the tenderhearted were consistent in their concern, *all* life must be saved.[16] Despite the evolution of our canine teeth, meat eating should cease, for farm animals have as much "right" to life as wild ones—they were, after all, wild once themselves. The commercial killing of wildlife should also stop, for in addition to the animals pursued, there are almost always other species that die as well; one example is that over 200,000 porpoises drown in the tuna industry's nets every year.[17] Finally, one should give up wearing leather shoes or using any product made from animal parts.

But even if we all became vegetarians, we would still be killing animals right and left.[18] The intensive production of any crop means clearing land and removing it as habitat for a myriad wildlife species. While some like bobwhite quail and mourning doves *might* continue to survive and even prosper, many others would be displaced. Because of greatly reduced habitat all over the country and the fact that eco-systems are usually filled to capacity with already existing birds and animals, any loss of habitat along the line means a permanent reduction in wildlife populations.[19]

The "awful" truth is that in order to live, all of us kill continually, directly or indirectly. While this fundamental fact is obvious to ecologists, it seems to have eluded many historians. They would prefer to condemn the gunner who shoots a dozen ducks every waterfowl season in a swamp that in many cases only sportsmen's money has preserved from the dragline and bulldozer,[20] rather than the developer who obliterates another swamp and takes it out of wildlife production forever. The former is often seen as little better than a criminal, while the latter is either applauded as the personification of "progress" or at least tolerated as an agent of the inevitable.

Sportsmen, those who supposedly "kill for the sake of killing," have become handy scapegoats for Americans unhappy with the declining populations of many wildlife species and the deterioration of the environment generally. The real causes for this wildlife reduction, "development," pesticide contamination, water pollution, etc., are generalized, amorphous phenomena that seem incapable of being controlled, while the hunter is a specific group that can be focused on and attacked.

A Ph.D. dissertation completed in 1973 by Dale L. Shaw, a student at Colorado State University, deals with the hunting controversy and offers some interesting findings. One of the techniques the author used was to poll a large number of college students. Of these, 55 percent of the males and 77 percent of the females stated their belief that "hunting endangers species"[21]—despite the fact that no species has ever become extinct in the United States as the result of sport hunting.[22] The overwhelming factors have been habitat alteration or destruction, killing by farmers and others who saw the species as a competitor, and *commercial* hunting. This explains why species that were rarely if ever hunted for sport, like the great auk and Carolina parakeet, have vanished from the earth. The ultimate irony here is that game species—because of the financial and political support of millions of sportsmen—are far better protected today than nongame species![23]

Shaw's dissertation also reveals that almost 40 percent of the students felt that movies and television programs were responsible for their negative attitudes toward hunting; the film *Bambi,* for example, was mentioned frequently.[24] One can only wonder if the attitudes of the students parallel their professors.

What is perhaps most significant about this study is the high degree of emotionalism found among those interviewed. The fact that there is a tradition, a code of ethics, even a "religion" of hunting, is completely lost on many who gave their opinions. "Killing is killing"; there is no need, therefore, to understand why millions of Americans find hunting enjoyable. Obviously, Pascal's statement that " 'the virtue of the hare is not in having it but in the pursuit of it' "[25] would be simply incomprehensible.

Shaw also discovered that what seemed to disturb spokesmen of anti-hunting organizations more than anything else was the idea that people got "fun" out of pursuing "small, defenseless animals."[26] Perhaps the Protestant ethic and national obsession with guilt have much to do with anti-hunter sentiment.[27]

Another important factor could be disenchantment with the human race itself. A number of writers have pointed out that self-proclaimed "animal lovers" are frequently those who seem to have difficulty relating to their fellow human beings.[28] Animals—particularly dependent, "cute" ones—may provide handy substitutes for the affection these people are unable to show others.

Whatever the origins of the virulent anti-hunting sentiment, at least one thing is sure. Groups like Friends of Animals and International Defenders of Animals are out to use every means at their disposal to destroy sport hunting. Here are a few representative statements from their publications: "It is wrong, immoral, and foolhardy to permit the hunting triumvirate [?] to warp the ecological fiber of our land"; "when public lands are open to hunters, they are private butcher shops, scenes of terror, murder and mayhem"; "hunters hold their blood-stained hands aloft and claim to be 'conservationists' when in reality their purpose is to provide a continuing and adequate supply of living targets to gratify their lust to kill"; "the wanton savagery that is being visited on wildlife must, inevitably, be turned on us"; "the minds of the young have been subverted and distorted by these perverts. They [seek] . . . to raise yet another generation in their image—strangers to pity, devoid of compassion, the personification of all that is vile and contemptible within the human frame."[29] Members of Friends of Animals even make a point of demanding that everyone "completely abstain from any association with businessmen, teachers, or churches which do not support a total ban on hunting, and that all children be kept out of the Boy Scouts because this group promotes hunting."[30]

If the reader thinks that such emotional propaganda is limited only to a "lunatic fringe," this effusion in the April, 1974, issue of the *Sierra Club Bulletin* proves otherwise: "In 1974, a single 'sportsman' can in a year joyride through a generation's worth of life and land. We cannot junk our heritage, our grand children's legacy, for dubious and temporary gain."[31] The Sierra Club is an organization with massive influence in academic circles, and its *Bulletin* is repeatedly cited by well-known environmental historians[32] like Roderick Nash and Wilbur Jacobs. (This is not to say that such historians are biased in favor of Sierra Club pronouncements but that the *Bulletin* has great influence among scholars, including very trustworthy historians.) Three other scholars concerned with the history of conservation even go so far as to introduce their new book with the dramatic declaration that "a large portion" of their royalties will be donated to the Sierra Club.[33] Their implication seems to be that it is *the* conservation organization, instead of only one of many.

Yet another manifestation of this association's strength is its supporters' continual stream of propaganda glorifying the club and particularly its founder, John Muir. As one dissenting historian has pointed out, it often seems as if every other conservation organization is morally lacking, while "the Sierra Club [alone] purveys chastity belts."[34] In reality, Muir's concrete contributions to conservation have been exaggerated, while the achievements of sportsmen like George Bird Grinnell and Charles Sheldon are simply mentioned in passing, if at all, by the journalists, commentators, and historians who cater to current fashion in environmental writing.

Even the great Aldo Leopold—who has been called the "father of ecology," the "father of scientific wildlife management," and the "father of the American land ethic"—has received less attention than Muir from recent historians. One can only wonder if this inadequate treatment is partly due to Leopold's *love* for hunting, a fact proven by many passages in his *Game Management* (1933), *Sand County Almanac* (1949), and *Round River* (1953).[35] The first book, in fact, is dedicated to his father—"PIONEER IN SPORTSMAN-SHIP"—and includes the "bags" of a number of Leopold's hunts.

Instead of trying to understand why so many of the forerunners of conservation were sportsmen, recent historians have ignored hunting as an unworthy topic for study, or found it an embarrassment that somehow taints their heroes. The outlook of these scholars seems to parallel that held by the wife of one of my colleagues, a recent convert to "pop" ecology. After reading, out of context, some of Leopold's writings, she informed me that he had become her mentor. But when told of other passages from his works that illustrate his dedication to hunting, she at once became distraught and declared that she would have to find someone else to inspire her. Then, after a pause, she closed with the statement that perhaps writer Joseph Wood Krutch "would be better," as she had heard that he was against killing.

Because moral issues, real or imagined, never lend themselves to objective analysis, many readers may find it impossible—regardless of the evidence presented—to even *consider* the role of sportsmen, particularly hunters, in the making of conservation. All the author asks is that they try.

II

Ever since the first decade of the twentieth century when President Theodore Roosevelt and his Chief Forester, Gifford Pinchot, made "conservation" a household word, the term has received a variety of definitions, and every group from the Sierra Club to the Army Corps of Engineers has claimed to be its one true representative. During the latter 1960s, the public discovered the word "ecology" and began to use it as if it were a more fashionable version of the older term. Though both words entered the American vocabulary in the late nineteenth century and are now used interchangeably—even by some historians[36]—they have in reality very different meanings.

As a discipline, ecology is "the study of the interrelationships of organisms to one another and to the environment."[37] Because this book deals with the nineteenth century, its human subjects cannot be called "ecologists." Even though many of them possessed an ecological orientation—perceiving the interrelatedness of wildlife and their habitats—they studied organisms (like birds) *or* environments (like forests) but rarely both simultaneously. Not until the twentieth century did ecology become a recognized science in the United States.

"Conservationist," not "ecologist," is the more precise term for the American pioneer of environmental concern. Long before 1907—when Gifford Pinchot claims to have been the first to perceive the interrelationship of all resource use[38]—an influential segment of the American population had come to understand that renewable resources like wildlife and forests could be exploited indefinitely as long as a certain amount of "capital" was maintained. Even nonrenewable resources like coal and oil could be made to last infinitely longer if managed on an efficient basis. Historically, conservation has not been a science like ecology but a reform movement using political and legal methods to obtain what Theodore Roosevelt called "wise use" of resources.

The confusion between ecology and conservation is only one of many ambiguities surrounding the origins of American concern for the environment. There is, in fact, no aspect of United States history more in need of revision than the historiography[39] of conservation.

One of the most important misconceptions is that no conservation movement existed until the twentieth century. Despite the publication of a number of books and essays purporting to treat the "origins" of the crusade, environmental historians invariably begin their works at the close of the nineteenth century, with perhaps a passing nod to a few "prophets" like George Perkins Marsh and John Wesley Powell. Conversely, this volume commences several decades earlier and shows that the movement originated in the 1870s. The work ends in 1901, when most historians of conservation are just "getting into" their studies. The first years of the present century have been chosen as the closing period because with the ascendancy of Theodore Roosevelt to the Presidency, a movement that began a generation before flowered into a fully developed federal program of resource management.

Another of the widely believed myths of conservation historiography is the result—like others we will discuss—of historians examining only the most available sources. Accepting at face value the political rhetoric of the Roosevelt administration, scholars through the 1950s pictured conservation as a movement of "the people" against the monopolistic control of resources by "special interests."[40] According to this thesis, conservation was an integral part of the early twentieth-century reform movement known as "progressivism."

The problems with this interpretation are immense. First is the fundamental question of whether there was really a progressive *movement* at all, or simply a myriad of different reform impulses later unified by historians under one all-encompassing label.[41]

Even if we accept the existence of progressivism, another impasse materializes when we try to bring conservation within its fold. Though historians of progressivism and conservation have described them as middle-class movements, this study will show that conservation, at least, began as an upper-class effort. If this is true, then how could conservation simply be one component of the larger progressive—supposedly middle-class—phenomenon? Of course, if conservation is to be seen as a democratic movement of "the people" against economic elites, then one *must* conclude that its base was middle class, since that socioeconomic group presumably makes up the majority of the American people.

An historian who has challenged the simplistic interpretation of conservation as the fulfillment of democracy is Samuel P. Hays. In *Conservation and the Gospel of Efficiency* (1959), he shows that the goals of leading conservationists commonly clashed with "grass-roots" democratic impulses. More often than not, "the people"—particularly in the West—opposed efforts aimed at keeping them from exploiting resources in the traditionally wasteful manner.

While Hays's thesis has received almost universal acceptance by professional historians, the notion it set out to destroy is still firmly embedded in the popular mind. Perhaps part of the reason is that he insists, like those before him, that conservation was a middle-class movement, despite the conspicuous roles played by upper-class individuals like Roosevelt and Pinchot.

There is, however, another, more significant problem with the Hays interpretation. Though his book only begins with the 1890s, he argues that the conservation movement started as the result of efforts by a small corps of engineers and physiographic specialists. During the Roosevelt Presidency, in the years from 1901 to 1909, a federal bureaucracy dealing with environmental issues came into being, and the engineers, geologists, and other "experts" Hays singles out were indeed important *by that time,* but they were not the group that originated the movement in the 1870s.

American sportsmen, those who hunted and fished for pleasure rather than commerce or necessity, were the real spearhead of conservation. Long before the period Hays and other historians choose to begin their works, sportsmen had initiated an environmental movement composed of thousands across the country.

With the establishment in the early 1870s of national newspapers like *American Sportsman, Forest and Stream,* and *Field and Stream,*[42] outdoorsmen acquired a means of communicating with each other, and a rapid growth of group identity was the result. Increasingly, gunners and anglers looked upon themselves as members of a fraternity with a well-defined code of conduct and thinking. In order to obtain membership in this order of "true sportsmen," one had to practice proper etiquette in the field, give game a sporting chance, and possess an aesthetic appreciation of the whole context of sport that included a commitment to its perpetuation.

The most obvious manifestation of the new self-awareness was the rapid growth of sportsmen's clubs and associations. While a desire for comradery was the underlying reason for their creation, one need only look at the names and constitutions of these organizations to understand that subjects like "game protection" and "fish culture" were important concerns of the members.

This early emphasis on the preservation and management of wildlife contains key implications for the historiography of conservation. Accepting the opinions expressed by Roosevelt and Pinchot in their autobiographies, historians have concluded that concern for the forests was the genesis of American conservation. Yet this work will show that the first challenge to the myth of inexhaustibility[43] that succeeded in arousing a substantial segment of the public was not the dwindling forests, but the disappearance, in region after region, of game fish, birds, and mammals.

While in the beginning, sportsmen as a group concerned themselves more with wildlife than woodlands, individual hunters and fishermen were among the most important pioneers of American forestry. Giants of forest conservation like Bernhard E. Fernow, Joseph T. Rothrock, and Gifford Pinchot were sportsmen long before they began their efforts to have the United States adopt a program of scientific timber management.

Regardless of which of the three main areas of early conservation we pick—wildlife, timberlands, or national parks—sportsmen led the way. During the 1870s and '80s, local and state associations forced one legislature after another to pass laws limiting and regulating the take of wildlife by market men and sportsmen alike. And in this same period, outdoor journals, particularly *Forest and Stream,* anticipated the later muckrakers in exposing the federal government's shameful neglect of Yellowstone National Park, the nation's first such preserve.

Finally, in 1887, Theodore Roosevelt, George Bird Grinnell, and other prominent sportsmen founded the Boone and Crockett Club, named after two of America's most famous hunters. Though almost ignored by professional historians, it—and not the Sierra Club—was the first private organization to deal effectively with conservation issues of national scope. The Boone and Crockett played an all-important role in the creation and administration of the first national parks, forest reserves, and wildlife refuges. In addition, "those Halcyon Days," as Roosevelt called the early Boone and Crockett period,[44] were the formative years of his development as the future leader of the conservation movement.

Before proceeding with the main body of this study, a few comments should be made concerning its origins. Research began in 1967, with an inquiry into the influence on conservation of *Forest and Stream*'s crusading editor, George Bird Grinnell. In the process of completing three works pertaining to him, an article, doctoral dissertation, and book, the writer extended his investigations to include the whole conservation movement. Except when appraising the conclusions of other scholars, I have based this volume on primary sources, most of which have been little used by professional historians and some not at all. This is one reason why the book is a new interpretation and not simply another "synthesis."

A second reason is the author's background. Because I am myself a sportsman, critics may charge that my treatment of nineteenth-century sportsmen is somehow biased in their favor—that I have exaggerated their part in the making of conservation. My response to such an assertion is that all historians, no matter how "scientific" their method,[45] choose what they study for largely subjective reasons, and the fact that I am a sportsman releases me from the prejudice which scholars have manifested toward that group.

Originally, this study was to be much longer, but it has been kept deliberately short in order that its thesis not be sidetracked by lengthy discussion of topics like commercial hunting and fishing, destructive logging practices, etc. Both the "Picture Album" and "Selected Bibliography" are intended, therefore, to illustrate ideas pertaining to subjects only briefly presented in the text.

During the seven years of research, the author has acquired many obligations. I would like to thank Northwestern University's history department for assisting me financially during the academic year 1968–69 with a University Dissertation Year Fellowship and during 1969–70 with a Hearst Fellowship and a James Alton James Fellowship. I would also like to thank the staffs of the following libraries and archives: Northwestern, Harvard, Yale, Princeton, Yellowstone National Park, Glacier National Park, the University of Miami, the Midwest Inter-Library Center, the American Museum of Natural History, the Southwest Museum, the New York State Library, the New York Historical Society, the New York Public Library, the National Archives, the Library of Congress, and the Theodore Roosevelt Birthplace National Historic Site.

Special gratitude is due James B. Trefethen, Director of Publications of the Wildlife Management Institute, for aid in the location of sources and the clarification of ideas. The late John P. Holman of Fairfield, Connecticut, was kind enough to allow me to use the Grinnell papers in his own possession and those in the keeping of the Birdcraft Museum of the Connecticut Audubon Society. It was a privilege to be the first professional historian to research this collection, as it may be the single most important source of unpublished materials pertaining to the early conservation movement. Beginning in the 1880s, the holdings include thousands of letters, and many of them are to and from prominent environmentalists.

Other individuals who also offered their help along the way are Roderick Nash, Robert H. Wiebe, Christopher Lasch, George M. Fredrickson, Frank Novak, David Lakari, Helen MacLachlan, Ruth M. Christensen, George W. Reiger, Barbara B. Reiger, Edwin L. Rothfuss, Raymond G. O'Connor, Ernest F. Dibble, William C. Eamon, Tom Rumer, Charlton W. Tebeau, Milan G. Bull, Thomas Minton, Sharon Halberstein, Theodore W. Cart, Pamela K. Schroth, and Henry A. Siegel. A number of publishers and photograph archives provided assistance, and they are acknowledged whenever one of their illustrations appears. For his invaluable editorial advice, I am deeply indebted to Robert Elman. Finally, there is Andrea, my wife, whose essential contribution is recorded in the dedication of this book.

ONE

American Sportsmen
and Their Code

T he appearance of a new monthly newspaper, the *American Sportsman,* in October, 1871, marks a watershed in environmental history. For this was the country's first national periodical to make the interrelated subjects of hunting, fishing, natural history, and conservation its primary concerns,[1] and the enthusiastic response the journal received proves that a segment of the American public was ready for its teachings.

The reasons behind its welcome reception can be found in the new attitudes arising in the 1860s regarding hunting and fishing. Before the Civil War, most Americans viewed these activities as acceptable only when necessary or helpful to the maintenance of a livelihood; one pursued game because he depended on it for food or pecuniary profit. If hunting and fishing were spoken of as "sports" at all, they were usually lumped together with diversions typified by chance and a purse, like horse racing, boxing, and cock fighting. An individual who acquired a taste for either to the point of practicing it as sport often found his "practical" neighbors regarding him as frivolous or worse. As the editor of one of the later outdoor journals put it, "a man who went 'gunnin or fishin' lost caste among respectable people just about in the same way that one did who got drunk."[2]

Not all Americans, however, regarded these activities in utilitarian or economic terms. For a minority who looked to the British Isles for their example, "correct" hunting and fishing increasingly became a chief means of distinguishing the "gentleman" in a postwar America best known for its Philistinism and commercialism. Across the Atlantic, the accepted ways of taking game were the products of traditions stretching back *at least* to the time of Izaak Walton[3] in the seventeenth century. Whether fly-fishing for trout in an English stream or grouse shooting on a Scottish moor, an aristocrat took his sport seriously. To be fully accepted by his peers, he had to have a knowledge of the quarry and its habitat; a familiarity with the rods, guns, or dogs necessary to its pursuit; a skill to cast or shoot with precision and coolness that often takes years to acquire; and most of all, a "social sense" of the do's and don'ts involved.

This last ingredient might be called the "code of the sportsman," and it was particularly important to nobility. Typical was Henry William Herbert, the English aristocrat who immigrated to America in 1831. A friend once said of him: "Like all true sportsmen, while fond of following the game in season with gun, dog and rod, he was a bitter and unrelenting enemy to all poachers and pot-hunters."[4]

In the late 1830s Herbert began writing a series of articles for William T. Porter's *American Turf Register and Sporting Magazine* that was expanded into a number of books, the first being *The Warwick Woodlands* published in 1845. Other writers of the antebellum period like John J. Brown, William Elliott, and Elisha J. Lewis also preached the need for adapting English sporting ethics to the American scene, but it was "Frank Forester"—as Herbert called himself—who had the greatest influence. In fact, Forester became the model for the rising generation of American sportsmen.

What is significant about all the writers mentioned above, particularly Forester, is that they did more than outline the basics of sporting etiquette; they also lamented the commercial destruction of wildlife and habitat and demanded that sportsmen join together to preserve their recreation. The notion that there was only one correct way to take game and that all other methods were "common," or even immoral, was a potential reservoir of reform that would play a key role in the making of the conservation movement.

What late nineteenth-century sportsmen and their journals had to fight was nothing less than the national myth of progress. An incredible rapidity of physical change, probably unexcelled in world history, was already the single most dramatic fact of the American experience. This impermanence had long been glorified as the essence of "progress"—that indefinable but inevitable something which was the trademark of the United States. In the words of one observer of the 1830s, "Americans *love* their country, not . . . *as it is,* but *as it will be.* . . . They live in the future, and *make* their country as they go on."[5] The truth of those statements is shown by the fact that from 1607 to 1907—scarcely more than four lifetimes by present expectations[6]—America would be changed from a couple of wilderness settlements into the most powerful nation on earth.

By the 1870s the country was well on its way to achieving that 1907 status. In fact, no period of American history, except perhaps our own, saw more physical change than the last generation of the nineteenth century. Rapid industrialization and urbanization, development of mass-production techniques and communication systems, and the building of a national railroad system all combined to effect speedy and dramatic alterations of the natural environment.

Particularly disconcerting to sportsmen were the obvious changes in what were once thought to be inexhaustible wildlife populations. Previously undeveloped regions, teeming with animals, birds, and fish, were made readily accessible to all, and improved guns, ammunition, and fishing gear, which the average man could afford, were produced in huge quantities. Hunting and fishing now became not only more practical, but also more profitable.

When *American Sportsman* came into being, the systematic, commercial exploitation of American animal life was everywhere evident. The nation's industry was on the move, and any natural thing that could be converted to cash was utilized. The taste buds of the American people also had to be satisfied, because it was now fashionable to eat wild game like canvasback duck and black bass. Though long in existence, the commercial hunter and fisherman were entering their "golden era." They killed big game for hides, waterfowl for flesh, wading birds for plumage, and ocean fishes for oil and fertilizer. Quick money, sometimes large amounts, could be made by men like the plume hunters who shot the snowy egret almost into extinction.

What is ironic about this dismal situation is that the same economic developments that made wildlife more accessible to the market hunter and fisherman also brought it closer to the sportsman. Indeed, a major reason for the rapid increase in the ranks of the latter group was because of improvements in transportation and equipment. An out-doorsman could now travel to his hunting and fishing spots in greater comfort and enjoy better sport when he arrived—that is, if market men had not already preceded him.

From the time of Elisha Lewis and Frank Forester in the 1850s, sportsmen continually complained of arriving on their favorite grounds only to find that all game had been killed or driven out by commercial hunters and fishermen.[7] Until sportsmen finally defeated the market men in the first quarter of this century and closed off the sale of game for all except some food fishes, this controversy between the two groups frequently approached a state of war. There were, in fact, some fatalities as a result of the conflict.[8] Sportsmen of the late nineteenth century would be little less than flabbergasted to discover that historians of today lump them together with commercial gunners and fishermen.

With the appearance of national periodicals like *American Sportsman* (1871), *Forest and Stream* (1873), *Field and Stream* (1874), and *American Angler* (1881), a new impetus was given to the sportsmen's struggle against commercial exploitation of wildlife. While the nation as a whole remained indifferent, these journals, in issue after issue, poured forth a steady stream of propaganda against the market men. Besides enumerating specific offenses, the main technique used was to teach the American public the ethics and responsibilities of sportsmanship.

A typical example of this approach is "What Constitutes A True Sportsman," an editorial in the November, 1872, issue of *American Sportsman*. In order to define "a *genuine* sportsman," says editor Wilbur F. Parker,[9] one need only refer to Frank Forester, the "prince" of sporting writers: "It is not the mere killing of numbers, much less in the mere killing at all; it is not in the value of the things killed, though it is not sportsmanship, but butchery and wanton cruelty to kill animals which are valueless [as food] and out of season; it is not in the inevitable certainty of success—for certainty destroys the excitement, which is the soul of sport—but it is in the vigor, science [correct technique], and manhood displayed—in the difficulties to be overcome, in the pleasurable anxiety for success, and the uncertainty of it, and lastly in the true spirit, the style, the dash, the handsome way of doing what is to be done, and above all, in the unalterable *love of fair play,* that first thought of the genuine sportsman, that true sportsmanship consists."[10]

But as complex as this definition is, the editor knows it is not complete. Thus, he cites two other unidentified writers. According to the first, "The pastimes of stream and woodland, champaign [flat, open country] and valley, are the characteristic exercises of many of the noblest properties of man's nature. They call into exertion courage, perseverance, sagacity, strength, activity, [and] caution; they are the wholesome machinery of excitement; of hope and fear, and joy and sorrow, regret and rejoicing; they are at once the appetite and the food of manhood. . . . *Instead of being antagonist[ic] meanings, the sportsman and the gentleman are [becoming] . . . synonymous terms.*"[11]

The second of these anonymous authorities, author of "a late and valued sporting work," explains that a true sportsman only "pursues his game for pleasure" and "makes no [financial] profit of his success, giving to his friends more than he retains, shoots invariably upon the wing and never takes a mean advantage of bird or man. It is his pride to kill what he does kill elegantly, scientifically, and mercifully. Quantity is not his ambition; he never slays more than he can use; he never inflicts an unnecessary pang or fires an [unnecessary] . . . shot." Nor does he look upon his quarry "as representing so much money value, . . . to be converted into it as soon as possible."[12]

No one will ever know what percentage of sportsmen adhered faithfully to these precepts—perhaps only a small minority. Yet, sportsmen of the 1870s came to adopt, at least rhetorically, all of these principles. And though they are barely even an adequate outline of the "code of the sportsman," they at least illustrate that "sport" was more than noncommercial hunting and fishing. It was, in fact, something approaching a "world view," even a religion.

Other *American Sportsman* editorials explaining the fine points of this "religion" have titles like "Shooting—Its Pleasures and Benefits"; "Influence of Field Sports on Character"; "Sporting Nomenclature"; "The Pre-Eminence of Field Sports"; and "The Passion of Sport." In addition to the ideas already cited, these didactic pieces explain how sport hunting and fishing inculcate appreciation of nature and knowledge of "the various habits of animals," improve physical health and mental alertness, and assure righteousness by removing one "from the noise and dirt and moral degradation incident to large towns."[13]

With the appearance of *Forest and Stream* and *Field and Stream* later in the 1870s and *American Angler* in the early '80s, Americans now had three more national newspapers to consolidate their ranks. While all followed the journalistic precedents set by *American Sportsman, Forest and Stream* proved to be the most innovative of the three and had the greatest impact.

Making its debut in New York on August 14, 1873, the weekly's course was determined by its wellborn editor, Charles Hallock, who "should . . . have credit for . . . establishing the policy of *Forest and Stream*."[14] That policy is suggested by the paper's subtitle: "A Weekly Journal Devoted to Field and Aquatic Sports, Practical Natural History, Fish Culture, The Protection of Game, Preservation of Forests, and the Inculcation in Men and Women of a Healthy Interest in Outdoor Recreation and Study." Looking over these topics, it is not difficult to see that Hallock's thinking was far ahead of his time. A century ago, he called for protection of watersheds and scientific management of forests; establishment of uniform game laws dictated by geography, habitat, and migration patterns, rather than judicial accident; creation of a science and industry of fish culture that would develop new strains of game fish and restock depleted waters; abatement of water pollution; and experimentation into methods for domesticating and "farming" fur-bearing animals.[15]

Like the editors of the other leading outdoor journals, Hallock, and later George Bird Grinnell, used *Forest and Stream* as a vehicle for importing the British concept of sportsmanship. For example, a regular column in the early years was "Sporting News From Abroad," which reported the experiences and viewpoints of aristocratic sportsmen. Other early features that reflect the English influence are "Woodland, Lawn and Garden," which related the advances of English landscape architecture, and "Athletic Pastimes," which kept track of competition, mainly at Ivy League colleges, in such games as polo and cricket. Although the names of the columns changed from time to time, and some eventually went out of existence, the standpoint they represent remained the same.

Why Hallock and Grinnell sought to emulate the English model is not certain, but their outlook may have been a manifestation of the new self-consciousness and Anglophilia that was sweeping the upper classes in the postwar era.[16] What is known—as will be shown later—is that what I have called the "code of the sportsman" became part of the thinking of many wellborn hunters and fishermen. When the moral element in their code was fused with their dissatisfaction over dwindling game and habitat, an important impetus to the conservation movement was born.

For now, all that Hallock could do was to remind the American public week after week of what rapid industrialization was doing to the natural environment. The blind worship of PROGRESS, the nation's secular religion, was at the root of the problem. Men must be taught to "enjoy the present earth and the present life, so that there shall be less necessity to look for the promised creation of 'a new heaven and a new earth.' "[17] Ultimately, it might even be possible "to restore the original Eden which was made perfect for our first parents."[18]

To work toward this goal, hunters and fishermen, the largest category of persons involved with the outdoors on a nonutilitarian basis, would be consolidated into a force for good. *Forest and Stream*'s first issue announced: "It is the aim of this paper to become a medium of useful and reliable information between gentlemen sportsmen from one end of the country to the other. . . ."[19] From the beginning, Hallock made it clear that his periodical was only for the "true sportsman" and not for those who would debase sport. In this second group were men who killed merely for the fun of killing, without appreciation and understanding of the quarry or its natural surroundings; the "pot-hunter," who committed such offenses as shooting grouse on the ground or geese on the water; the "meat hunter," who took wildlife only to fill his stomach and knew nothing of the subtleties of sport; the poacher, who killed without regard to season or sex, often trespassing in the process; and worst of all, the market man, who destroyed everything from trout to elk for the money they would bring.

To ensure that none of these individuals would think that *Forest and Stream* was for them, Hallock declared that his weekly "will pander to no depraved tastes, nor pervert the legitimate sports of land and water to those base uses which always tend to make them unpopular with the virtuous and good."[20] Herein lies the underlying thrust of *Forest and Stream*: Hallock sought to define, and ultimately to "legitimize," the proper mode for pursuing field sports and the enjoyment of their natural surroundings. While his immediate purpose was to bring together those already in the true sportsman category—by giving them their own vehicle of communication—he also hoped to set an example so compelling as to cause the ignorant and unethical to give up their ways and join the ranks of the initiate.

Less than seven years after Hallock began *Forest and Stream,* his natural-history editor and business partner, George Bird Grinnell, bought him out and became the owner and editor in chief of the newspaper.[21] It was a monumental event in the history of conservation. From an old and wealthy Eastern family, Grinnell was already well-known in both scientific and sporting circles.[22] Controlling *Forest and Stream* until 1911, he would pour forth a continual stream of muck-raking editorials, which when combined with his private efforts, made his influence on conservation incalculably great.

Upon assuming his new post on January 1, 1880, Grinnell lauded the accomplishments of the weekly and implied that he would follow Hallock's precedents: "It only remains now for it [the paper] to hold its vantage ground and signal success which continue to follow it."[23] Retaining the same subtitle and most of the columns, he continued to emphasize that "sportsmanship" was the chief ingredient of hunting and fishing. Its essence, he maintained, was a concern, not for the size of the bag, but whether the game was taken in season, by legal methods, and with the idea of noncommercial use.[24] He asked his fellow outdoorsmen to join him in scorning the "pot-hunter" and "trout hog," those unprincipled enough to shoot ducks on the water and catch trout on the spawning beds. But he thought they were no worse than the so-called "honorable sportsman," who shoots ducks in the correct manner but leaves them in the cattails to rot, or catches trout also in "a perfectly scientific way," all of which, however, happen to be fingerlings.[25]

Grinnell went to the heart of what was troubling him in "The Corruption of Sport." He lamented that America was in the "money-making stage" of her history, when "the mighty dollar is the controlling agency in every branch of social and public life." Perhaps, he continued, "this generalization may sufficiently account for the mercenary element of so many forms of alleged sport" in which the "sordid clutching after purses, gate money, entrance fee or prize" seemed the main attraction.[26] Even competition in rifle and trapshooting was being prostituted in this way. He asked that all competitors contend only for "well earned and respected superiority in quick sight and steady aim, [and] not for a paltry sum of money."[27] Only then would these last preserves of men of quality be kept from being "cast into a disrepute which will bar gentlemen from enjoying in them and reaping their benefits."[28]

Like Hallock before him, Grinnell was clearly attempting to define, and ultimately to legitimize, the proper mode for pursuing field sports and the enjoyment of their natural setting. Both men seemed to feel that an older, more refined way of life was passing out of existence under the assault of rapid industrialization and its accompanying Philistinism, and that "correct" hunting and fishing were two of the ways of differentiating the gentleman.

Hallock and Grinnell came from old family, highly educated, monied backgrounds, and they shared a contempt for what they thought America was becoming—a society of Philistines, noted only for their pursuit of material success. Indeed, the two men seem to be prime candidates for what historian Richard Hofstadter calls the "status revolution."[29] One might surmise that they felt threatened by the challenge presented to their class values by the "new men": the Vanderbilts, Rockefellers, Harrimans, and their lesser-known peers. According to Hofstadter, the recently acquired fortunes of these individuals gave them so much power and prestige that they were supplanting the older elite in basic decision-making. In addition, their wealth enabled them to assume without difficulty the life style of the upper class: landed estates, art collections, and opera tickets could all be easily purchased. But, as has been illustrated, the understanding and appreciation of field sports and their outdoor surroundings could not be bought—one almost had to be "bred" to them. Perhaps Hallock and Grinnell were subconsciously attempting to keep at least one representative element of the older elite's world free from the encroachment of the *nouveaux riches*. In a sense, the preservation of genuine field sports and their natural setting was also the retention of the life style and environment of an otherwise vanishing order.

At first glance, it would seem that the backgrounds of Hallock and Grinnell fit the requirements of the "status revolution" thesis. But when analyzed, their attitudes are more representative of the revision to Hofstadter's theory offered by a number of historians. One of these is George M. Fredrickson. In describing jurist Oliver Wendell Holmes, Jr., he suggests that Holmes was concerned, not with status anxieties, but "with the fact that so many of his fellow Brahmins had retained their status at the price of joining the Gilded Age[30] as successful businessmen, thereby denying themselves the possibility of being a noncommercial aristocracy."[31] Grinnell's father, interestingly enough, seems to fit this generalization perfectly; after the Civil War bankrupted the family's textile firm, he went to work for none other than Commodore Vanderbilt, recouped his fortune, and made another in the process.[32]

Perhaps the younger Grinnell's disdain for business in his early adult years and his flight from a career in his father's company[33] show that he was trying to "rise above" his father's surrender to the new commercial order. In any case, it will be shown that he possessed no status anxieties in regard to the men of new wealth. Instead, he thoroughly absorbed the ideology of the business world, thereby fulfilling the second part of Fredrickson's analysis: "It would seem in fact that the 'mugwumps' [the name Hofstadter gives to the old elite] acted as spokesmen for a large segment of that [business] community, articulating the prevailing attitude of businessmen toward government, education, philanthropy, etc."[34] Grinnell later applied these conceptions to the problems of natural resources, discovering that they could be "managed" like a firm. In fact, his successful handling of *Forest and Stream* and the companies inherited from his father show that he was, himself, a consummate businessman.[35] As will be made clear, what threatened Grinnell, Hallock, and others of their class was not one particular group of individuals, but rather the whole, multifaceted trend toward commercialism and Philistinism that was accompanying the rapid industrialization of American society.

Whether or not the wellborn sportsman socially resented the new plutocracy, there is little doubt that he and his less privileged fellows deeply regretted the loss of "their" hunting and fishing grounds to the insatiable appetite of commerce. While most other Americans, including farmers and ranchers, saw land only as a commodity of capitalism, sportsmen viewed it as the necessary context of their sport.

Every hunter and angler had his own favorite microcosm composed of woodlots, swamps, ponds, and other topographical features. On a larger scale the little world of the sportsman might be a whole geographical entity like the Adirondacks in New York State or Currituck Sound in North Carolina. But whatever and wherever his "territory," it was part of the fiber of every sportsman's existence. While in its midst, he watched the change of seasons, shared the joys of friends, made discoveries about nature and himself, and experienced other sensations too mystical to put into words. Then, as now, many walked onto old hunting and fishing grounds with some of the same emotions felt by a devout Christian entering the door of his church. If that statement sounds like an exaggeration, one need only read the works of John Krider, Samuel H. Hammond, Thaddeus Norris, or Henry Van Dyke.

In their love for the outdoors, sporting authors of the last century were, of course, influenced by the same Romantic movement that touched every major American writer from Thomas Jefferson to Walt Whitman. Sportsmen, too, paid tribute to nature and derived inspiration from wild grandeur. Even when it came to basic guidebooks, hunting and angling locations were continually rated in terms of their picturesque qualities.

But despite these similarities, there were significant differences between the Romantic movement and the sporting tradition as they evolved in the United States. For one thing, the Romantic movement in the arts originated in Germany and France late in the eighteenth century, while the American sporting tradition originated in the British Isles and dates back at least to Izaak Walton in the seventeenth century—indeed, many would take it back to the ancient world.

Another difference is that Romantics often seemed content merely to stroll through a "sylvan glade" and contemplate the "beauty" around them, while sportsmen wished to involve themselves personally in the rhythms of nature by pursuing and capturing a momentary fragment of that beauty in the form of a ruffed grouse or brook trout.[36] The Romantics appear almost voyeuristic,[37] while the sportsmen were participants.[38]

This is undoubtedly one reason why the latter group often combined serious scientific inquiry with their love of nature, while Romantics were usually little more than dilettantes in science and sometimes—as in the case of Ralph Waldo Emerson—even hostile to it because of the fear that its application might unravel the mysteries of nature.[39]

Another example of the voyeur-versus-participant analogy is the fact that most Romantics only had eyes for the "beautiful" and "scenic" in nature. Like their modern counterparts, they had little use for "ugly" topography like inland swamp and coastal marsh.[40] To the sportsman, however, so-called wastelands were frequently the repositories of fond memories and keen anticipations. Indeed, the word "swamp" is still a synonym for worthless land, a place often considered to be fit only for dumping garbage. As their financial support proves, twentieth-century waterfowl hunters have had a very different notion of its value.[41]

The despair felt by early sportsmen at the loss of precious hunting and fishing grounds and their denizens constitutes one of the basic themes in sport history. Its most common form was a nostalgia for the past, when game was still abundant and its habitat unmarred by "improvements." This continuous wail, which I call the "good-old-days lament," is evident even in the antebellum period, and the protests have a remarkably modern ring.

In 1846 William Elliott, a planter of Beaufort, South Carolina, related that "I cannot but perceive with regret that there are causes in operation which have destroyed, and are yet destroying, the game to that extent that in another generation, this manly pastime [of hunting] will no longer be within our reach. . . . Undoubtedly, the most obvious cause of the disappearance of the deer and other game is the destruction of the forests—that of the river swamps especially. . . ." Because of "the wanton, the uncalled-for destruction of forests," "the trampling and cropping of the shrubs and undergrowth" by cattle, and "the practice of burning the woods in spring to give these cattle more luxuriant pasturage," all cover for wildlife had been eliminated, and the game abundance Elliott knew in former years was no more.[42]

Elliott's lament was echoed by John J. Brown, a New York fishing-tackle dealer, who wrote *The American Angler's Guide* (1845). In a later edition of that popular work, he asked his fellow outdoorsmen if they thought their sport would last and answers his own question by declaring:

> You who have trod the mossy bank in pursuit of trout, and warred against the swift current when the striped basse was the object of

your sport, will answer emphatically *no*. You are painfully assured that the well known haunts wherein in happy boyhood you took many a "silver side," are deserted, and the overarching banks of your favorite streams conceal your spotted friends no longer. You know that at your note grounds you take few and still fewer fish, and that some of your former places are now never visited by the sought for game. It is the commonest complaint of the old anglers that fishing nowadays is uncertain; that it is much more difficult to take a mess of fish; there are too many after them; in short, that "times are not as they used to be," and so also says the gunner of his favorite sort of game.[43]

By the 1860s, Robert Barnwell Roosevelt, well-known sportsman and the uncle of Theodore Roosevelt, complained that "streams in the neighborhood of New York [City] that formerly were alive with trout are now totally deserted. The Bronx, famous alike for its historical associations and its once excellent fishing, does not now seem to hold a solitary trout, or indeed fish of any kind. The shad that a few years ago swarmed up the Hudson River in numbers incomputable, have become scarce. . . ." And "on every portion of our sea-coast, in spite of replenishment from the mighty ocean, the same diminution is visible, while many of our confined inland waters are absolutely depopulated."[44]

In this period the West, of course, was the most dramatic example of rapid environmental change, and America's best-known narrative historian, Francis Parkman, introduced the 1872 edition of his classic, *The Oregon Trail* (1847), with a lament for the hunting grounds of his youth. Where once he had joyfully pursued the buffalo,[45] one now heard "the disenchanting screech of the locomotive" and found hotels, gambling houses, and even "woman's rights"! For Parkman, much of the West had already passed under the rule of "triumphant commonplace."[46]

By the time the national outdoor journals appeared, the good-old-days lament was a well-established characteristic of the "sporting mind." Most issues of the "big four" newspapers contain evidence of its strength. In early 1875, for example, Wilbur F. Parker, editor of *American Sportsman,* rhetorically asked his fellow Americans what they had to brag about as the nation's centennial approached: "Shall we boast that where the deer, the buffalo, the salmon, and the feathered game . . . were once plentiful . . . , we may now tramp for many a long summer day and not find a specimen. Shall we take credit for our predatory instinct that as individuals we have wasted natural gifts not exceeded in any other part of the world, and that as a nation we have been so intent on multiplying the almighty dollar that we have given over our streams to pollution, our fish to destruction, and our land and water to the poacher and exterminator: that with our immense domain and our boundless endowments we are now poorer in this particular of national wealth than the thickly settled countries of Europe. . . ?"[47]

One of the more ironic examples of the good-old-days lament appears in the same note in October, 1876. The Reverend William H. H. Murray, whose *Adventures in the Wilderness* (1869) is credited by local historians with "opening up" the Adirondacks as a fashionable resort,[48] now complains that nonsporting tourists have overrun much of the region. Because of the need to supply the new hotels with trout and venison, the game had all but vanished. The sporting region Murray had glorified only a few years before was now "worthless" for sportsmen: "The trout are entirely gone, practically so, and the deer are going as fast as stupid greed [market hunting] can destroy them."[49]

One last example of the good-old-days lament is from an 1882 editorial in *American Field,* the same journal as *Field and Stream* but with a new title.[50] Like all such material in the sporting journals, the piece is unsigned, but is presumably by the paper's editor, Nicholas Rowe. Describing the Long Island (New York) of his youth, he recalls that:

> Not longer than twenty-five years ago, and even less, large bags of quails, woodcocks, ruffed grouse and water fowls [sic] could be made; and very fair deer hunting could be had. Then more birds could have been brought to bag in one day than in one week now. . . . To the young generation of sportsmen who live in the vicinity of Long Island these statements must seem almost incredible; but there are numbers [of hunters] living who can substantiate them. We have shot from one end of Long Island to the other, and as we look back through the vista of years memory fondly brings back some of the happiest days of our life, and we almost feel like a boy again. Of all the shooting we have had, those days spent on Long Island are the greenest in our memory. Whether July woodcock shooting, or in August basking in the hot sun on Moriches or Shinnecock bay

shooting bay [shore] birds, or in September on Mountauk [*sic*] Point
shooting plovers, or on the North Side [Shore] shooting Fall wood-
cocks, or in the brown October days quail and ruffed grouse shooting,
or in November duck shooting, we enjoyed ourselves as only one
can who delights in the sports of the field. We have always thought
Long Island possessed a charm for sportsmen such as no other place
that we have seen . . . , and it is to be deeply regretted that its glory
has departed.[51]

Almost everywhere in the sporting literature of the postwar generation, one will find similar protests. And what is notable for our story
is that sportsmen did more than lament—they also acted.

For most, the first step was to join with their brothers and form
a club or association. Though these organizations can be found as
early as the eighteenth century,[52] they were few and far between until
the 1870s.[53] Then, with the establishment of the national sporting
journals, a movement began that immediately resulted in the formation of scores of new associations across the nation. Before long, this
"club movement"—the term the sportsmen themselves used—en-
gendered not only many local clubs but state and national organizations as well. As conservationist John B. Burnham pointed out later:
"All at once, in the winter of 1874–75, . . . it seemed to penetrate
the consciousness of the readers of those . . . journals that they had
a responsibility for the game, a feeling that was accentuated by the
disappearance or decrease of the game in many parts of the country.
At any rate, for the first time they not only realized but assumed
their responsibility, and in that winter of 1874–75 nearly 100 sportsmen's organizations were organized all over the country, ten or twelve
state associations and one national association."[54]

The incredible growth of the club movement after this initial spurt
of activity is documented in Charles Hallock's *American Club List
and Sportsman's Glossary* published in 1878. *Forest and Stream*'s editor enumerated thirty-four organizations "devoted chiefly to the
pleasure of angling and the protection and propagation of fish,"
among them the Illinois State Fish Culturists' Association and the
American Fish Cultural Association,[55] of which Hallock was a prominent member. Most were in the Northeast, but a number of states
outside that region, including California, had at least one club. Sepa-

rated by Hallock from these associations are what he calls the "Sports-men's Clubs," those "organized either for field shooting, or for shoot-ing and fishing combined," as well as "the preservation of game and the observance and enforcement of laws governing close[d] seasons." These now numbered 308, more than a threefold increase since 1874–75. Virtually every settled portion of the United States was rep-resented, though the Northeast was again most prominent.[56]

Some of the clubs' names are especially interesting. Two were named for John James Audubon, five for Frank Forester, two for Hallock himself, and eight for *Forest and Stream*.[57] The latter two groups reveal the influence Hallock's paper had already wielded in its efforts to get readers to form associations.

It should also be mentioned that these 308 do not include a long list of what Hallock calls "Gun Clubs"—those that, "technically speak-ing," are devoted mainly to trapshooting—even though "many Gun Clubs also engage largely in Field Shooting." Neither does it include the angling clubs mentioned above, even though many combined hunt-ing as well, nor fourteen fox-hunting associations concerned with rid-ing to the hounds.[58]

Because all of the 308 associations, and the thirty-four angling clubs as well, claimed to be committed to the perpetuation of wildlife and their habitats, the editors of the "big four" newspapers performed a real environmental service by fostering what they called the "club idea." While only a small minority of these organizations had an im-portant influence on conservation, the general effect of the movement was to increase sportsmen's awareness—and the nation's as well—of the damage being done by American economic growth.

On a more concrete level these associations also acted as centers for discussion and, in many cases, as lobbies for better enforcement of already existing laws and passage of new ones.[59] Except for sports-men, only a tiny number of Americans had any real interest in con-servation before the turn of the century. As we will see later, historians have given these individuals labels like "nature lover," "expert," "sci-entist," "naturalist," or "preservationist," when many could be cate-gorized as "sportsman" just as easily.

To see how fashionable the club idea had become by the 1870s, the reader need only leaf through the sportsmen's journals, the main vehicle of communication for what they called the "fraternity." In an age that historians claim was devoid of environmental consciousness outside of a few "prophets" like John Wesley Powell and John Muir, one is surprised to find organizations cropping up everywhere whose avowed purpose is the preservation of wildlife and natural areas. Typical is an entry in the *American Sportsman* issue of October 25, 1873. Under the heading of "New Sportsmen's Associations," correspondent Frederick W. Jones informs the editor that "An association of gentlemen has been formed in Orange Co., N.Y., under the name of the Summit Lake Association for the purpose of propagating fish and game of various kinds." After giving the acreage controlled by the club, Jones, its president, adds: "We have the lake well stocked with black bass, obtained from Seth Green [the noted fish culturist]. . . ."[60] Another example of an entry under this heading, taken from an issue in the following month, is a letter from a correspondent in Missouri Valley, Iowa, who tells the editor that "At a meeting of the sportsmen of our town on Tuesday evening, December 2d, 1873, a sportsman's club was formed for the purpose of enforcing the game laws, the protection of game, and elevating the standard of . . . sportsmen, to be known as the Missouri Valley Sportsman Club."[61]

By the following year, the paper's editor, Wilbur F. Parker, could already report a "marked and radical . . . change in popular feeling" that "has brought field sports up from being deemed a pursuit for loafers only, to their present estimation as a matter of manly honor and credit to men of the highest rank and position. The asceticism and puritanic[al] condemnation of everything which does not directly tend to the accumulation of the almighty dollar, has fortunately for our good sense and physical improvement given way to a more liberal sentiment." Now, "a professional man who desires a few days' recreation with rod or gun [a]mid the haunts of Nature, is no longer obliged to steal away 'like a thief in the night,' but can go forth openly, and on his return proclaim his success with a flourish of trumpets, if so inclined, without suffering either in purse or reputation thereby. A few years since a sportmens' [sic] club was a thing unknown;[62] now they may be counted by scores, and exist in almost every important city in the Union, encouraging and fostering a true sportsman like [sic] spirit. . . ."[63] At last, "the sportsmen of America are . . . roused to the importance of banding themselves together for the purpose of checking and controlling the wanton and wasteful destruction of nature's best gifts intended for the heritage of universal man, and not for the benefit of the reckless and greedy few. . . ."[64]

As Parker believed, this was only the beginning. With the steady encouragement of the sporting journals, the coming years would witness the establishment of an increasing number of local, state, and national associations, and together they would exert a massive influence on both the attitudes of the general public and the history of conservation.

From what has already been said, it is obvious the author feels that the importance—and often even the existence—of these early organizations has been overlooked by professional historians. If this is true, then it can only follow that historians have also ignored the individual gunner and angler, despite the fact that hunting or fishing was a part of the lives of most American males in the late nineteenth century.

The nation was still overwhelmingly rural, and even those living in big cities usually had only a short distance to go before reaching woods, fields, streams, or other kinds of topography suitable for gunning and angling. While the landscape, particularly around big cities, had already been dramatically altered, it often still possessed a kind of countrylike atmosphere. Even the environs of New York City, the nation's largest urban center, offered hunting and fishing opportunities throughout the century.

In a world without automobiles, urban sprawl, and all the other wonders created by twentieth-century ingenuity, people were unable to insulate themselves from the reality of nature. The slight awareness of the natural world so evident today in urban and even suburban America was a very rare phenomenon a century ago.

This does not mean, of course, that most Americans were then appreciative of nature, but only that its presence was infinitely more apparent than in recent times. The great majority still possessed at least some feeling of hostility toward forces that could wipe out their crops overnight, make their roads impassable, and produce a hundred other unpleasant possibilities.

But regardless of how an individual felt toward the natural world, the important thing for us was that it was the most obvious and accessible sphere for recreation, particularly for youngsters. Costing nothing, the outdoors was free to rich and poor alike, and the few who have studied the history of American recreation agree that nineteenth-century youth, especially males, took full advantage of its possibilities. Fishing in early boyhood and hunting in adolescence seem to have been almost universal.

In the early part of the century purely recreational angling and gunning, even for juveniles, was still frowned upon in the North, but the same "thaw" in the compulsive practicality of Americans that helped sportsmen benefited boys everywhere; more time now could be taken up by hunting and fishing without fear of censure or punishment. In the South youngsters escaped for the most part the puritanical heritage of their Northern counterparts. Although fishing was never as popular there as in the North, hunting, even for recreation, always seems to have been a central part of the socialization process for males.

Because professional historians, including those writing biographies, have considered these activities of little significance, it is often extremely difficult to discover whether or not a particular conservationist—who is not already well known as a sportsman—ever hunted or fished in his youth. The author has made an attempt to track down this information, and he has found that an extraordinarily large number of the nineteenth-century leaders of conservation were gunners or anglers some time during their lives. Many, like John F. Lacey and Gifford Pinchot, retained throughout their years the love for sport first acquired in boyhood, while others, like George Perkins Marsh and Robert Underwood Johnson, were extremely fond of angling or hunting in youth but later discontinued these activities.

Why they gave them up is hard to say, but the most obvious hypothesis is also the most likely. Probably the press of business—of achieving status in their chosen fields—simply left them with little time for purely recreational pursuits. Still, this does not explain why others, like George Bird Grinnell and Theodore Roosevelt, managed to combine active careers with an outdoor life. For many, the vitality of the sporting tradition was such that it counterbalanced cultural pressures to give up the "innocent" pursuits of childhood for the "practical" endeavors of adulthood. But others, like George Perkins Marsh and Spencer Fullerton Baird, had to camouflage their old love for the pursuit and capture of wildlife by calling it "scientific collecting," despite the fact that the same techniques were used and the same pleasure experienced. Even though some gave up their youthful interest in hunting or fishing, or chose to systematize it in the name of science, most looked back on their early experience as gunners or anglers with the deepest affection, and one can only assume that it played an important part in fashioning these individuals' love for the natural world and the desire to see it preserved.

As we have seen, the responsibility for wildlife and habitat inherent in the code of the sportsman explains much about why outdoorsmen like Seth Green and John F. Lacey should devote themselves to conservation. But it would not seem to tell us much about those who gave up these recreations later in life, or those who (as far as we know) never pursued them at all. Yet the interesting fact is that many in both categories also believed in the code of the sportsman, particularly that aspect that claimed hunting and fishing built health and character in the individuals who followed them. One example is George Perkins Marsh.

In his 1857 *Report* to the Vermont legislature advocating the adoption of a fish culture program—a study initiated by sportsmen who wanted to restock the state's depleted waters[65]—Marsh asserted that "the chase is a healthful and invigorating recreation, and its effects on the character of the sportsman, the hardy physical habits, the quickness of eye, hand, and general movement, the dexterity in the arts of pursuit and destruction, . . . the courage and self-reliance, the half-military spirit, in short, which it infuses, are important elements of prosperity and strength in the bodily and mental constitution of a people. . . ." And though "it must be admitted that angling and other modes of fishing are under few circumstances attended with as great moral and physical benefits as the pursuit of the larger quadrupeds, . . . they are nevertheless analogous in their nature and influences, and as a means of innocent and healthful recreation at least, they deserve to be promoted rather than discouraged by public and even legislative patronage."[66]

This affirmation of the benefits attending hunting and fishing antedates by seven years the publication of his famous *Man and Nature* (1864), which has been called the "fountainhead of the conservation movement"[67] because it was the first detailed description of Americans' destruction of natural resources. In the 1857 study Marsh lamented the passing of Vermont's wildlife, including fish,[68] and the knowledge he gained researching that *Report*[69] was incorporated into

Man and Nature. It would appear, therefore, that an interest in wild-life preceded his later concern for all natural resources.

Another example of the nonsportsman's commitment to the code of the sportsman is the case of John W. Noble, Benjamin Harrison's Secretary of the Interior and one of the pivotal figures in the early conservation movement. A shadowy figure, Noble left almost nothing pertaining to his private life, and although he later belonged to the Boone and Crockett Club, he never states, one way or the other, that he had any personal experience with hunting or fishing. Yet, in an obituary of his old chief, Noble argues that Harrison's experience in sport hunting helps to explain the latter's success as a lawyer.[70] As will be shown later, Noble also seems to have been greatly influenced by friends in the Boone and Crockett Club, particularly William Hallett Phillips.

Regardless of whether Noble ever hunted or fished himself, the point here is that a majority of the nineteenth-century pioneers of environmental concern, who have left any substantial record of their recreational interests, engaged wholeheartedly in one or both of these activities sometime in their lives. And this is just as true for those individuals whom historians have pigeonholed as "preservationists" (persons supposedly concerned only with preserving natural areas and wildlife *untouched*) as it is for those they have categorized as "conservationists" (persons supposedly concerned only with the *utilization* of resources). Given in alphabetical order, the following list of eighty names is representative of this fact:

John Quincy Adams	John Burroughs
Stephen H. Ainsworth	George Catlin
Joel A. Allen	Frank M. Chapman
George S. Anderson	Galen Clark
Chester A. Arthur	Grover Cleveland
John James Audubon	DeWitt Clinton
Spencer Fullerton Baird	James Fenimore Cooper
Albert Bierstadt	Charles B. Cory
William H. Brewer	Elliott Coues
William Brewster	Samuel S. Cox
John J. Brown	William Dutcher
William Cullen Bryant	George F. Edmunds

Daniel G. Elliot

William Elliott

Barton Warren Evermann

Bernhard E. Fernow

Edward H. Forbush

"Frank Forester"

Theodatus Garlick

George Brown Goode

Madison Grant

Horace Greeley

Seth Green

George Bird Grinnell

Charles Hallock

Samuel H. Hammond

William C. Harris

Benjamin Harrison

Joel T. Headley

Cornelius Hedges

William T. Hornaday

Emerson Hough

Washington Irving

William H. Jackson

Robert Underwood Johnson

David Starr Jordan

Clarence King

John F. Lacey

Charles Lanman

Elisha J. Lewis

William Ludlow

George Perkins Marsh

Fred Mather

C. Hart Merriam

Thomas Moran

William H. H. Murray

Thaddeus Norris

Frederick Law Olmsted

Wilbur F. Parker

Francis Parkman

William Hallett Phillips

Gifford Pinchot

John Wesley Powell

Robert Ridgway

Robert Barnwell Roosevelt

Theodore Roosevelt

Joseph T. Rothrock

Nicholas Rowe

Carl A. Schenck

Ernest Thompson Seton

George Oliver Shields

Livingston Stone

Henry David Thoreau

Frederick Jackson Turner

Henry Van Dyke

George G. Vest

Daniel Webster

Alexander Wilson[71]

The primary interests of nineteenth-century environmentalists were "nature appreciation," wildlife, parks, and forests, and whether in artistic, literary, political, or scientific form, all of the individuals listed made a lasting contribution to one or more of these subject areas. Most of the names should be familiar to environmental historians.

While this compilation is not all-inclusive—it could have been much longer—the list does contain a fair number of better-known individuals from a wide variety of fields. And what is most interesting is that not only did all these men pursue hunting or fishing at one time, but the great majority retained that interest through much of their lives. All but a handful of the eighty gunned or angled for recreation at least occasionally after reaching adulthood.

Though most of those enumerated fit the definition of "sportsman," historians have habitually labeled them as "nature lovers," "nature writers," "naturalists," "scientists," or "experts." Yet the main thing these diverse individuals had in common was a shared experience as anglers or hunters. Surely that personal involvement with the rhythms of nature on a nonutilitarian basis—unlike farmers and ranchers, for example—must have played a crucial part in the fashioning of their love and concern for the outdoors. How many know that forestry pioneer, John Quincy Adams, ruminated on the difficulty of achieving wildlife conservation in a democratic society while out hunting one evening in 1787; that scientist Spencer Fullerton Baird loved wildfowl hunting in his youth to the point of envying wealthy sportsmen-naturalists who were able to spend all their time shooting; that artists Albert Bierstadt and Thomas Moran were accomplished sportsmen; that author and artist Charles Lanman loved angling; that one of the greatest moments in the lives of photographer William H. Jackson and explorer-scientist Clarence King was the shooting of a grizzly bear in the Great West; that the favorite pastime of "nature writers" John Burroughs and Henry Van Dyke was fishing; that on October 23, 1873, ornithologist Elliott Coues told the readers of *Forest and Stream* that he had long thought of starting a hunting, fishing, and natural-history periodical like theirs; that ornithologists William Brewster, Charles B. Cory, and Daniel G. Elliot also loved bird shooting; that the intellectual father of Yellowstone National Park, Cornelius Hedges, was an avid trout angler; that the two major Congressional defenders of the Yellowstone preserve, George G. Vest and Samuel S. Cox, were enthusiastic sportsmen; that editor Robert Underwood Johnson and scholar George Perkins Marsh considered their youthful angling excursions among the most cherished experiences of boyhood; that artist George Catlin, perhaps the first American to conceive of the idea of a national park, hunted buffalo for sport; that John James Audubon—like Louis Agassiz Fuertes, Lynn Bogue Hunt, and many other bird painters of a later day—loved hunting the birds he illustrated; that C. Hart Merriam, mammalogist and founder of what became the United States Fish and Wildlife Service, was a hunter and active member of the League of American Sportsmen; that Galen Clark, who was a key figure in the early history of what became Yosemite National Park, explored the area while on hunting trips; that ichthyologists Barton Warren Evermann, George Brown Goode, Seth Green, David Starr Jordan, Fred Mather, Thaddeus Norris, and Livingston Stone were all enthusiastic anglers before and after they became "scientists"; that Gifford Pinchot believed that a fishing trip to the Adirondacks in his youth had much to do with his later decision to become a forester; that Joseph T. Rothrock, pioneer in forestry at the state level, was a frequent contributor to sportsmen's periodicals on the subject of hunting; that Samuel H. Hammond, perhaps the first individual to make a specific recommendation for the creation of an Adirondack preserve, did so in a work relating his hunting and fishing adventures in that wilderness region; that zoo director William T. Hornaday, often quoted by historians for his attacks on hunters was an avid hunter himself; that "preservationist" Frederick Law Olmsted once hunted whooping cranes and later belonged to a fox-hunting club; that Theodore Roosevelt claimed that he would never have become President if it had not been for his experiences in the West, which began with a buffalo hunt; that on a trip to Maine's Mt. Katahdin region, Henry David Thoreau became so excited by the prospect of angling for trout that he was unable to sleep and arose before anyone else in camp in order to get a jump on the finny tribe; that Grover Cleveland wrote a philosophical book on the joys of hunting and fishing; that the only bill angler Daniel Webster introduced in his one term as a Massachusetts state legislator was an act to preserve trout; that William Dutcher, founder of what became the National Audubon Society, was a bird hunter; or that Frederick Jackson Turner, considered by some to be America's greatest interpretive historian and author of the famous "frontier thesis," was a devoted sportsman his whole life?

The author could provide numerous other examples of the same theme, but enough is enough. The point is that hunting or fishing for pleasure was almost universal among early environmentalists; men like John Muir and Franklin B. Hough, who never seem to have had any interest in these activities or were even hostile to them, are clearly the exception. For most, the pursuit of wildlife seems to have provided that crucial first contact with the natural world that spawned a commitment to its perpetuation. Instead of ignoring sportsmen, or treating them with contempt, scholars might do better to acknowledge and investigate the role played by sport in motivating environmental reforms and achievements. The only result can be a fuller, truer picture of the history of American conservation.

TWO

Conservation Begins
with Wildlife

If the reader were to pick up virtually any work on the history of conservation, he would find the same matter-of-fact statement that concern for the nation's forests initiated American conservation. First asserted by Theodore Roosevelt and Gifford Pinchot and later re-affirmed by forestry spokesmen and their supporters, the claim has now achieved a kind of sacrosanct quality that makes it almost un-assailable. Even the title of the only scholarly history journal to empha-size conservation, *Forest History,* suggests the strength of what is, in fact, an erroneous assumption.

Roosevelt and Pinchot were actually late-comers to conservation. This statement may sound incredible today, but it is nevertheless true. By 1901, when these two dynamic men teamed up to make "conserva-tion" a household word, a less dramatic, but still influential, movement had already been in existence for a quarter of a century. From the 1870s on, sportsmen had been working for the restriction of commer-cial hunting and fishing, the adoption of a national fish-culture pro-gram that included efforts to control water pollution, the establishment of adequately protected game preserves, and the passage of new game laws and the better enforcement of old ones. As it turned out, indi-vidual sportsmen would also pioneer in forest preservation and management, but the bulk of outdoorsmen were concerned first with wildlife.

Because Roosevelt and Pinchot were both extremely proud men, it is only natural that they would have liked to believe that little occurred before *they* arrived on the scene.[1] Even though Roosevelt's administration established five national parks, seventeen national monuments, and over fifty wildlife refuges, its focal point was the forests, as the most all-inclusive, "practical" issue in conservation. In a nation overwhelmingly utilitarian in its outlook, the *only* political approach they could take was to claim that the forests were being preserved and managed in order to protect watersheds and ensure a never-ending supply of building materials. To do anything else would have been to court political defeat for their whole conservation program, particularly in the fiercely democratic West where the administration's new forest reserves were set aside.[2] Yet Roosevelt knew that while millions of acres of timberland were being preserved, the big game he cherished so much would also find sanctuary, and he was right.[3] Outside of Yellowstone and Glacier National Parks, the majority of Western woodland mammals still live in the "national forests," as the forest reserves were called after 1907.

Historians have tended to follow the Roosevelt-Pinchot "line" in considering timberlands first in importance and wildlife second. Those two men *had* to take that approach—regardless of their personal feelings—but historians have followed them simply because they have not considered animals, birds, and fish as anything but minor subjects in the history of conservation. Not understanding that wildlife is an index to environmental quality and that in many areas it is worth more economically, as a recreational resource, than the value of potential board feet of lumber, most scholars have been taken in by the same "practical-mindedness" that has always plagued American attempts to develop a sound natural-resource policy.

This is undoubtedly a major reason for their habitual tendency to look upon wildlife as an issue that hardly even competes with the "important" resources like forests and minerals. A major result of this "tunnel vision" is that they have overlooked the massive efforts of sportsmen to conserve wildlife long before Roosevelt and Pinchot appeared on the scene.

It is not difficult to prove that in the minds of a substantial segment

of the American people, wildlife preceded forests as the most important environmental issue. As we have seen, in the 1870s hundreds
of sportsmen's organizations—including state and national associations—were formed across the country with the express purpose of
preserving and propagating game. In addition, several national periodicals with the same objectives came into existence. Where in regard
to the forests was there a comparable movement? The answer is nowhere. There were no forestry clubs scattered all over the nation;
no forestry journals appealing to a national audience; and before
the 1890s, no more than a scattering of individual forest proponents,
many of whom were sportsmen like George Bird Grinnell and
Bernhard E. Fernow. Only one organization existing in the 1870s
might, at first glance, seem to be an exception to the above statements;
this was the American Forestry Association, established in 1875 by
John A. Warder. But historians admit that it never showed any life,
and the group faded out of existence in 1883.[4]

Of all the conservation efforts relating to wildlife, probably the most
popular for sportsmen and nonsportsmen alike was fish culture. As
early as the 1840s, Frank Forester had called for the restoration of
game fish to waters depleted by dams and pollution.[5] Many today
seem to think that these last two issues are recent problems, but American sporting literature proves otherwise. After Forester's initial protests, he was joined in later years by Robert Barnwell Roosevelt,
Thaddeus Norris, and Genio C. Scott. Their works, and the volumes
of the national sporting periodicals, are replete with protests against
the dumping of sawdust, mine wastes, factory chemicals, and other
pollutants into the country's waterways; demands for fish ladders at
dams so that migratory fishes could pass around these obstructions;
and attacks on commercial fishermen whose nets, it seemed, were
staked across every important river, lake, and sound in the nation.[6]

As with every other nineteenth-century conservation issue, American
pioneers in fish culture modeled their first efforts on English or Continental precedents. France, in particular, had long devoted herself
to this subject, and early American fish culturists like Theodatus
Garlick and Thaddeus Norris studied French discoveries in order to
adapt them to the United States. By the 1870s, American culturists
were making many new discoveries of their own and the movement
was in full swing. Hatcheries were put in operation from New York

to California, important species like shad and brook trout were restored to waters barren only a few years before, and new species were established in regions where they had never existed. Perhaps the outstanding beneficial example of the latter achievement was the establishment of shad and striped bass on the West Coast, while the outstanding harmful example was the spread of the Old World carp[7]—after its first introduction in 1832[8]—to every part of the United States.

Even though it has been overlooked by most scholars, the fish-culture movement was the very first environmental crusade to capture a significant percentage of the American public. Seven years before George Perkins Marsh published his famous *Man and Nature* (1864), the Vermont legislature—at the request of sportsmen (Chapter 1)—commissioned him to study the feasibility of restoring the state's depleted fish stocks. Sportsmen and nonsportsmen alike had become alarmed over the disappearance of game and food fishes; the salmon and shad runs that had once made the Connecticut River famous, providing both recreation and a cheap source of protein, had been eliminated by nets, pollution, and especially dams. Marsh's report advised that the runs could be restored if cooperative action was taken by every state through which the river passed.[9]

The effort to protect the Connecticut River fishery was by no means an isolated case, as shown by the controversy over New England's saltwater fishery a few years later. By the late 1860s, coastal hook-and-line fishermen, who included both sportsmen and "meat fishermen,"[10] had become so incensed by what appeared to be a diminishing supply of fish that they petitioned the legislatures of Connecticut, Rhode Island, and Massachusetts to put a stop to the ravages of commercial netters.[11] From Massachusetts alone, petitions and protests signed by almost 11,000 people poured into the legislature in early 1870.[12]

As a result of the uproar, the United States Fish Commission—the first federal agency created to deal with the conservation of a specific natural resource—was established in 1871 and called in to settle the dispute.[13] Headed by Spencer Fullerton Baird, the Commission made extensive investigations and arrived at some interesting conclusions. In its *Report,* published in 1873, the agency detailed the incredible destruction of coastal and freshwater fishes (a section on the Great Lakes was also included) by commercial netters. Other factors like pollution and bluefish predation were discussed, but Baird concluded that the impact of the netters was the most important reason for the apparent diminution of fish stocks. Predicting the virtual disappearance of some inshore species, he went so far as to threaten federal intervention if the states failed to pass proper legislation against the netters.[14]

Baird was certainly ahead of his time in understanding that migratory wildlife species should be under the authority of the federal government, even though nonmigratory species must remain under the control of the individual state in which they are found. Not until the Federal Migratory Bird Act and Treaty were passed in the first quarter of this century was this principle firmly established. Ironically, despite the implications of Baird's stand a century ago, the concept of federal responsibility for migratory fishes that pass through several states has still not been accepted.

Although the Fish Commission's *Report* failed to produce any action against the netters, hostilities between them and their hook-and-line opponents ceased with a return to abundance of the same species Baird claimed were passing out of existence—the Commissioner had simply failed to comprehend the importance of cycles in fish populations.[15] While the nets did take a fearful toll, the tremendous surpluses produced by wildlife, especially fishes, allow large harvests without any permanent damage to the stocks. Apparently, when the clamor to stop the netters began, several New England species were at a low point in their cycles, and with the return of the fish to abundance, the controversy died away.

Despite nature's resolution of this specific issue, general interest in the preservation and propagation of fish grew apace. By the mid-1870s it was already approaching "mania"[16] dimensions. Soon, every part of the nation was clamoring for its fair share of the millions of food and game fish being produced by the hatcheries. Congressmen were continually besieged by their constituents to get the United States Fish Commission to supply them with fish stocks, particularly carp, while the leading private fish culturists, like Seth Green and Fred Mather, were working overtime to provide their fellow sportsmen with adequate quantities of game fish.[17] It seemed that there was hardly a lake, river, or bay that missed being stocked with native or foreign species. As an indication of the movement's strength, the following is a partial list of the quantities of freshwater and saltwater species

produced by the New York State Fish Commission from 1870 to 1881:
53,609,000 shad; 10,990,000 "salmon trout" [lake trout]; 2,438,000
whitefish; 5,375,000 brook trout; 1,288,700 "California trout" [rain-
bow trout]; and 900,000 "frost fish" [Atlantic tomcod].[18]

As usual, sportsmen had led the way in fish culture. Every one
of the leading private culturists were self-proclaimed anglers as well
as "scientists,"[19] and those who have left any substantial record of
their lives indicate that boyhood angling experiences initiated their
fascination with fish.[20]

With the establishment of the sportsmen's journals, fish culture had
been given a tremendous boost. *Forest and Stream,* for example, was
the official organ of the American Fish Culturists' Association,[21] and
that body's concrete achievements are further proof that wildlife, and
not forests, was the first major issue in conservation history. Thaddeus
Norris, Seth Green, and Fred Mather ran fishing-fish culture columns in the sporting papers, and virtually all the important "scientists"
involved with the subject, including the leading government culturist,
Spencer Fullerton Baird, used the outdoor periodicals as their forum.[22]
In addition, all the major papers furthered the movement by constant
references to its achievements and potentialities.

Why the "fish culture idea" took hold with such success is not difficult to ascertain. For sportsmen, it meant a restoration of angling
opportunities; for farmers and ranchers, it meant a profitable sideline,
for the United States Fish Commission repeatedly claimed that carp
could be raised more cheaply than hogs and with equal or better
economic returns; for commercial fishermen, like shad netters, it meant
never-ending profits despite systematic exploitation of the resource;
and for the nation as a whole, it meant cheap food for the masses.

By the end of the century, it was clear to many that fish culture
was not quite the bonanza it was first thought to be. Sportsmen found
that the introduction of black bass and German brown trout often
resulted in a drastic reduction of native brook trout; farmers and
ranchers found that their promised profits never materialized; commercial fishermen found that fish propagation did not eliminate their
responsibility for the resource because each ecosystem only supports
so many fish, regardless of how often it is stocked; and the nation
as a whole found carp an indifferent food and rejected it as anything
but a last resort.

Twentieth-century fish culturists began to understand that the best way to produce more fish was to provide a healthy habitat, for fish always increase to the limit of their food supply, available cover, suitable breeding locations, etc. Still, in heavily fished streams with a small capacity for natural production, hatchery-bred fish introduced on a "put-and-take" basis do provide recreation for countless thousands of anglers, and the successful planting of Pacific-coast salmon in the Great Lakes in recent years—which has created a multi-million-dollar sport fishery[23]—proves that fish culture is still an important component of wildlife conservation.

In addition to their public services in stocking the nation's waters and protecting them from dams, pollution, and nets, sportsmen also made an important contribution in the private sector by establishing numerous game preserves. Virtually all of the sportsmen's clubs controlled, by leasing or direct ownership, large acreage that was kept in natural condition, thereby maintaining the ecosystems of those areas. Because each association enforced its own rules, in addition to state laws, game stocks were preserved; where game already had been reduced before the creation of the club, artificial propagation often filled the void. Nongame species also benefited by having their habitats guarded against "improvements." In many areas the only substantial acreage remaining in an undeveloped state was the land controlled by sportsmen's clubs.

Game preserves (in fact if not in name) date back to early Colonial days, and these "deer parks," as they were called, were considered by many in Virginia and Maryland to be an essential part of any country estate.[24] One of the more noteworthy deer parks of a later period was owned by Judge John D. Caton, a sportsman-naturalist who wrote frequently for both *American Naturalist* and the sporting press. About 1858, near Ottowa, Illinois, he set aside a sanctuary that eventually encompassed 200 acres and stocked it with white-tailed deer, elk, and other species. From studies made on these herbivores, Caton wrote his important work, *The Antelope and Deer of America* (1877).[25]

With the increase of sportsmen's self-consciousness in the 1870s, impetus was given to the game-preserve idea. Undoubtedly, the same British example that played such an important part in the development of American "sportsmanship" also was a factor in the creation of preserves, for the latter had long been used by English sportsmen as an instrument of conservation.

Another, more important, factor in the establishment of preserves was outdoormen's desire to perpetuate game and habitat in spite of the utter indifference of a nation seemingly obsessed with economic development. Instead of waiting for the indolent state and federal governments to assume their responsibility for natural resources, sportsmen decided to take the initiative themselves. Two of the earlier, better-known preserves were Blooming Grove Park and the Bisby Club.

According to T. S. Palmer, the leading authority on the subject, "the first game preserve belonging to an incorporated association was that established by the Blooming Grove Park Association in 1871, for the purpose 'of preserving, importing, breeding, and propagating game animals, birds, and fish, and of furnishing facilities to the members for hunting, shooting, and fishing on its grounds.' One of the important features was a deer park [of 1,000 acres]."[26] Located in Pike County, Pennsylvania, the Blooming Grove property consisted of 12,000 acres "in one of the wildest and most picturesque portions of the State."[27]

The founders of Blooming Grove were Fayette S. Giles, a wealthy jeweler; Genio C. Scott, author of *Fishing in American Waters* (1869); and Charles Hallock, future editor of *Forest and Stream*. Their idea of establishing "a grand park or inclosure . . . where game might be bred and protected" was based on an old European precedent, their specific models being "the grand forests of Fontainebleau and the Grand Duchy of Baden." (Giles had been a resident of France for six years and had "engaged actively in field sports, both in the forests of Fontainebleau and in Germany. . . .")[28]

In addition to the preservation and management of game animals, fish-culture and forestry programs were also initiated. The latter endeavor is particularly noteworthy. *It was probably the first attempt to establish systematic forestry in the United States.*

As Hallock noted in 1873, "the cultivation of forests . . . and the selling of timber and surplus game of all kinds [will] . . . compensate in some degree for the frightful waste which is annually devastating our forests and exterminating our game."[29] It should be noted here that Gifford Pinchot is universally credited with initiating "the first systematic forest management" in the United States.[30] Though his work was far more extensive than that done in Blooming Grove, it did not begin until 1892, twenty years later.

Only one historian, Theodore W. Cart, seems to have perceived the importance of Blooming Grove Park in the history of conservation:

> The concept and execution of the Blooming Grove plan provided the first large-scale demonstration of integrated natural resource planning for primarily recreational purposes in America, something that would not be approached in the public sector for twenty years. . . . Yellowstone Park, created in the next year [1872], had no effective game protection until 1894 and had no plan to cultivate its timber. . . . Blooming Grove had no public counterparts until the national forest system provided for multiple use of timber and game resources. . . .[31]

The success of Blooming Grove encouraged sportsmen in other areas to emulate its example. One of these was the Bisby Club, established in New York's Adirondack Mountains. Believing "that the state would never take any action which would result in creating a grand park out of this vast wilderness" and feeling "an interest in preserving the forest from the incursions of civilization," a group of prominent sportsmen in 1877 leased a large tract of land in "the Northern Wilderness . . . to convert it into a park or preserve . . . where they might fish and hunt without molestation by the general public."[32] Its president was Richard U. Sherman, one of the state's commissioners of fisheries, and other well-known sportsmen who became regular or honorary members were Thomas R. Proctor, banker; Seth Green, fish culturist; Horatio Seymour, ex-Governor; and Verplanck Colvin, surveyor.[33]

By the spring of 1882, the club held lease to 9,000 acres of Herkimer County that embraced nine separate lakes, as well as some smaller waters. A spacious clubhouse had been built, and the waters stocked with game fish and planted with wild rice to attract waterfowl.[34]

In the early 1890s the Bisby Club merged with the much larger Adirondack League Club, which controlled 179,000 acres, and ceased to exist. The newer association "was organized in 1890 by a number of gentlemen of sporting proclivities, for the purpose of establishing a game preserve in a chosen quarter of the Adirondack wilderness and to put into practice the system of rational forestry prevailing on the continent of Europe, which reconciles the preservation and continual reproduction of forest areas with a continual and increasing income."[35] One of the prominent trustees of the club, and its "forestry adviser,"[36] was none other than Bernhard E. Fernow, Chief of the Division of Forestry of the United States Department of Agriculture. Describing the new association, guidebook-writer S. R. Stoddard stated that Fernow "is in . . . active management of its forest policy. A contract for the removal of the spruce above 12 inches in diameter at a stumpage price, which already guarantees the Club an income from this source of $30,000 a year, is in operation. . . ."[37]

Stoddard was probably writing in 1893, during the same period Pinchot was establishing his forestry program on George W. Vanderbilt's huge estate in western North Carolina. Even though it was planned in 1890, the Adirondack project was probably not put into operation until after Pinchot began his work in early 1892.[38] Nevertheless, it deserves mention, because it was one of the three earliest attempts to manage timber systematically and because it took place—like the Blooming Grove effort twenty years before—on a preserve established by sportsmen.

While these preserves allowed wealthy sportsmen to maintain their "world" despite the ravages of progress, hunters and anglers were not content merely to retreat into their sanctuaries and forget their responsibilities to the nation. Instead, they chose to establish a system of laws regulating virtually every facet of gunning and angling. And it should be emphasized that, contrary to popular belief, sportsmen urged these restrictions upon themselves, for no individual, group, or government agency forced them to limit their "bags," hunting and fishing seasons, or any other aspect of sport. If sportsmen failed to regulate themselves, no one else would, for they lived in a country characterized, first, by a Judeo-Christian tradition that separated man from nature and sanctified his dominion over it;[39] second, by a *laissez-faire* economic order that encouraged irresponsible use of resources; third, by weak institutions, including the federal government, that seemed unwilling or unable to protect wildlife and habitat; and fourth, by a heritage of opposition to any restraint on "freedom," particularly that vestige of Old World tyranny, the game law.

American laws pertaining to wildlife appeared as early as the seventeenth century, but most of these statutes were not for the purpose of protecting wildlife but for killing it.[40] By paying Americans to destroy wolves, squirrels, crows, and other fauna, the bounty system was supposed to save livestock and crops. In reality, this unfortunate inheritance from England only wasted money and wildlife without resulting in any substantial benefits for the farmer. Even though it has been demonstrated time and again that bounties are worse than worthless as a wildlife-management technique, they have persisted even into recent years.

Sportsmen, too, originally supported the bounty system, but for them it was only one of many approaches to game preservation. For nonsportsmen, however, bounties represented the typical American orientation toward wildlife. Unless an animal or bird served some utilitarian purpose—usually economic in character—the usual question was: "What good is it?"

Farmers and ranchers made poor nature lovers, seeing wildlife only as competitors or sources of profit. Sportsmen, on the other hand, regarded most animals and birds with nonutilitarian motives.[41] Not depending on nature for a livlihood, sportsmen were the only *large* group of Americans who came to woods and fields for mainly recreational and aesthetic reasons. It is no wonder, then, that they would take the initiative in preserving nonsporting species as well as those traditionally pursued as game.

From Colonial days, sportsmen had monopolized legislative efforts in regard to wildlife, and by the 1870s these "game laws"—as all wildlife regulations were called—had proliferated into a tangled mass of confusing and often contradictory statutes. For this reason Charles Hallock, and later George Bird Grinnell, used *Forest and Stream* to demand "uniform laws for contiguous States which lie in the same isothermal belts."[42] Though ahead of its time, this idea would become the basis for determining the opening and closing dates of hunting and fishing seasons. Clearly, the editors of the leading outdoor journal of the time understood that the states had to cooperate with each other in the establishment of game laws if anything of permanent value was to be achieved.

Before efficient game laws could be passed, the public had to accept the necessity for legislation and be motivated to abide in it once enacted. Accordingly, at least once a year, the Forest and Stream Publishing Company printed a booklet containing the nation's game laws with a section explaining the purpose of the regulations. The pamphlet was distributed without charge.

In the effort to obtain respect for statutes protecting wildlife, one major obstacle the sporting journals had to overcome was the status resentment of nonsportsmen. Repeatedly, they received letters like the one printed in *Forest and Stream* on November 25, 1880. Ranting against the "aristocratic trespassers" who were invading the farms of East Rockaway, Long Island (New York), with no other claim to hunt and destroy property than that they belonged to the "wealthier classes," a farmer condemned these "encroachments . . . upon the liberties of the people."[43] Other letters were sent to *Forest and Stream* protesting that sportsmen exploited farmers and that game laws were only for the benefit of the rich, who had the time and money to pursue the game protected by the legislation.[44]

To counter these charges, Grinnell formulated his theory of democratic game protection. In an editorial in March, 1881, he denied the charge "that *Forest and Stream* was 'aristocratic' or that it favored measures which would make the enjoyment of legitimate sport by the poor man more difficult."[45] He argued, in fact, that it was the person of small income who most benefited by the enactment and enforcement of strict game laws. For "the rich man can travel to distant fields where game is plenty, and can have his shooting whether the laws are enforced or not. With the poor man it is not so; he has to take his day or half day in the field when he can get it, and has neither the time nor the money to travel far in search of game. It is, therefore, the man of modest means who is or should be interested in game preservation even more than he whose fortune is ample."[46] However, Grinnell noted, "no question of class or fortune should enter. . . ."[47] In a later editorial, " 'We, the People,' " he stressed that "laws prohibiting the destruction of game in its breeding season and of fish on their spawning grounds are not for the advantage of any narrow clique. They are for the good of us, the people." *Forest and Stream,* he added, takes the "broad tenable ground" of "the greatest good to the greatest number."[48]

Whereas Hallock had emphasized the need for additional game laws of a uniform kind, Grinnell put his stress on law enforcement. Shortly after becoming editor, he observed that game protectors for years had claimed that more legislation was the solution to wildlife depletion. The fact was, he asserted, most states had plenty of legislation, and some too much. What was really needed was not more statutes, but adequate enforcement of those already on the books.[49]

To accomplish this, he advocated the creation of a county game constable (now warden) system to be financed by small fees from each hunter. After all, he reasoned, "Those who dance must pay the fiddler."[50] Particularly important was that the office of the constable be nonpolitical and filled through appointments by the states rather than local citizen groups. He wanted the officers to be free from local pressure, so that their work could be performed efficiently and without interruption.[51]

The notion that the traditionally free and unstructured activity of hunting must now be financially supported by the sportsmen themselves and regulated by the states was a new idea. In the years ahead, however, it would become the cornerstone of game management. What was perhaps most significant about Grinnell's proposal was the insistence on the necessity of continuity—on a continual *process* of administration. This concept would become the basis of conservation itself.

Probably the most ambitious task *Forest and Stream* set for itself in the area of game legislation was its attempt to revolutionize the public's attitude toward lawbreakers. The paper had to struggle against massive indifference. Even those offenses which were generally condemned—like shooting deer at night after they were stunned by the glare of an artificial light—were not reported because of fear of retaliation by the relatives or friends of the poacher. Invariably, the informer would be visited by that ubiquitous fiend, the barn burner. *Forest and Stream* reported that "this deterrent fear of burning barns is not confined to any particular locality. We hear the same story from the West, from the Adirondacks, [and] from persons dwelling within five miles of New York City. . . ."[52]

Despite public opposition, the sporting journals never wavered in their efforts to pass good game laws and change American attitudes toward them. One of the more important goals the periodicals set for themselves was to end hunting of waterfowl and shore birds during the breeding season. Beginning in the late '70s, *Forest and Stream* and *American Field* (the later name of *Field and Stream*) ran editorial after editorial attacking the traditional practice of spring shooting and censured individual sportsmen who were slow to adopt the new creed; even President Cleveland was not immune from such public criticism.[53] As shown by the opinions of correspondents, sportsmen increasingly came to accept this latest piece of self-denial, even though it was not until the twentieth century that the practice was completely stopped.

Market men, of course, had little regard for the campaign against spring shooting or any other "cause" that might reduce their profits. Sportsmen naturally felt frustrated to find their conservation efforts continually thwarted by the activities of commercial hunters and fishermen. They gradually came to realize that the biggest threat to game was its commercial, *systematic* exploitation, for even when habitat remained more or less intact, species like the elk and Eskimo curlew could be overharvested to such a degree as to imperil their very existence. Allowing them to be killed for market was the same as placing a bounty on their heads. Where the sportsman might shoot a dozen ducks or a pair of bison, market gunners often killed a hundred ducks and a score of bison. While the surpluses all wildlife produce allow a certain amount of utilization without endangering breeding stock, market men rapidly exhausted surpluses and began cutting into stocks as well. Possessing no code of the sportsman to regulate the amount of wildlife killed or the methods used, market men saw no motive in killing other than the economic one.

All wildlife, no matter how elusive under ordinary circumstances, is highly vulnerable when unsporting methods are employed. Wild turkeys, for example, were easily baited with corn and captured in log traps, and deer were driven to water with dogs, forced to swim, and then clubbed to death from the bow of a canoe. Less wary species like passenger pigeons and bison were killed by the *millions*. With their nets, "pigeoners" usually caught hundreds of birds at one time. Descending on breeding grounds that might cover forty-five square miles, commercial pigeon hunters slaughtered so many they filled freight cars with their stiff bodies. Once numbering in the hundreds of millions—some say billions—this magnificent species was already scarce in most areas by the 1880s, and the last of its race died in the Cincinnati Zoo on September 1, 1914.[54]

The dramatic decline of wildlife species like the passenger pigeon and buffalo piqued the conscience of Americans and shattered their previous faith in the inexhaustibility of resources as did no other issue, including forest destruction. As late as 1870, the bison still numbered anywhere from six million to well over thirty million, depending on which authority you accept. Yet, this symbol of Western expansion was utterly wiped out in thirteen years. With the close of 1883, the "thundering herds" were reduced to a pitiful remnant staggering on the edge of extinction.

The passenger pigeon and bison were merely the most famous examples of the devastation wrought by a capitalistic democracy that treated wildlife resources as mere articles of commerce, available to everyone for the taking. Less well known today, but just as alarming to conservationists of the late nineteenth century, was the destruction of nongame birds for mindless fashion. Already disturbed by the systematic exploitation of wildlife, particularly the buffalo and the wild pigeon, environmentalists discovered a new menace in the "taste" of American women.

Beginning in the late 1870s, the style of wearing hats stuffed with feathers, and even the birds themselves, became a craze. Countless American women, many of whom undoubtedly considered themselves animal lovers, saw no inconsistency in creating a demand that resulted in the slaughter of hundreds of thousands of birds. Even after the formation of the Audubon societies, it was not unusual for their female members to arrive at meetings wearing hats festooned with bird parts![55]

Because the plumage of egrets was most valuable in the breeding season, and because many bird species are concentrated at that time, nesting sites were invaded, the adult birds killed, and the young left to starve, fry in the sun, or be eaten by predators. Colony after colony was wiped out, and before many years passed, it began to look as if several species were headed for extinction. Yet with the price of some plumes higher than an equal weight of gold,[56] there was no stopping the slaughter. Like the "mountain man," hide hunter, "pigeoner," and commercial meat gunner, the man who shot for the millinery trade was no more responsible for the destruction than the society that spawned him. They were equally culpable, a fact often overlooked by environmental historians.

Despite the oft-repeated statement that sportsmen have only been interested in wildlife because they wanted a never-ending supply of

targets, it was the sportsman-naturalist who led the movement to preserve nongame species as well as those ordinarily pursued for sport.
Because the commercialization of any species was against the code
of the sportsman, it was only natural that his periodicals would be
full of editorial attacks on the slaughter of bison, passenger pigeons,
and nongame species like warblers, terns, and egrets.[57]

The real importance of sportsmen in ending the market hunting
of song, sea, and wading birds has been obscured by the failure of
historians to see that most of those they have labeled as "ornithologists," "scientists," or "nature lovers," could just as easily be categorized as "sportsmen." An example of this problem is the recent doctoral
dissertation by Theodore W. Cart that studies the events leading to
the passage in 1900 of the Lacey Act, which ended the market hunting
and interstate shipment of wildlife or wildlife products taken in violation of state law. Separating those who agitated in behalf of this legislation into "sportsmen," "scientific naturalists," "humanitarians," and
"nature-lovers," Cart neglects to mention that many, if not most, of
those in the "scientific naturalist" and "nature-lover" categories were
also sportsmen; indeed, many were "killers" of birds and mammals,
as well as fish. Nor does he make clear that John F. Lacey himself
was an avid hunter and fisherman who appealed to the code of the
sportsman in the Congressional speech advocating his bill.[58] Even with
his arbitrary categorization, Cart admits that sportsmen were the most
influential of his four groups in passing this landmark legislation.[59]

Although it may be difficult for some to accept, the great majority
of the "ornithologists" who crusaded against bird destruction for millinery were sportsmen before and after they attained "scientist" status.
Virtually all of those who founded the Nuttall Ornithological Club
in Cambridge, Massachusetts, in 1873 were self-avowed bird hunters,
as were those who created the American Ornithologists' Union in
1883.[60] In fact, the latter association grew out of the Nuttall Club,
though it was modeled on the British Ornithologists' Union.[61]

From John James Audubon to Frank Chapman, leading bird students made that critical first contact with the natural world through
the vehicle of the gun. And most never lost their love for the hunt.
The writings of Audubon, William Brewster, Elliott Coues, Robert
Ridgway, Edward H. Forbush, Daniel G. Elliot, Charles Cory, Chapman, and others contain numerous references to recreational hunting

as well as "scientific collecting." And Brewster and Coues were just two of the ornithologists who wrote extensively for sportsmen's journals.

Because the ornithologist's chief tool was the shotgun, he often used the same techniques and experienced the same feelings as the sportsman.[62] In fact, it is literally impossible much of the time to make a clear distinction between the ornithologist and the sportsman. A better term might be "sportsman-naturalist," because ornithologists' works are replete with hunting instructions and reminiscences; ornithologists often hunted for pleasure; the ornithologist's joy in "collecting" a rare specimen resembled in every way the pleasure experienced by the sportsman who bagged an unusual species of game bird for the first time; sportsmen themselves commonly kept "natural history cabinets" and collected for museums;[63] and the level of the "scientific" papers in the best-known sporting books and periodicals often equaled that of journals like *The American Naturalist* and *The Auk* for the simple reason that they were written by the same men.[64]

It was this "sportsman-naturalist" group that spearheaded the crusade to end destruction of song, sea, and wading birds for mindless fashion. The American Ornithologists' Union and League of American Sportsmen played major roles in formulating and passing the Lacey Act of 1900, which was the "beginning of the end" for the "feather trade."[65]

In the earliest years, however, the most influential element in the movement was the Audubon Society, founded by sportsman-naturalist George Bird Grinnell in 1886. While there had been one or two prior organizations named after the great bird painter, these had been established by sportsmen for the perpetuation and propagation of game species. Grinnell's association, on the other hand, was solely for the preservation of nongame species, a category of wildlife all but ignored up to that time. Once again, sportsmen-naturalists took the initiative in filling the void left by public indifference. Personal involvement with the natural world on a nonutilitarian basis and adoption of the aesthetic component in the code of the sportsman caused many sportsmen-naturalists to be almost as concerned with the destruction of nongame birds as with those traditionally pursued for sport.

Grinnell announced the formation of his new society in *Forest and Stream* on February 11, 1886. Entitled "The Audubon Society," this front-page editorial is an important document in the history of conservation and is here quoted in full:

> Very slowly the public are awakening to see that the fashion of wearing the feathers and skins of birds is abominable. There is, we think, no doubt that when the facts about this fashion are known, it will be frowned down and will cease to exist. Legislation of itself can do little against this barbarous practice, but if public sentiment can be aroused against it, it will die a speedy death.
>
> The *Forest and Stream* has been hammering away at this subject for some years, and the result of its blows is seen in the gradual change which has taken place in public sentiment since it began its work. The time has passed for showing that the fashion is an outrageous one, and that it results very disastrously to the largest and most important class of our population—the farmers. These are injured in two ways; by the destruction of the birds, whose food consists chiefly of insects injurious to the growing crops, and of that scarcely less important group the Rapaces[66] which prey upon the small rodents which devour the crop after it has matured.
>
> The reform in America, as elsewhere, must be inaugurated by women, and if the subject is properly called to their notice, their tender hearts will be quick to respond. In England this matter has been taken up and a widespread interest in it developed. If the women of America will take hold in the same earnest way, they can accomplish an incalculable amount of good.
>
> While individual effort may accomplish much, it will work but slowly, and the spread of the movement will be but gradual. Something more than this is needed. Men, women and children all over our land should take the matter in hand, and urge its importance upon those with whom they are brought in contact. A general effort of this kind will not fail to awaken public interest, and information given to a right-thinking public will set the ball of reform in motion. Our beautiful birds give to many people a great deal of pleasure and add much to the delights of the country. These birds are slaughtered in vast numbers for gain. If the demand for their skins can be caused to fall off, it will no longer repay the bird butchers to ply their trade and the birds will be saved.
>
> Statistics are as yet wanting to show the proportions to which this traffic has grown in North America, but we know that it reaches well into the hundreds of thousands. Some figures published in *Forest and Stream* of Aug. 4, 1884, showed that in a three months' trip

a single taxidermist collected bird skins to the number of 11,018, which, including specimens too badly mutilated for preservation, and skins spoiled in the making, would perhaps represent a destruction of 15,000 birds. This same person states that he handles annually about 30,000 bird skins, almost all of which are used for millinery purposes. A single middleman who collected the spoils of the shooters in one small district, brought to the taxidermist's in four months about 70,000 birds.

The birds of the fields, the birds of the woods, the birds of the marshes, and those of the sea, all suffer alike. It is needless to repeat the oft-told story of destruction. How can we best go to work to combat this great and growing evil, what means can we best employ to awaken at once popular feeling against it?

We desire to enlist in this work every one who is interested in our birds, and we urge all such to take hold and assist us.

In the first half of this century there lived a man who did more to teach Americans about birds of their own land than any other who ever lived. His beautiful and spirited paintings and his charming and tender accounts of the habits of his favorites have made him immortal, and have inspired his countrymen with an ardent love for the birds. The land which produced the painter naturalist, John James Audubon, will not willingly see the beautiful forms he loved so well exterminated.

We propose the formation of an association for the protection of wild birds and their eggs, which shall be called the Audubon Society. Its membership is to be free to every one who is willing to lend a helping hand in forwarding the objects for which it is formed. These objects shall be to prevent, so far as possible, (1) the killing of any wild birds not used for food, (2) the destruction of nests or eggs of any wild bird, and (3) the wearing of feathers as ornaments or trimming for dress.

To bring this matter properly before the public at large, we shall employ every means in our power to diffuse information on the subject over the whole country. Those who are willing to aid us in our labors are urged to establish local societies for work in their own neighborhood. To such branch societies we will send without charge circulars and printed information for distribution among their neighbors. A little effort in this direction will do much good. As soon as the association shall have a membership and shall be in position to organize and shall have attained an existence, we will hand the books and any funds which it may have, over to its members, who will thereafter take charge of it.

The work to be done by the Audubon Society is auxiliary to that undertaken by the Committee of the American Ornithologists' Union;[67] and will further the efforts of the A.O.U. committee, doing detail[ed] duties to which they cannot attend. Those who desire to join the Audubon Society, established on the basis and for the purpose above set forth, should send their names at once to the *Forest and Stream,* 40 Park Row, New York.[68]

The Audubon Society proved to be an instant success. Well-known Americans, most of whom were also sportsmen, immediately joined the organization and endorsed it in the pages of *Forest and Stream.*[69] In turn, they attracted a large number of followers—so many, in fact, that by the fall of 1888 the society had nearly 50,000 members.[70]

Paradoxically, the very success of the Audubon Society caused its demise. So many joined the new organization that Grinnell found all his time being consumed by its functions. Only by discontinuing it in 1889 could he maintain *Forest and Stream* at the high level he demanded.[71]

Despite the dissolution of Grinnell's organization, its efforts were hardly in vain. The movement it had set in motion continued to grow, and in 1896, sportsman-naturalist William Brewster founded the Massachusetts Audubon Society, the first permanent state association to model itself after Grinnell's original society.[72] Many other state groups came into existence, and after they joined together in 1905 to form the National Association of Audubon Societies, now the National Audubon Society, Grinnell became a director of the new body.[73] Interestingly enough, the men who did most to establish the first state associations, and the national organization as well, were all hunters of birds—just like their societies' namesake.[74]

The slaughter of birds to adorn ladies' hats was merely one more example of the havoc wrought by a capitalistic democracy that gave everyone the "right" to exploit commercially animate and inanimate natural resources without the slightest regard for the needs of future generations. By the 1890s, some sportsmen had decided it was time the nation accept a major component of their code by putting an end to the commercialization of game. Though long in the making, *Forest and Stream*'s announcement of this principle on February 3, 1894, represented the most revolutionary statement up to that time on the subject of wildlife conservation.

Written, evidently, by George Bird Grinnell and his managing editor, Charles B. Reynolds,[75] the front-page editorial called "A Plank" is a watershed in the history of conservation. Here, in its entirety, is what it said:

This is 1894. We have just been celebrating the four-hundredth anniversary of the coming to this continent of men equipped with firearms. For four centuries, from the time of Christopher Columbus to that of Charles Delmonico [presumably a reference to a member of the famous family of *restaurateurs*], we have been killing and marketing game, destroying it as rapidly and as thoroughly as we knew how, and making no provision toward replacing the supply. The result of such a course is that for the most part the game has been blotted out from wide areas, and to-day, after four hundred years of wanton wastefulness, we are just beginning to ask one another how we may preserve the little that remains, for ourselves and our children.

With all the discussion of the subject in the columns of the *Forest and Stream* from 1873 to 1894, there has been and is a general consensus of opinion that the markets are answerable for a larger proportion of game destruction than any other agency or all other agencies combined. The practical annihilation of one species of large game [the bison] from the continent, and the sweeping off of other species from vast regions formerly populated by them, have not been brought about by the settlement of the country, but by unrelenting pursuit for commercial purposes. The work of the sportsman, who hunts for the sake of hunting, has had an effect so trivial, that in comparison with that of the market hunter it need not be taken into consideration. The game paucity of to-day is due to the skin hunter, the meat killer, [and] the market shooter.

From the beginning wild game has played an important part in the development of the country. It has supplied subsistence when there was no other food for the pioneer and the settler. Buffalo and elk and deer and grouse and quail and wild goose and wild duck have sustained the men who first cut into the edge of the unbroken forests of the continent, who blazed the trails westward, and pushed their way, directed as mariners at sea by note of sun and stars, across the billowing prairies. Many a halt would have been made by these advancing hosts, had they been compelled to depend upon sutler trains, instead of foraging on the abundant game resources of the country as they took possession of it. For generations, then, it was right and proper, and wise and profitable that game should be killed for food; that every edible creature clothed in feathers or in fur should be regarded as so much meat to be spitted or potted or panned.

But times have changed. Conditions are not what they were. Game still affords food for the dweller in the wilderness, for those who live on the outskirts; and for people in such situations venison is a cheaper commodity than beef. But for the vast and overwhelming multitude of the people of the continent game is no longer in any sense an essential factor of the food supply. It has become a luxury, it is so regarded, and it is sold at prices which make it such. With the exception, perhaps, of rabbits or hares, the supply of wild game as marketed is not such as to reduce the cost of living to persons of moderate means. The day of wild game as an economic factor in the food supply of the country has gone by. In these four hundred years we have so reduced the game and so improved and developed the other resources of the country that we can now supply food with the plow and reaper and the cattle ranges cheaper than it can be furnished with the rifle and the shotgun. In short, as a civilized people we are no longer in any degree dependent for our sustenance upon the resources and the methods of primitive man. No plea of necessity, of economy, of value as food, demands the marketing of game. If every market stall were to be swept of its game to-day, there would be no appreciable effect upon the food supply of the country.

Well, then, why not recognize this, and direct our efforts, in line with such a recognition, toward the utter abolition of the sale of game? Why should we not adopt as a plank in the sportsman's platform a declaration to this end—*That the sale of game should be forbidden at all seasons?* To share and express the sentiment is one thing, to put it into execution is quite another. Perhaps the time is not ripe for such stringent measures. Yet this very rule of no game traffic holds in certain county laws in this State [New York]; and one of these days it will hold in every State, East and West, North and South. It may not be brought about in our day, but the present moment is none too soon to adopt the plank as a working principle and to work for it.

That which stands in the way of the present prohibition of the sale of game in the larger cities is the magnitude of the commercial interests involved. The traffic is one of large proportions, much capital is invested, and the business not one which would readily be sacrificed. No one of these considerations, however, can withstand a campaign of education and the creation of a public sentiment which will surely follow when that education shall have taught the community the true place of wild game in the economy of the civilization of the present.[76]

Because *Forest and Stream*'s "plank" struck at the American economic system itself, many thought it an impossible dream. Yet the paper continued to demand its acceptance, and outdoorsmen began rallying to its standard. With the passage of the Federal Migratory Bird Act and Treaty in the first quarter of this century—both of which were achieved largely through the efforts of sportsmen[77]—a custom as old as the country ceased to exist. No other single principle, before or since, has had as beneficial an effect on the continent's wildlife.

THREE

The Early Fight
for the Forests

W hile their first concern was wildlife, sportsmen quickly perceived that the effort in behalf of mammals, birds, and fish was a solution to only half the problem. It would do little good to preserve wildlife if its habitat continued to shrink, for eventually both would be gone. That part of the environment most immediately threatened was the forest.

Without power saws, bulldozers, or any other modern machinery, nineteenth-century Americans proved amazingly adept at timber destruction. Whole forests of live oak, white pine, redwood, and other species were cut down and burned over, and by the latter part of the century almost every wooded section of the country had experienced a logging boom. While these lumbering operations provided a boost to the local economy, the prosperity rarely lasted, and when the loggers moved out, they left in their wake a denuded landscape.

Paradoxically, a certain amount of deforestation improved wildlife habitat. Ruffed grouse, wild turkeys, and white-tailed deer are among the many species that profit by selective cutting which opens up clearings in deep woods. In fact, the abundance of these species in wilderness inhabited "only" by aborigines proves that the American Indian had already made his mark on the land long before the white man arrived. With the use of stone implements and fire, aborigines had altered the ecology of vast regions, and unwittingly enhanced the habitats of numerous animals, birds, and fish. When the white invaders began pushing west from the Atlantic, they duplicated, and extended, the Indian's earlier alterations of the land, harming some species but benefiting many others.

While in its initial stages lumbering may have helped some wildlife, widespread systematic logging operations, combined with the huge conflagrations that frequently followed them, ultimately did far more harm than good to the ecosystems involved. Soil damage and erosion, elimination of watersheds and wildlife cover, and siltation and flooding were only some of the adverse effects produced by the cut-and-run mentality of a nation that often looked upon trees as little more than overgrown weeds and bragged about how many farms its citizens had worn out in their lifetimes. To many Americans of the nineteenth century, uncut woodlands were an offense to their "Manifest Destiny," for this was a society whose self-image was defined in terms of physical change and material success. Consequently, some of its leading folk heroes were "skinners" of natural resources—real men like Buffalo Bill Cody or mythological ones like the giant lumberjacks who figured in humorous tall tales until, after the turn of the century, they were synthesized into the single mighty character of Paul Bunyan.

Sportsmen, however, manifested a different orientation. Possessing an Old World code, they saw forests not as a challenge to the American mission of progress, but as one of the essential settings for that important activity called sport. Free from the prejudices of the frontiersman, farmer, and logger, sportsmen viewed trees as something more than a hiding place for Indians, an obstacle to ploughing, or a source of financial gain. Woodlands were both the home of their quarry and the aesthetic backdrop for that avocation which many considered more rewarding—in a noneconomic sense—than their vocation. Regrettably, few historians have understood that an individual's recreation often tells us as much about him as his occupation.

The importance placed on woodlands by those who were, or had been, hunters or fishermen is revealed in their efforts to draw attention to forest destruction. Once again, this group led the way with protests that began long before the Civil War. In one way or another, the following called for timber preservation in the antebellum period:

James Fenimore Cooper, Washington Irving, DeWitt Clinton, John Quincy Adams, John James Audubon, William Elliott, Frank Forester, Elisha Lewis, William Cullen Bryant, Horace Greeley, Henry David Thoreau, Charles Lanman, and Samuel H. Hammond.[1] While Cooper, Adams, and Bryant seem to have engaged in gunning or angling only in youth, the rest pursued these recreations in adulthood as well; in fact, most of this latter group were enthusiastic sportsmen.[2]

After the Civil War, organized efforts in behalf of forest preservation and propagation increased, though not at the same rate as those in regard to wildlife. There was no national "timber movement" comparable to the crusade for fish culture, sportsmen's clubs–wildlife preserves, and better game laws. Nor were there any national periodicals devoted wholly, or in part, to forest conservation like those dealing with wildlife. One significant indication of the earlier public interest in wildlife is the fact that the states and the federal government established fish commissions before forest commissions.

The interest in woodlands did grow in the post-bellum period, however, with much of the activity centered in the federal government. The Timber Culture Act of 1873 represented one approach, though it can hardly be called a conservation measure. Based on the dubious notion that the planting of trees on the Great Plains would reduce the aridity of the region, the purpose of this legislation was to expand settlement by increasing rainfall.[3] The supposed climatic benefits obtained from tree planting also played a part in the 1872 suggestion of Nebraskan J. Sterling Morton to dedicate April 10 of every year as "Arbor Day."[4] Like the Timber Culture Act, Arbor Day was little more than a gesture that had only a vague relationship to forest conservation.

Fortunately, the Timber Culture Act was not the only federal activity relating to forests in the 1870s. More worthwhile was the 1876 Congressional appropriation of $2,000 to the Commissioner of Agriculture for the employment of an agent to investigate the rate of consumption of forests and the best methods for renewal.[5] Franklin B. Hough received the assignment on August 30, 1876, and according to one scholar, "thus began the first action by the federal government toward a forest policy."[6] Hough had become aware of forest destruction as superintendent of the 1870 United States census, and it was he who alerted the American Association for the Advancement of

Science, who in turn submitted the petition to Congress that resulted in the 1876 appropriation and Hough's appointment.

After he received his assignment, Hough traveled widely in the United States and Europe studying forests and forestry. As a result of these investigations, he published a number of official reports that helped lead to the establishment in 1881 of the Division of Forestry of the United States Department of Agriculture.[7] Yet, apart from the work of Bernhard Fernow, who became its Chief in 1886, this understaffed and underfinanced bureau accomplished little until the end of the century. Despite the bureau's lack of early achievements—in contrast to the tremendous environmental efforts of sportsmen, and the establishment of an active United States Fish Commission ten years before the Division of Forestry—the *Concise Dictionary of American Biography* states matter-of-factly that Hough's "activities paved the way for the successful conservation movement of later years."[8] Thus, we have yet another example of the omnipresent, but erroneous, twin assumptions that no conservation movement existed until the turn of the century and that concern for the forests initiated that movement.

Although the national government was establishing a poor record in regard to forest conservation, a few federal officeholders did attempt to arouse the public on this issue. Carl Schurz, who was something of a gunner in his youth,[9] was one of these men. In his position as Secretary of the Interior during the years 1877 to 1881, he advocated the adoption of a wide-ranging program of forest conservation, including the creation of forest reserves, a federal forest service, and a national forestry commission. Like the other German-born pioneers of American forestry, Bernhard E. Fernow and Carl A. Schenck, Schurz hoped to introduce into the United States what was essentially an Old World patrician concept of state responsibility for resource stewardship. In a country that made a fetish of freedom, it was inevitable that Schurz's ideas would be attacked as aristocratic and un-American.[10]

Other federal officeholders who expressed a concern for the forests were Presidents Arthur, Cleveland, and Harrison, all of whom were eminent sportsmen. Arthur was reputedly one of the finest fly-casters and salmon anglers America has ever produced; Cleveland loved freshwater fishing and bird shooting equally, and his classic *Fishing and Shooting Sketches* (1906) reveals much about a man who believed that the sporting life bestowed physical, mental, and spiritual benefits upon its followers; and Harrison had a penchant for duck hunting that knew no bounds, particularly when the canvasbacks and redheads were flying. As leading members of the "fraternity" possessing the British-derived code of the sportsman, all three of these Presidents shared to a degree Carl Schurz's Old World perspective on natural resources. Undoubtedly, the responsibility for the *total* natural environment inherent in the sportsman's code played a part in their official statements calling for forest protection.

While a number of federal officeholders cited the need for timber preservation in the 1880s, easily the most important pioneer in this area was Bernhard E. Fernow, who became Chief of the Division of Forestry of the Department of Agriculture in 1886. Despite Gifford Pinchot's efforts to bury his predecessor by ignoring him, Fernow's achievements as head of the Division were substantial, and they were obtained despite a woeful lack of financial support. He helped to keep the subject of forestry alive, and according to historian Sherry H. Olson, his approach was, in many ways, superior to his successor's; Fernow, for example, stressed the need for research in wood technology, while Pinchot's primary concern was simply to obtain ever-increasing timber production.[11]

In sum, Bernhard Fernow has been underrated by those who have accepted Gifford Pinchot's later claim that little of note occurred in conservation before *he* arrived on the scene. Fernow was the preeminent leader of the incipient forestry movement of the 1880s, and his conception of the state, which has been described by one environmental historian "as the highest expression of the social organism and the promotion of academics and professionals in government service," would later be adopted by the Roosevelt-Pinchot conservation team. As that scholar correctly observes, Fernow's belief in federal responsibility for resource husbandry was one of the vehicles by which "the conservation movement merged with the evolving doctrine of the welfare state."[12] It is important to note that Fernow, Roosevelt, and Pinchot were all distinctly upper-class in background, for despite the use of democratic rhetoric and the need to make frequent political compromises, the conservation program of the Roosevelt administration would manifest a patrician, *noblesse oblige* conception of the need, and the right, to manage the people's natural resources for their own good, whether or not they desired such stewardship.[13]

Besides his similar vision of the state's purpose, Fernow had something else in common with Roosevelt and Pinchot, for he, too, was very much a sportsman. In his native Germany, professional foresters often pursued hunting and forestry simultaneously, and Fernow was no exception.[14] Like another German-born forester, Carl A. Schenck, Fernow would bring his penchant for sport with him to the United States.[15]

Both men found out that forestry and hunting were also compatible in America. As we have seen, Fernow first practiced forestry in the United States on the game preserve of well-to-do sportsmen. Schenck's experience was somewhat similar. On Gifford Pinchot's recommendation, he was appointed in 1895 as forester of George W. Vanderbilt's 120,000 acre Biltmore estate in North Carolina, but on arriving in America to consult with Pinchot, Schenck found that avid sportsman more interested in talking about hunting and fishing than forestry.[16] Later, hunting excursions on the estate helped cement their friendship.[17]

Like Great Britain, Germany had a long sporting tradition, at least among the aristocracy. One may surmise that the responsibility for the natural environment inherent in the British sportsman's code—which had already influenced American sportsmen like Gifford Pinchot—had its counterpart in the German tradition. If so, it would help to explain the origins of the commitment to conservation that Fernow and Schenck brought with them to the United States and helped to establish here.

Thus far, we have concentrated mainly on the genesis of the federal government's work in forest preservation and management, but the greatest amount of activity in this area during the earliest years was performed by private citizens. One of these individuals was William Henry Brewer, professor of agriculture at Yale's Sheffield Scientific School from 1864 to 1903. In former years he had assisted Josiah Dwight Whitney in his geological survey of California and combined deer hunting with geology on a number of occasions.[18] One reason Brewer is considered to be an outstanding pioneer of forest conservation is because in 1873 he began offering at Yale what were probably the first lectures on forestry ever given at any American university.

In addition, he was on the committee of the American Association for the Advancement of Science that petitioned Congress in 1874 to recognize the importance of forest preservation and cultivation. As noted previously, Franklin B. Hough was appointed in 1876 to investigate that subject.

Of all the private groups interested in timber preservation in the 1870s, none were more active than sportsmen. It has already been shown that even before the Civil War began, a number of outdoorsmen had attacked forest destruction. In the post-bellum period these scattered protests became an organized agitation, not as widely popular as the crusade for wildlife, but powerful nonetheless.

As in the case of wildlife depletion, the appearance in the early '70s of the first national sporting periodicals, *American Sportsman, Forest and Stream,* and *Field and Stream,* helped focus sportsmen's anger over woodland eradication and unite them against it.[19] While Brewer was offering his lectures at Yale, these journals were giving their own lectures, and to a far greater audience. When *American Angler* appeared in the next decade, another voice for forest preservation was added to the sporting press. Like the other journals, *American Angler* endeavored to keep its readers informed of the most up-to-date information on "natural history," and that included the disastrous effects of unregulated logging and pulp-mill production on rivers and their inhabitants. In addition to the attacks on water pollution already cited (Chapter 2), the paper also explained in detail how uncontrolled lumbering ruined fishing waters by causing such habitat changes as bank erosion and higher water temperatures.[20] Like the other periodicals, *American Angler* illustrated a remarkable understanding of ecological principles.

Of the four major papers, *American Sportsman* and *Forest and Stream* proved to be most concerned with forest preservation. Founded in 1871, the former journal repeatedly lamented the extent and ramifications of woodland destruction, and as a solution to the problem, it suggested that European forestry techniques be adapted to American timberlands.[21]

When *Forest and Stream* was founded in 1873, it quickly proved that it was even more dedicated to forest conservation than its predecessor. Editor Charles Hallock stated every week in *Forest and Stream*'s subtitle that his paper was "Devoted to . . . Preservation

of Forests," and he lived up to that claim by frequently calling attention to the depletion of timberlands and the need for their protection.[22]
Hallock's interest in this issue may have been spawned, in part at
least, by George Bird Grinnell. Although Grinnell did not join the
paper's staff until 1876, he was associated closely with it from the
beginning as a writer, financial supporter, and natural-history adviser.
Since his graduation from Yale in 1870, he had also kept in touch
with scientific developments through his close association with Othniel
C. Marsh, a sportsman and paleontologist who was then one of the
university's most prominent faculty members. Grinnell assisted Marsh
on his 1870 fossil-collecting expedition to the Far West, entered Yale's
Sheffield Scientific School in early 1874, and received a Ph.D. under
Marsh in 1880.[23] Undoubtedly, Grinnell knew of William Brewer's
forestry lectures at Sheffield, then a tiny institution, and it seems prob-
able that he would have advised Hallock of their significance.

As we have seen, Grinnell first concentrated on defining "sportsmanship" and preserving wildlife after becoming *Forest and Stream*'s editor and owner. It did not take long, however, for him to understand
that more was also needed on the subject of forest conservation. In
April, 1882, therefore, he began his editorial drive to transform the
nation's orientation toward its woodlands. Years earlier, Hallock had
pointed the way by drawing attention to how rapidly the timberlands
were being depleted and by suggesting Europe's system of managed
forests as an alternative to the wasteful methods of American lumbering. But Grinnell went far beyond his predecessor in publicizing the
European science of forestry.

In "Spare the Trees," the opening editorial of his campaign in
behalf of the forests, he manifested awareness of the interrelationship
of all natural resources. "If we have the most perfect code of game
and fish laws which it is possible to devise," he wrote, "and have
them ever so thoroughly enforced, what will they avail if there is no
cover for game nor water for fish?"[24] Employing the ideology of the
business-farm community, he called for Americans to use their
"proverbial thriftiness and forecast" to achieve "the proper and sensi-
ble management of woodlands." The forests must be seen as a
"crop . . . which is slow in coming to the harvest, but it is a sure
one, and is every year becoming a more paying one."[25] In addition,
"it breaks the fierceness of the winds, and keeps the springs from dry-

ing up, and is a comfort to the eye. . . . Under its protecting arms
live and breed the grouse, the quail and the hare, and in its shadowed
riles swim the trout. . . ." Although the lesson was a simple one,
it had not yet been learned by the American people: "No woods,
no game; no woods, no water; and no water, no fish."[26]

In perceiving the subtle interconnection of all life, Grinnell foreshadowed the science of ecology. By his use of terms like "harvest,"
"crop," and "management," he articulated the gospel of the efficient
administration of natural resources, an ideology taken from the scientific and business communities which would eventually become the
core of the national conservation movement. As so often would be
the case, Grinnell manifested a knack for advancing new ideas that,
in time, would become the dominant ideology. Because of his belief
in the environmental responsibilities inherent in the code of the sportsman and his incomparable training in paleontology, with its obvious
lessons in the vulnerability of animal and plant species, it is not surprising that he was in the forefront of the American minority that was
knowledgeable about the growing crisis in natural resources. And that
awareness was enhanced, poignantly, in the period 1870–83 by seeing firsthand the destruction of the "Great West," a land originally
typified by huge bison herds and free-ranging Indians. All of these
formative influences dovetailed when Grinnell became editor of the
leading outdoor journal of the time. From that position, he received
new information, as well as feedback, from all sources concerned with
the natural world, putting him at the nucleus of the intellectual evolution of conservation.

Ever since the early days of *Forest and Stream,* the weekly's editors
had been interested in the possible applicability to American conditions
of European developments in sport, natural history, and science. Particularly significant in this regard was the Europeans' attitude toward
their woodlands. In an 1883 editorial, "Forestry," Grinnell reported:
"In parts of Europe forestry is a science, and officers are appointed
by the governments to supervise the forests; and only judicious
thinning of young trees and cutting of those which [have] attained
their growth is allowed. . . ."[27]

He pointed out that the system was used not only on government
lands but on private holdings as well, "the theory being that the individual will pass away, but the forest must remain forever."[28] He con-

trasted the Continental emphasis on continuous resource management with the situation existing in America, where the sovereignty of private ownership allowed an individual to "buy a tract of land in the great water producing region of the State and for his own pecuniary benefit render it forever sterile."[29] Grinnell suggested that laws regulating forest use, like those already existing in Europe, should be immediately passed in the United States. As in the case of game legislation, he believed that statutes protecting the forests would have democratic results and "work well for the people at large."[30]

In 1884 *Forest and Stream* stepped up its campaign to educate the American people in the principles and methods of forestry. Grinnell argued on pragmatic rather than aesthetic grounds that European practices be tried in the United States. Relying on figures supplied by the Canadian statistician James Little and the Harvard dendrologist Charles Sprague Sargent, Grinnell claimed that the "awfully wasteful modern methods of lumbering" cost the nation one billion dollars annually.[31] He noted that in the process of felling and transporting one mature tree, an average of fifty saplings were killed. In addition, dead brush was always left behind, resulting in a serious fire hazard.[32]

Unlike the pure preservationist, who wanted forest tracts set aside that would remain undisturbed, Grinnell realized that this essentially negative approach was only a "holding action." Other possible approaches included substituting for wood when possible, using "economy in cutting and marketing," and protecting from fire and livestock grazing. He knew that all these suggestions had their place, "but after all, the great dependence must be upon reproduction. . . ." To have a healthy, productive forest, it had to be cared for by thinning mature and dead trees. To leave the timber untouched was "wasteful," an adjective used repeatedly in *Forest and Stream*.[33]

In March Grinnell used the recent floods of the Ohio and Mississippi Rivers as illustrations of "the terrible effects of our criminal waste of woodlands."[34] He asked for massive reforestation along the rivers' banks and the creation of state and federal forestry commissions.[35] Later that spring, he went further and demanded that the national government immediately appoint "A Competent Forestry Officer," a "trained professional" to lead in "the inauguration of a system of forest conservancy."[36] Because there were no American forestry schools, only foreigners had the requisite training. As one qualified for the job, Grinnell suggested Charles F. Amery, an alien residing in America, who had over fourteen years of experience in the forest bureaus of Germany and elsewhere.

Grinnell noted that despite the increasing awareness of the "necessity of doing something for the maintenance of a permanent timber supply, action is paralyzed by the difficulty of deciding how best to set about it." Although the federal government had created a Division of Forestry several years before, the bureau remained tiny and inactive. Grinnell believed that "the appointment of such a man as Amery on the staff of the forestry department would be regarded as [proof] . . . that the Government had at length come to . . . face the problem squarely." The fact that Amery was an alien was an advantage in a sense, for it guaranteed an apolitical perspective.[37]

Although Grinnell's recommendations were not adopted, the editorial reveals that he now perceived that the natural resources of the nation must be *administered* on a continuous and efficient basis, and that the removal of all political considerations was a necessary prerequisite for achieving this goal. In time, this view would become the cornerstone of the conservationist faith.

In the five-part series, "Forests and Forestry" (1884–85), Grinnell consistently used almost the entire front page of his weekly to explain the fundamentals of the European science. He argued that forestry's concepts were applicable to every country. While American trees and soils were not exactly like those in Germany and France, the Continent's expert foresters were "capable of adapting general principles to changed conditions."[38] And "pending the theoretical and practical training of young Americans," these foreign professionals should staff the forestry bureau.[39] Under their direction, it could become an animated, functioning department.

If the administration of a "systematic conservancy" was established, it would not only protect water supplies but also produce a perpetual, annual supply of four-billion board feet of lumber. According to Professor Sargent, this was the "capacity" of the American forests.[40] In other words, if the government were to "husband" its "timber stock" intelligently, the woodlands of the nation would be perpetuated while, at the same time, producing wealth.

Although Grinnell's sophisticated understanding of forestry came mostly from European sources, some Americans also contributed. One, as we have seen, was Charles Sprague Sargent, whose statistical estimates Grinnell used. More important was George Perkins Marsh, whose *Man and Nature: or, Physical Geography as Modified by Human Action* (1864) influenced all subsequent thinking on natural resources. He was the first to go beyond the Romantics and argue that forests should be preserved, not because they were aesthetically pleasing, but because they were necessary for human survival.[41] This basic fact seemed so obvious to Marsh that he found it incredible that "man has . . . forgotten that the earth was given to him for usufruct alone, not for consumption, still less for profligate waste."[42]

Applying his ideas to the great wilderness north of New York City, the Adirondacks, he argued that the water-holding properties of these woodlands made it imperative that they be retained in a wild state. The spongelike quality of the forest floor slowed and regulated the release of moisture, guaranteeing the continuous flow of water to the south.[43]

From the first numbers of *Forest and Stream,* Hallock had publicized Marsh's conclusions, including his thesis that the decline of Spain and other countries was in part caused by their thoughtless destruction of forests.[44] Hallock's desire to have the Adirondacks preserved probably grew out of the sportsman's code and the Romantic tradition, but as historian Roderick Nash has pointed out, he employed the watershed argument because it was the most likely to succeed.[45]

After Grinnell became *Forest and Stream*'s editor, he continued fighting for the Adirondacks on the basis of the Marsh-Hallock watershed defense. The area had to be set aside because it protected the sources of the Hudson River and other water supplies upon which New York City depended. If uncontrolled lumbering of the region continued, these supplies would wither away, and the future of the state would be imperiled. This is what Grinnell meant when, in "Save the Adirondacks," he declared: "The reasons why the forests should be preserved are not sentimental, but very practical."[46] From late 1883 on, he kept up a steady barrage of editorials on the subject, directed mainly at businessmen.

As with all later issues relating to natural resources, the dialogue on the future of the Adirondacks suffered from the abysmal ignorance of legislators. In March, 1884, a bill to preserve the region was being debated in the New York Assembly, and a number of members were in vehement opposition. One announced that the watershed argument was absurd, since the Hudson was an arm of the sea and did not depend on drainage from the Adirondacks. Instead of trying to ensure the continued flow of water into the river, he thought that all its tributaries should be blocked off to eliminate the expense of dredging the channel![47]

Grinnell did not despair, however, for there were a few in the Assembly who took an intelligent position on the issue and stuck to it. One of these was the young Theodore Roosevelt. Although the two men had already met, they still knew each other mainly by reputation: Roosevelt, the dynamic legislator, and Grinnell, the editor of the leading journal on hunting and natural history, two of Roosevelt's favorite subjects. Referring to the assemblyman who wanted to dam the Hudson's feeder streams, Grinnell wrote: "In agreeable contrast to the utterances above quoted are those of Mr. Roosevelt and a few other gentlemen, who in all matters pertaining to the public good, take liberal and advanced views. It is satisfying to see, now and then, in our legislative halls a man whom neither money, nor influence, nor politics can induce to turn from what he believes to be right, to what he knows to be wrong."[48] Never known for his self-effacement, Roosevelt undoubtedly appreciated this public tribute. More importantly, the reference reveals that his interest in the future of natural resources existed earlier than indicated by historians.

When Grinnell editorialized in behalf of the Adirondacks, he at first simply repeated the Marsh-Hallock watershed argument. Soon, however, he thought of using the wilderness as a testing ground for the theories of European forestry.[49] On January 17, 1884, he urged: "Protection and conservation, now, prompt, adequate—this is what the Adirondack forests demand, not restoration years hence, after the damage from unregulated lumbering shall have been wrought and ruin has followed."[50] This was the first time Grinnell used the expression "conservation," which, it should be remembered, did not become the catchword for dialogue on natural resources until more than twenty years later. Yet, the term's juxtaposition in the editorial, and his other, concurrent writings on forestry, make it clear that he was already employing the word in its modern sense: as the wise *use* of resources so as to make them last indefinitely.[51]

In the above passage, the "protection" of the Adirondacks would be accomplished when they were set aside and the fire hazard controlled. This was the static aspect of Grinnell's plan for the region. "Conservation" was the dynamic part, the *process*; it would only be achieved when the woodlands were systematically managed on a continuous basis.

The watershed argument, although valid, did not go far enough. The problem was that most of its supporters, including New York City business groups, felt that if the Adirondack "preserve" were established, it should be kept in a wild state. After all, they reasoned, was it not the lumbering of the forests that threatened the watershed's usefulness? Grinnell, however, thought it impractical to attempt to keep an area the size of Connecticut in a permanently inviolate condition; in time, pressure to utilize it economically would become too great to resist. Why not, therefore, have the future of the Adirondacks shaped realistically from the beginning by illustrating that protection of the drainage area and exploitation of its timber were not incompatible? Grinnell probably reasoned that since the watershed defense was favorably received by the state's businessmen, they would be doubly impressed when shown they could "have their cake and eat it too." Increasingly, this was the appeal he used to justify the creation of an Adirondack reserve.

Addressing himself to those who wanted to keep the territory undisturbed, Grinnell wrote: "It is now generally well understood that forests are not to be maintained in good order by excluding the axe, but that the great economic aim of forest administration is to raise the productive yield of the forests to the highest capacity of the soil."[52] Put another way, the woodland as a whole would be improved by harvesting dead and mature trees. Grinnell was so determined that the Adirondacks be used as a proving ground for forestry that he editorialized *against* setting aside a larger portion of the region than could be efficiently administered.[53]

With the New York Chamber of Commerce and other business organizations now demanding its passage,[54] Governor David B. Hill, on May 15, 1885, signed a bill establishing a 715,000-acre Forest Preserve.[55] Having first been told that lumbering of the Adirondack drainage area endangered their economic future, the businessmen of the state found it difficult to readjust their thinking to Grinnell's later argument that the region's forests should be harvested. Instead, their continued support of the proposed reservation had been based on the understanding that it would be kept inviolate. This attitude prevailed, and the act creating the preserve stipulated that it would remain forever "as wild forest lands."[56]

Grinnell was pleased that the area would now be protected from wasteful lumbering, but because it had been put in a kind of quarantine, with no provision for forestry, he remained unsatisfied. In later years, Gifford Pinchot would express the same unhappiness over the status of the Adirondack forests, and for the same reason.[57] Ironically, *Forest and Stream* shared much of the responsibility for instilling in the public a suspicion of all those who used an axe. Grinnell would have an uphill fight convincing New Yorkers that with forestry, the timber could be cut, the watershed protected, and the woods, as a whole, made healthier.

The distrust of the lumber companies, of course, was warranted. After interest in setting aside the Adirondacks had become widespread, the loggers in the region had worked at an ever-faster pace to fell its timber, "their object being to get as much on the ground as possible before any law interfering with them shall be passed."[58] Having no understanding of forestry, their only "policy" was the making of short-term profit.

Even after the preserve had been established, the companies continued to lumber indiscriminately within its borders. In June, 1885, Grinnell attacked them by demanding: "Who are the forest skinners?" The answer, he said, was obvious: "They are capitalists who are taking away for a mess of pottage the birthright of the people." And "Who is responsible for the people's loss? First, the people themselves; and second, the men sent by the people to Albany to take care of the people's interest." In Grinnell's view, their indifference put both groups at fault.[59]

His application of the "skinner" image was apt, for the lumberman who stripped the forest cover from the land and the market gunner who flayed the hides from big game were from the same mold. Both were creations of rapid industrialization, and both regarded the natural world only as a source of quick profit. Incidentally, it should be noted that Theodore Roosevelt, many years later, would also use the "skinner" image, and in exactly the same way.[60]

It was characteristic of Grinnell to see the use—or misuse—of resources as part of a common pattern. If the ideology and organization of American business was so effective that the forests and big game of vast regions could be exploited into oblivion within a few years, then the only way to stop the depletion of natural resources was to adopt that same ideology and organization.

When, for example, he demanded that the nation adopt a systematic approach to its timberlands based on the principles of forestry, he sometimes employed the analogy of the corporation.[61] The federal government would act as the manager of the corporation, administering the forests for the benefit of its stockholders, the American people. Each year, it would be calculated how much of the woodland could be cut without infringing on the "capital." The resulting income would be a continuous source of revenue. As will be shown, his solution to the problem of diminishing game was similar. Only the "interest" of each animal population would be spent by hunters, leaving sufficient breeding "stock" to produce the next generation. Here again, perpetual revenue would be produced, directly, through taxes on licenses, guns, and ammunition, and indirectly, through increased incomes for local businessmen servicing visiting sportsmen.

As we have seen, Grinnell played a central role in alerting Americans to the need for stewardship of timberlands. But it should be stressed that while his editorial drive probably represents the earliest, extended campaign of any national newspaper in behalf of forest preservation *and* conservation, that effort was based on many earlier precedents. In regard to the specific issue of New York's Adirondack watershed, sportsmen had long been calling for the region's protection. Although angler DeWitt Clinton made a general recommendation for the preservation of Adirondack forests as early as 1822,[62] the first specific proposal seems to have been presented by another sportsman, Samuel H. Hammond. In 1857 he suggested that the nation "mark out a circle [in the Adirondacks] of a hundred miles in diameter, and throw around it the protecting aegis of the constitution." A prophet of the "wilderness idea," Hammond requested that this preserve be kept free of logging and settlement, "a forest forever" in which "the old woods should stand . . . always as God made them."[63]

Two years after Hammond made his recommendation, a sportsmen's organization, the Northwoods [Izaak] Walton Club, requested legislation that would protect "our Northern Wilderness." If such a law were passed, the nation would possess a "vast and noble preserve" where game could thrive and where "no screeching locomotive [would] ever startle . . . Fauns and Water Sprites."[64]

To the members of this club, and to many other outdoorsmen as well, the Old World concept of the game preserve or park for noble sportsmen seemed like an idea worthy of emulation in the New World.[65] Across the Atlantic, huge tracts had been set aside for centuries to provide aristocratic disciples of the chase with a hunting ground untouched by civilization. Deliberately kept in a wild state to ensure game propagation and protected from poachers through the vigilance of gamekeepers, these preserves might have been an injustice to "the people," but they protected forests and wildlife that would have been quickly exhausted by a society possessing the freedoms of the United States.

This is not to say that the Old World precedent was copied exactly. The fundamental differences—a better word might be antagonisms—between aristocracy and democracy forbade it. The closest representation was the private sportsmen's association possessing its own preserve or park. Made up of wealthy outdoorsmen, these organizations often maintained comfortable clubhouses and large protected tracts where their members could enjoy hunting and fishing without concern for "No Trespassing" signs, "improvements," and other hindrances to sport. Blooming Grove Park and the Bisby Club, already discussed, are merely two of the best-known examples of this kind of association.

But even in the case of this latter group, the sportsmen's organizations were more New World than Old World in character. Though often upper-class in membership, the clubs reflected American political and economic customs. Officers were usually selected by majority rule, and while some associations required merely an initiation fee and yearly dues, others operated like joint-stock companies.[66] Thus, an aristocratic, precapitalistic precedent was altered to fit a democratic, capitalistic culture.

Another example of the desire to adapt the game-preserve idea to American conditions was the 1858 recommendation of Henry David Thoreau. Discussing Maine's northern wilderness in an article in *Atlantic Monthly*, he referred to the European tradition of setting aside hunting preserves for nobility and asked: "Why should not we . . . have our national preserves . . . in which the bear and panther, and some even of the hunter race [aborigines], may still exist, and not be 'civilized off the face of the earth'—[and] our forests [saved] . . . not for idle sport or food, but for inspiration and our own true recreation?"[67]

Obviously, Thoreau had a different object in mind than the members of the Bisby Club or Blooming Grove Park. Though an experienced angler,[68] a hunter in his younger days,[69] and an admirer of the aesthetic aspects of hunting and fishing,[70] he never considered himself a member of the sporting fraternity and occasionally even expressed hostility toward that group.[71] The Romantic movement, rather than the sporting tradition, inspired his aim of adapting the Old World precedent of the game preserve to the United States.

Fortunately for the history of the Adirondacks, sportsmen did more than engage in Romantic fantasies of sanctuaries where the Indian and his game would remain forever in a primitive state of suspended animation. As in the case of other wild regions—like Florida's Everglades, Montana's northern Rockies, and Alaska's coast and Mount McKinley area[72]—sportsmen had been among the first to explore, map, and study the Adirondacks.[73] While not nearly as pristine as the other regions mentioned, New York's northern mountains still qualified as *bona-fide* wilderness, and sportsmen had been establishing preserves there since at least the 1850s.[74] By the '70s, these sanctuaries dotted the wilderness, and the sportsmen who maintained them led the movement to create a huge public preserve occupying much or most of the Adirondacks. Only in that way could the borders of their own reserves be protected from the encroachments of loggers, sawmill operators, and others bent on exploiting the forests for short-term gain.

From the early '70s on, sportsmen's newspapers called for the creation of a vast Adirondack reservation.[75] In other words, almost a decade of agitation preceded Grinnell's editorial campaign for forest conservation. While lacking the national appeal of the movement for wildlife, particularly fish culture, the efforts in behalf of the Adirondacks had been publicized enough to make the sporting fraternity receptive to the arguments presented by *Forest and Stream*.

As it turned out, however, most outdoorsmen accepted only half of Grinnell's proposal, rejecting his plan for scientific forestry. Historian Eugene J. O'Neill is correct in arguing that the drive to set aside an Adirondack forest preserve and the repeated rejections of recommendations for the introduction of forestry after the reservation was established were mainly based on aesthetic and recreational considerations rather than the desire for efficiency in the utilization of resources. Even the New York City civic and business groups that joined—but did not initiate—the crusade wanted the region forever barred to economic development. As O'Neill observes, Samuel Hays's widely accepted thesis on the origins of conservation proves erroneous when applied to this seminal issue in environmental history.[76]

Yet, one may argue that Hays's thesis does apply, at least in part, because the aim of the 1885 law setting aside the reservation "was the preservation of wilderness, but for commercial ends."[77] Those holding this view can claim that the main reason for the victory of wilderness advocates was the utilitarian desire to protect New York City's economic life by maintaining the source of its water supply. It should be stressed, however, that sportsmen, and not downstate business interests, began the crusade, and they remained a key element in the campaign—even after the businessmen joined. As in the case of other early conservation issues, concern for wildlife preceded concern for forests. Sportsmen wanted the preservation of their game and sporting grounds for aesthetic and recreational reasons, but they knew that the best way to accomplish their purpose was to couch it in utilitarian terms. Charles Hallock and George Bird Grinnell, for example, were *primarily* interested in protecting game and habitat for the enjoyment of future generations of sportsmen. Yet they admitted that in a society like the United States another, more "practical" argument must be used. As Hallock observed in "The Adirondack Park," an editorial appearing in September, 1873, "Our hope is that the whole subject [of an Adirondack reservation] will be placed before them [the members of the state legislature] in a practical way. We do not urge here the tourist or hunting question. As much as the *Forest and Stream* advocates the preservation of game, we would give it a secondary place, though the preservation of the woods is the life of the game." And elsewhere in the article, Hallock argues that the only way to ensure the legislators' interest "is to have them look at the preservation of the Adirondacks as a question of self-interest."[78] It was an accurate appraisal of the utilitarian instincts of most of his countrymen, and sportsmen-conservationists from George Bird Grinnell to Theodore Roosevelt would employ the same "practical" approach, regardless of their deeper motives.[79]

While most historians of conservation grant sportsmen a place in the crusade to save the Adirondacks, the latter group's true importance has been obscured not only by the tendency to take outdoorsmen's public statements at face value but also by scholars' failure to identify leaders of the drive as sportsmen. In his work on the early history of conservation in New York State, Marvin W. Kranz, for example, cites name after name of those who pioneered Adirondack preservation without seeming to be aware that many of these individuals were sportsmen before they were conservationists. Included in this group are Verplanck Colvin, Charles E. Whitehead, Abram Hewitt, and Grover Cleveland. Even Bernhard E. Fernow, who helped draft the 1885 law establishing the Forest Preserve; James Husted, who steered the bill through the New York Assembly; and Governor David B. Hill, who supported and signed it, were all sportsmen.[80]

The creation of the 715,000-acre Adirondack preserve marks a high point in the early history of American environmental concern. As in the case of the game preservation–fish culture movement going on at the same time, sportsmen had initiated the effort to save New York's timberlands. Pragmatic arguments to the contrary, a desire to perpetuate wildlife and habitat for recreational and aesthetic enjoyment inspired both campaigns.

FOUR

Development of
the National Park Concept

As we have seen, the responsibility for the total natural environment inherent in the code of the sportsman aroused hunters and fishermen to work in behalf of nongame and forests as well as those animals, birds, and fish traditionally pursued for sport. It should not be surprising to learn, therefore, that outdoorsmen also played a leading role in the creation—and protection—of national parks. Even though these reservations sometimes lacked good fishing and would eventually prohibit hunting entirely, no group was more important in their early history than the American sportsman.

In fact, the first to suggest the national park idea—so far as we know—was hunter George Catlin. Although best known as a student and painter of Indians, he was also a self-proclaimed sportsman who combined recreational hunting with his studies of the Western aborigines.[1] Preceding by a quarter of a century Thoreau's call for "national preserves" (Chapter 3), Catlin proposed in 1832 that the federal government establish "a *magnificent park*" to house the Indians, buffalo, and wilderness—"a beautiful and thrilling specimen for America to preserve and hold up to the view of her refined citizens and the world, in future ages!"[2]

Like Thoreau's later recommendation, Catlin's idea was probably based on the Old World precedent of large game parks where aristocratic sportsmen preserved wildlife and habitat intact for their own personal enjoyment. And also like Thoreau, Catlin hoped to "freeze" the Indian and his game, particularly the buffalo, in a state of suspended animation.[3]

This fanciful goal suggests, however, that Catlin and Thoreau wished to alter the Old World precedent to fit New World circumstances. Like Thoreau, Catlin wanted "A *nation's Park,* containing man and beast, in all the wild[ness] and freshness of their nature's beauty!"[4] In other words, both men apparently envisaged a preserve for the whole country—for "the people"—instead of merely for the enjoyment of a privileged class. Aside from the impossibility of keeping aborigines ignorant of the civilization outside, one can only wonder how Catlin and Thoreau thought a wilderness park could be for the whole nation and still remain in a pristine state.

That problem, of course, has never been solved. Today, many in the National Park Service seem to understand that unless visitors' freedoms are restricted, the preserves will be damaged irrevocably by overuse.[5] Yet, the debate continues between those who see a national park as untainted wilderness where an individual must find his own pleasures in his own way and those who see it as a recreational area necessitating blanket automobile access, hotels, restaurants, and every other kind of convenience. Like the efforts in behalf of game laws and forestry, the attempt to adapt what was originally an aristocratic precedent—in this case the game preserve or park—to the requirements of a democratic society proved to be only partially successful.

Despite one or two earlier examples of federal action to set aside natural areas for public use,[6] the first real national park was Yellowstone, established in 1872. White men had been passing through the region, though not necessarily in the park proper, since at least the time of John Colter, a hunter for Lewis and Clark. A later visitor was that ubiquitous mountain man, Jim Bridger, who stumbled across the wondrous land of geysers, waterfalls, and hot springs in 1830. Although he told the outside world of his find, everyone knew that mountain men were notorious storytellers, and "Old Jim Bridger's lies" were long a source of amusement.[7] Not until forty years later did the real "discovery" of the region occur, "by which is meant its full and final disclosure to the world."[8] After the return of two expeditions made in 1869 and 1870, Bridger was no longer ridiculed.

The second of these explorations played a direct role in the creation of America's first national park. Led by Henry D. Washburn and Gustavus C. Doane, a party of nineteen men traveled through the Yellowstone wilderness in August and September of 1870 and discovered for themselves the geysers, hot springs, and other marvels first described by Jim Bridger.

On September 19 the expedition camped where the Firehole and Gibbon Rivers join to form the Madison, and around the evening fire its members discussed the future of the Yellowstone. While most expressed an intention to file claims in the area to profit from future tourism, one of the party, Cornelius Hedges, had a different opinion. Rather than to have the "wonders" exploited for private gain, he proposed the creation of "a great National Park" to insure that future generations would enjoy these natural objects in their original form.[9] While Hedges's idea may not have been entirely new[10] and only envisaged the provision of small buffer zones around the geysers and along the rims of the canyons,[11] it is generally regarded as the beginning of the effort that resulted in the establishment of Yellowstone National Park.

Like so many other prophets of environmental concern, Hedges was a cultivated, extremely well-educated Easterner. In an age when only two percent of the American population received the advantages of a secondary-school education,[12] Hedges held a Bachelor's degree from Yale and a law degree from Harvard. Coming to Montana in the early 1860s, he became one of Helena's leading citizens.

Although historian Aubrey L. Haines asserts that Hedges "was not an outdoor type of person,"[13] an examination of the diary he kept on the expedition yields a very different interpretation. Hedges was, in fact, the most enthusiastic and accomplished angler of the party.[14] While the general influence of the Romantic movement undoubtedly had much to do with Hedges's proposal for "a great National Park," the code of the sportsman may also have played a part. A highly literate, even scholarly individual, Hedges had probably seen the writings of Frank Forester, Samuel Hammond, or other well-known authors who stressed the aesthetic aspects of fishing and hunting and reminded outdoorsmen of their responsibility for the natural environment.

After returning to civilization, Hedges and another member of the expedition, Nathaniel P. Langford, publicized the national-park idea and succeeded in inducing a small interest in the project. One of those to be stimulated was Ferdinand Vandiveer Hayden, director of the Geological and Geographical Survey of the Territories, who decided to lead an expedition through the Yellowstone in the summer of 1871.[15] Among those he chose to accompany him were photographer William Henry Jackson and landscape artist Thomas Moran. These two gathered a pictorial record that would soon play an important role in the history of the region.

Like most expeditions to the Great West in those early years, Hayden's 1871 survey offered numerous opportunities for recreational as well as utilitarian hunting and fishing. Although many historians give the impression that these activities were pursued only to provide the camp with food, a close reading of the personal diaries and journals of expedition members proves otherwise. Often, simply the appearance of a big-game animal like an elk or grizzly bear caused the excited explorers to break formation and give chase. On the Hayden survey none were more enthusiastic in their sporting interests than William Henry Jackson, who shot a trophy grizzly,[16] and Thomas Moran, who repeatedly proved his expertise as a trout angler.[17]

On returning to the East, Hayden joined forces with Nathaniel P. Langford and Montana's Congressional delegate, William H. Clagett, in an effort to establish a reservation in the Yellowstone. One who came to their support was Jay Cooke, banker, financier, and angler.[18] Actually, the latter had been interested in establishing a park in the Yellowstone months before the Hayden expedition visited the region. A financier of the Northern Pacific Railroad through Montana, Cooke hoped the creation of a park would result in a lucrative tourist business for the line.[19] In early 1871 he had helped to subsidize several lectures given by Langford in behalf of a Yellowstone preserve, and later he also defrayed the expenses incurred in pushing the park legislation through Congress.[20]

That body's consideration of the proposed bill began on December 18, 1871. The brief Congressional debate revealed a general disinterest in the subject,[21] though at least one Senator expressed a fear that the park would take potential farm land out of cultivation.[22] Once again, environmentalists found that they had to use a "practical" approach, and they claimed that the Yellowstone region's high altitude and cold climate would make farming impossible.[23] As with future national parks, the Yellowstone could be set aside only after it was successfully argued that the area was essentially worthless for economic development.[24]

Using this strategy, plus the claim that the government would incur little expense for the preserve's maintenance, park proponents managed to slip their bill through Congress. They received invaluable aid from Jay Cooke, whose money helped finance the effort; Nathaniel P. Langford, whose published articles on the Yellowstone were copied and distributed to the legislators before they voted; and especially William Henry Jackson, whose magnificent photographs, given out at the same time as Langford's articles, backed up the claim that the Yellowstone's wonders were absolutely unique and must be set aside.[25] Soon, Thomas Moran's paintings would add another visual dimension to Americans' appreciation of the Yellowstone[26] (and other scenic areas as well) and play no small part in increasing public support for the creation of national parks.[27]

Finally, on March 1, 1872, President Ulysses S. Grant signed the bill establishing—at least on paper—"a public park or pleasuring-ground."[28] As we shall soon see, it took many years of agitation by environmentalists to define just what had been created by the stroke of Grant's pen.

The deep involvement of sportsmen like Cornelius Hedges, William Henry Jackson, and Thomas Moran in the effort to establish and publicize a Yellowstone preserve was only the first of many such campaigns. Those who had avidly fished or hunted for recreation would also play a vital role in the founding of many later national parks, among them Yosemite (1890), Glacier (1910), Lassen Volcanic (1916), Mount McKinley (1917), Grand Canyon (1919), Great Smoky Mountains (1930), Isle Royale (1940), and Everglades (1947).[29]

But the treatment of all these preserves was based on precedents established in the handling of Yellowstone National Park, long the nation's only such reserve. After the latter's "creation" in 1872, over two decades would pass before the government and general public of the United States began to view a "national park" in the way many now take for granted: as an essentially inviolate wildlife and wilderness sanctuary.

Spearheaded by George Bird Grinnell's *Forest and Stream,* sportsmen initiated a movement that aimed, first, to define the meaning of Yellowstone Park for the American people and, second, to establish for it an effective administration. The 1872 act creating the reservation had for its object the protection of a natural "museum" of "wonders"—geysers, hot springs, and canyons.[30] The park was *not* intentionally preserved either as a wilderness or a game refuge.[31] The only concern of those few interested in the area was that the "curiosities" be made available to the public as soon as possible.[32] Instead of believing that the park should remain in a pristine state, most of these individuals assumed that it would soon be "improved" by a multitude of hotels, roads, and other conveniences.

During the rest of the 1870s and the very early '80s, most of Congress, as well as the general public, virtually forgot about the park. Because there was no convenient access to its vicinity, the reserve's only visitors were hide hunters, sportsmen, and members of expeditions.

The statute creating the reservation provided that it "is hereby reserved and withdrawn from settlement, occupancy, or sale . . . and set apart as a public park or pleasuring-ground for the benefit and enjoyment of the people."[33] The Secretary of the Interior was authorized to draw up regulations to "provide for the preservation from injury or spoliation, of all timber, mineral deposits, natural curiosities, or wonders . . . and their retention in their natural condition."[34] This proclamation could be given a variety of interpretations. Clearly, however, the one held by the Secretary of the Interior would be crucial. The rules he promulgated would largely determine how Americans conceived of their first "national park." In the same way, the degree of enforcement of these decrees would indicate which infractions, if any, the government considered threats to the meaning of the park, and which it looked on as insignificant. In time, the failure to prosecute the latter would make what they prohibited accepted practices. Eventually, such practices would receive the sanction of tradition, making them almost unalterable.

Because of its inaccessibility, there was at first little danger to the park outside of the depredations of commercial hunters. But by 1881, the tracks of the Northern Pacific Railroad had approached the vicinity of the reservation. "Soon after," George Bird Grinnell recalled in his autobiography, "its [the railroad's] President, . . . [Henry] Villard, took out a special train carrying a number of guests—railroad men, capitalists, and scientific men—to show the public the country traversed by his road. Among those who then visited the Park were some men who saw its possibilities as a pleasure resort, and realized that the privileges offered to lessees through the Act establishing the Park would have a money value to those who might secure them."[35] Soon these men would begin their efforts to exploit the reserve, inspiring Grinnell to launch a campaign aimed at protecting the park by clarifying its status.

In large measure, Grinnell's crusade was the outgrowth of his experience in the West. Because the boundaries of Yellowstone Park were drawn with little real knowledge of the terrain, a number of expeditions were sent into the region to see exactly what Congress had, in fact, preserved.[36] One of these was an 1875 reconnaissance led by engineer and sportsman[37] William Ludlow. As the expedition's official naturalist, Grinnell became thoroughly familiar with the park and its problems, the most obvious of which was hide hunting.[38]

Although all species of big game were being systematically slaughtered, he was most alarmed by the destruction of the buffalo, in this, their last stronghold. For seventy years, the dream of Western expansion had fed on buffalo meat, and the animal had become the symbol of the new land, the game Old World aristocrats and New World patricians—Grinnell[39] and Roosevelt[40] among them—had to shoot, as a kind of initiation rite into frontier Americanism.

Long before Grinnell first saw the animal on its native grounds in 1870, hunters George Catlin and John James Audubon had expressed the hope that this representative of the West would never die out.[41] Now, with the establishment of Yellowstone National Park, there appeared to be a possibility that the bison might be preserved, though the founders of the park had not conceived of it as a game refuge.

Perhaps the first to envisage the national park as a preserve for keeping the buffalo from extinction was Theodore B. Comstock, who made the recommendation in *American Naturalist* in early 1874.[42] Three years later, Grinnell, independently of Comstock, also suggested the game-preserve idea. In the very popular *Sportsman's Gazetteer and General Guide* (1877) he observed that "the rapid and appalling diminution in their [the buffalo's] numbers and range is owing entirely to their wanton and useless destruction by skin-hunters and pseudo-sportsmen." While governmental protection during the breeding season would be a help, "another and better method for saving the few remaining herds from utter annihilation may be suggested; namely, by forming a buffalo reservation." The ready solution, he pointed out, lay in Yellowstone Park, where "we have the necessary territory, and it is already stocked; but the skin-hunter, that ruthless destroyer of game, must be kept at a distance, if we would hope to save this species."[43]

For several years, Grinnell wrote nothing more on the refuge concept. Perhaps he was waiting to see how the Secretary of the Interior and Congress would handle the park. In the meantime, he continued his attacks on the market gunner, that camp follower of industrialism's advance into the Western wilderness. In 1880 he observed: "There is nowhere in the world such systematic, business-like and relentless killing as on the buffalo plains."[44]

By early 1881, he had decided that the government did not intend to protect the park buffalo. In the March 17th issue of *Forest and Stream*, he reiterated the view that the survival of the bison, as a species, depended on those in this reservation and said that it was mandatory, therefore, that the federal government appoint at least six wardens to watch over the animals.[45]

The wardens were not appointed, and the reserve continued to be treated as a bonanza for hide hunters. Pseudo-sportsmen also took their toll. In 1882 *Forest and Stream* reported "The Very Latest," the incredible story of the "Yellowstone Valley Hunting Club." The group advertised that on payment of a fee, it would guarantee trophies for Eastern tourists. All guns, ammunition, and other requirements were supplied, and the game was even located ahead of time, so that the "pilgrim" could kill his prize without the slightest delay. Grinnell's weekly satirized the operation by suggesting the adoption of a kind of burglar-alarm system which could "intersect all the ravines, plateaus and hills in the Yellowstone Valley with wires, all converging to the club room, so that every time a brute stirred anywhere in the territory covered by the club, an alarm would be given, and the exact whereabouts of the game shown by an indicator in the club room." Another possibility was that "a large stock of game might . . . be corralled in substantial enclosures, where the timid tourist could pump away with his repeating rifle. . . . Or the animals might be roped and tied to a post and then slaughtered by proxy." What was fantastic to Grinnell was that the managers of the "club" failed to see that their project was self-defeating, for soon the game would be exterminated and they would be out of business.[46]

In response to Grinnell's editorial attack, the president of the club, H. S. Back, wrote to the editor of *Forest and Stream* on June 15, 1882. Not aware of Grinnell's Western experience, Back called him a "tenderfoot" and mocked his supposed ignorance of the Yellowstone region and its game. He finished by asserting that "Eastern hunters have no idea of the extent of this Territory or of the amount of game there is in the Northwest; and we give you the laugh when you talk of exterminating the game in this country."[47]

Despite the Westerner's assurances, in the next few years the buffalo would vanish, several subspecies of larger mammal forms would become extinct, and many others would dwindle to precariously low levels. What Back's letter exemplifies is the hostility and utter lack of communication between East and West, which would continue to plague the efforts of environmentalists, mostly Easterners like Grinnell, to save the West from its own destructive inclinations.

Although Grinnell's conception of the national park as a wildlife preserve was articulated as early as 1877, it took several years for him to realize that if his idea was to become a reality, something more was required than sporadic protests. On December 14, 1882, he provided that "something more" by launching a crusade in *Forest and Stream* to define the status of Yellowstone National Park and protect it from commercialization. Only after a continuous campaign of a dozen years would his goal be achieved.

The first editorial, "Their Last Refuge," covered the whole front page and was both a plea for the buffalo and a detailed analysis of the deficiencies in the act creating the reserve. He pointed out that the statute put the destiny of the reservation completely in the hands of the Secretary of the Interior. This official had the power to grant leases to private persons and corporations for the purpose of building roads, hotels, and other facilities, and to decide what regulations should be devised for the park. With regard to wildlife, only their "wanton destruction" with "the purpose of merchandise or profit" was specified as one of the offenses the Secretary was to "provide against."[48]

Grinnell's editorial made it clear that the vagueness of the act subjected it to a number of interpretations and left huge loopholes for those who sought to use the reserve for their own profit.[49] An example was the section on wildlife, which seemed to suggest that individuals or corporations could kill all the game they wished, just so long as they were not too "wanton." The greatest deficiency, of course, was that the act provided no machinery for carrying out any regulations the Secretary of the Interior might promulgate. As Grinnell later recalled, the Secretary's rules "soon came to be regarded as a dead letter. Anyone was at liberty to cut down the forest, kill the game or carry away natural curiosities, and all these things were constantly done. . . ."[50]

He cogently summed up the problem in the 1882 editorial: "This 'great and glorious government' has again stultified itself by enacting laws without supplying the means to enforce them. The Park is overrun by skin-hunters, who slaughter the game for the hides, and laugh defiance at the government. . . . The curse of politics has entered into the management of the reservation, and the little money appropriated for its maintenance is wasted by incompetent and ignorant officials. It is leased to private parties, who desire to make a peep show of its wonders."[51]

In this editorial Grinnell also expressed regret that the park's potential as a wildlife sanctuary was not yet realized. He asked that the recommendation he made in the *Report* of the 1875 Ludlow reconnaissance to end hide hunting be followed at last.[52] He also repeated the proposal made by Ludlow in the same publication that the reservation be transferred to the War Department and guarded by troops,[53] for, as Grinnell emphasized, nothing could be expected from the Department of the Interior, "that sink of corruption." A final suggestion was that the park be extended to the east as far as Cedar Mountain, which would almost double its area while preserving crucial big-game habitat.

The editorial closed with an urgent plea for the retention of at least one place as it was before the coming of the white man. In his own time Grinnell had witnessed "the tide of immigration [into the West], once small, like a tiny mountain stream, move forward, at first slowly, and then, gathering volume and strength, advance with a constantly accelerated power. . . ." But "there is one spot left, a single rock about which this tide will break, and past which it will sweep, leaving it undefiled by the unsightly traces of civilization." Most importantly, "here in this Yellowstone Park the large game of the West may be preserved from extermination; here . . . it may be seen by generations yet unborn. It is for the Nation to say whether these splendid species shall be so preserved, in this their last refuge."[54]

With the arrival of a new year, *Forest and Stream* stepped up its drive to have the park legislatively defined as a wildlife and wilderness preserve, all commercialism excluded, and a mechanism of enforcement established. In "The Park Grab," an editorial of January 4, 1883, Grinnell exposed the scheme of the so-called "Yellowstone Park Improvement Company," the main group involved in exploiting the reserve for private gain. The corporation was endeavoring to obtain a lease of seven tracts in the park, all but one of which was to be 640 acres in size. For the tiny annual charge of $2.00 per acre, the company would be entitled to build hotels, stores, stage and telegraph lines, raise cattle, and have unlimited use of all water, timber, and arable land. Grinnell found it incredible that "the only National Park possessed by the American people" could be so flagrantly appropriated for the benefit of a few commercialists.[55]

There was some cause for optimism, however. Opposition to the "monopolists" had already been expressed by a few in Congress, notably Senator George G. Vest of Missouri. But because "it is whispered that his interest in the subject has on a sudden ceased," Grinnell urged the Senator to remove this doubt by reasserting his original position.[56] The editor's fear was unjustified, for Vest would prove to be the staunchest defender of the park in Congress. A member of the Woodmont Rod and Gun Club of western Maryland,[57] he was also an enthusiastic outdoorsman and a believer, apparently, in the environmental obligation intrinsic to the code of the sportsman.

Despite the efforts of *Forest and Stream*, the "Improvement Company" succeeded in getting the requested lease from the Assistant Secretary of the Interior.[58] It covered Mammoth Hot Springs, Yellowstone Canyon and Falls, and all the larger geyser basins.[59] But the corporation was not to go unscathed. Grinnell's attack on January 4 was resumed the following week. In an editorial that occupied almost the whole front page, he revealed that in order to construct a 600-room hotel at Mammoth Hot Springs, the company had established a sawmill that was busily cutting up the reserve's trees. The park's wildlife was also in danger. In order to feed the large labor force that was to be in the area through the winter, "the company called for bids from contractors to furnish 20,000 pounds of wild meat. . . ."[60]

Still, there was a positive side to the situation. Senator Vest had renewed his opposition to the corporation and had even introduced a bill that incorporated many of the demands Grinnell had made in his editorials. The proposed legislation would extend the park east to Cedar Mountain and south to the 44th parallel, adding about 3,344 square miles to its size; detail troops within its borders if found necessary; provide heavy fines for traffic in game; and establish a force of ten wardens, accountable to a regularly paid superintendent of the park.[61]

The friends of the preserve appeared to be achieving results in other areas as well. The January 18th number of *Forest and Stream* printed a letter received from Secretary of the Interior Henry M. Teller addressed to the Superintendent of the Park. Dated the 15th, it prohibited "the killing, wounding or capturing at any time" of the reserve's wildlife and forbade, in addition, the cutting of timber without the Secretary's authorization. Grinnell thought these orders might not be too late, if only they could be enforced.[62]

Concerning the proscription on animal destruction, he argued that if put into effect, it would perpetually maintain good hunting in the region surrounding the preserve. Protected in their natural nursery, the big game would quickly increase. This reproductive spiral would be amplified by animals coming from the outside, which, in their search for safety, would concentrate within the reservation's borders. The wildlife inside the park would continually reproduce and spill over its edges to restock depleted adjacent territory.[63]

Here was another application of the concepts of business management to resource use. The reserve's wildlife would act as capital stock to produce interest for reinvestment in other areas. In the years ahead, Grinnell often repeated this theory. It added a "practical" touch to the battle over the park's future that would appeal to Western sportsmen. And it worked precisely as he predicted, making Theodore Roosevelt, among others, an enthusiastic endorser.[64]

The January 18th issue of *Forest and Stream* contained another seminal idea on the meaning of the nation's first national park. In

"The People's Park" Grinnell emphasized that the reservation was *owned* by the American public as a whole rather than by the few commercial groups which were in the process of taking it over.[65] Since this idea is now the heart of the national park philosophy, it is difficult to envisage a time when public ownership was not a universally accepted truth.

Although the act setting aside the Yellowstone region had provided the basis for this view, by describing its product as "a public park or pleasuring-ground for the benefit and enjoyment of the people," this clause could just as well have sanctioned the creation of another Coney Island. Like the side shows of a carnival, the attractions of the Yellowstone were, for most, its "freaks and phenomena of Nature."[66]

Others looked to the example of Europe. In March, 1883, George G. Vest announced in the Senate that there was nothing new in Yellowstone Park, for "France has such a park, Germany has such a park, England has her royal parks, and why should not America have her republican park. . . ."[67]

Vest's statement illustrates the continuing influence of Old World ideas on the development of New World environmental concern. As discussed earlier (Chapter 3), the first national-park proposals in American history were probably based on the precedent of the European and English game preserve or "park" set aside for aristocratic sportsmen. What is particularly interesting about the Senator's comment is that a number of the best-known city parks of Europe and England were originally the hunting preserves of nobility—London's Hyde and St. James Parks, for example.[68] It would appear that the evolution of the park concept on both sides of the Atlantic—whether in the form of a well-ordered, formal park like those in London and later in American cities like New York and Chicago or the wilderness parks created by the United States—can be traced back to a concern for wildlife first exhibited by Old World sportsmen.[69]

In view of this complex, somewhat shadowy history, it is no wonder that the "true" meaning of the American national park took many years to develop. The people of the United States had to be *taught* that they were the owners of the Yellowstone, and that their preserve was not to be an amusement park or a well-ordered, formal park. Instead, it was to be a great wildlife and wilderness sanctuary. Again, the basis for this interpretation was contained in the act establishing the reserve; the stipulation that the Secretary of the Interior "shall provide against the wanton destruction of the fish and game" would, in time, be construed as a prohibition against *all* killing of wildlife, and the phrase "their retention in their natural condition," as applied to "all timber, mineral deposits, natural curiosities, or wonders," would later justify the *total* exclusion of all but the most necessary of man's works. The battle over the future of Yellowstone National Park was, in a sense, a battle over the language of the act that created it. The strict constructionists, led by Grinnell, eventually won out. This was fortunate, not only for this one reserve but for the future of the entire park system in America and, indeed, the world.[70]

When Grinnell began his editorial crusade, he had a somewhat naive understanding of the difficulties and setbacks he would have to overcome before achieving success. At the end of January, 1883, *Forest and Stream* headlined "The Park Saved." The weekly printed a letter from Secretary of the Interior Teller to Senator Vest stating that he would not grant the lease of the Improvement Company until Congress had taken action on the Senator's bill or until the session closed. With premature enthusiasm, Grinnell exclaimed, "This ends the fight. The grabbers are defeated. The people's rights are to be protected. The Yellowstone Park is not to become a second and greater Niagara" [i.e., a commercialized tourist attraction].[71]

Vest's bill, however, was not passed. Actually, the fight was only beginning, and Grinnell would have to battle over a decade longer to have the reserve adequately governed. But the struggle *Forest and Stream* had initiated was now joined by other periodicals, among them *American Field* (the later name of *Field and Stream*), *Harper's Weekly,* and the New York *Times* and *Herald.*[72]

In February Grinnell expressed the hope that Vest's bill would pass in the future and asked that it be amended to include the scenic Tetons to the south.[73] This proposal, introduced by the paper, would not become a reality until the establishment of the Grand Teton National Park nearly a half-century later.

The next month, Grinnell kept the issue alive by quoting in detail the lively Senate debate on the amendment to the Sundry Civil Service Bill submitted by Vest. The proposal was for a $2,000 annual salary for the Superintendent of the Park and $900 each for ten assistants, to be appointed by the Secretary of the Interior. They, as well as the Superintendent, were to reside permanently in the reserve, and their job would be "to protect the game, timber, and objects of interest therein." The Secretary of War, at the request of the Secretary of the Interior, would be authorized to detail troops in the park. Public access would be improved by new roads and bridges. Finally, a limitation would be placed on the power of the Secretary of the Interior to grant leases; they could not cover a larger area than ten acres, nor be near any geysers or "other objects of curiosity or interest."[74]

The view of the West was typified by Senator John J. Ingalls of Kansas, who condemned the amendment as a waste of money. The park, he asserted, was already becoming a burden on the federal government. He thought it should be surveyed and sold as other public lands were sold. Declaring "I do not understand myself what the necessity is for the Government entering into . . . show business in the Yellowstone National Park," he advised handing the reserve over "to private enterprise, which is the surest guarantee for proper protection for such objects of care as the great national curiosities in that region."

Sounding very much like earlier sportsmen, Vest defended his amendment by proclaiming: "Mr. President, the great curse of this age and of the American people is its materialistic tendencies. Money, money, l'argent, l'argent, is the cry everywhere, until our people are held up already to the world as noted for nothing except the acquisition of money at the expense of all esthetic taste and of all love of nature and its great mysteries and wonders."[75] The Senate responded to this attack on the materialism of the times and approved Vest's amendment. Future events would prove, however, that the park was still a long way from having an adequate administration.

In late March *Forest and Stream* reported that the Secretary of the Interior had asked the Secretary of War for a detail of troops for the park: "Things are, therefore, marching along in very satisfactory shape."[76] But the troops never arrived, and the dismal situation remained unchanged.[77] In November the weekly's editor argued that the unenforced and unenforceable laws of the Wyoming and Montana territories against big-game destruction should be shored up by "a Federal law, backed by the power and resources of the Federal Government."[78] The state of the reservation continued to deteriorate, and by the end of 1883, *Forest and Stream* was informing its readers that the Superintendent of the park was either dishonest or incompetent, or both, and his assistants were not the experienced Westerners required but corrupt Easterners who were augmenting their income by selling the geyserite and game they were supposed to be protecting![79]

The beginning of a new year brought the news that the meager steps already taken to provide a government for the park could not be carried out. The Secretary of the Interior announced that because most of the reservation was in an unorganized county of Wyoming Territory, his regulations were null and void. Without a judge to try cases, vandals and market gunners could only be censured—they could not be prosecuted or even expelled from the park.[80] The Improvement Company had taken advantage of the situation—increasing the pasturing stock, killing the game with abandon, and even threatening to remove the helpless Superintendent if he failed to cooperate.[81]

Forest and Stream bitterly complained that "an effort has been made to care for the Park, and this effort has proved wholly abortive. The Government is now the laughing stock of the Improvement Company and the skin-hunters and trespassers."[82] Now, as never before, the paper's editor was convinced that only the Army could fill the void until a permanent administration was established.

Though disappointed, Grinnell had by no means given up. In the months ahead, he re-emphasized the idea that the American people owned the reserve and were, as a result, responsible for it—"its geysers, its forests, its game, must be preserved for its owners."[83] He went so far as to claim that "public opinion" demanded a government for the park,[84] which was hardly the case. At this early date, the public had not the slightest concern for the area. Nevertheless, Grinnell was on the right track. The sanctity of private property was at the heart of the American value system. When the people eventually learned that they owned the Yellowstone, they became anxious to save it. The warning to the country that its property was rapidly being used up by commercialists and "monopolists" would prove one of his most effective appeals.

In March, 1884, a bill passed the Senate which, if it had become law, would have incorporated most of the provisions *Forest and Stream* had been advocating. These included extension of the park on the east and south, authorization for the use of troops to capture and expel lawbreakers, inclusion of the reserve within the judicial jurisdiction of Gallatin County, Montana, and the provision of fines for the destruction of game.[85]

As happened time and again, the bill passed the Senate only to be killed in the House by amendments for "improvements." The lobbyists of the Improvement Company were working diligently to get sections of the park removed for commercial development. Their assault on the reservation had been joined by mining interests in Cooke City. Located just outside the northeastern corner of the park, the town wanted a rail connection with Gardiner, Montana, the terminus of the Northern Pacific. Spokesmen for the Cinnabar and Clark's Fork Railroad Company had succeeded in having riders added to Vest's bill which would have granted a right of way across the reserve.

Grinnell was particularly alarmed by this new menace.[86] He knew that if the railroad were built, a precedent would be set leading to the construction of others. Soon, the stillness of the wilderness would be broken by the whistle of locomotives and the babble of tourists. In addition, sparks from passing trains would be a perpetual fire hazard.

Partly as a response to the railroad threat, Grinnell now added another dimension to his rationale for wanting the park protected. If the Yellowstone region were seen as a vital watershed, the fire danger presented by sparks flying from passing locomotives would make it mandatory that railways be excluded from the reservation. In the simultaneous battle he was carrying on for the Adirondacks, the watershed argument was proving very effective. Why not apply it to the Yellowstone? Here, too, it would prove a powerful defense, so much so that it would become for many the primary justification for having the region protected.

One of these was Arnold Hague. From a distinguished New England family and a professionally trained geologist, he had been with Clarence King on his 1870 Survey of the Fortieth Parallel and in 1883 had taken charge of the Geological Survey work in Yellowstone Park. Grinnell's contributions to the *Report* of the Ludlow reconnaissance and his newspaper crusade for the reserve brought him to Hague's attention. The two became acquainted, and Hague asked

Grinnell to accompany him on his 1884 summer survey of the park. This was the first of several such trips they made together,[87] the result of which was a friendship that would last their lifetimes.

While camped in the wilderness, the two had long talks about their hopes for the park,[88] and they found that they were in basic agreement. Undoubtedly, Grinnell spoke of the success the watershed rationale was having in gathering support for the Adirondacks, and Hague probably affirmed the validity of its application to the Yellowstone region. After their return to the East, they increasingly talked of the reserve in terms of its importance as a drainage area.

Grinnell led the way with a letter to the New York *Times,* published on January 29, 1885. He argued that the reservation's forests must remain inviolate, because they were situated on the watersheds of both the Missouri and Snake Rivers, and correctly predicted that the continued flow of these rivers would become important to the West as their potential for irrigation was realized. Hague followed Grinnell's example in a letter to a member of the Senate's Committee on Territories, published in *Forest and Stream* and in an article in *The Nation.*[89]

It is important to note that the watershed defense did not become Grinnell's sole argument for preserving the Yellowstone in an undisturbed condition; it was only *added* to the game-refuge idea and is one more illustration of the fact that conservation began with a concern for wildlife. An editorial appearing in *Forest and Stream* the same day the *Times* letter was printed combined these reasons in arguing for the park's protection.[90]

What is significant about Grinnell's position on the Yellowstone is how much it differed from his interpretation of the purpose of the Adirondacks. Although the campaigns for these areas were going on at the same time, the editor of *Forest and Stream* differentiated—from the start—between the state forest, which he hoped would be systematically exploited according to the principles of scientific forestry, and the national park, which, though serving a similar purpose as a watershed, must remain an unaltered wilderness. Grinnell was not the pure "preservationist" who wished to leave all timberlands in a completely undisturbed condition, whether they were state forests, national forests, or national parks. Nor was he the purely utilitarian kind of "conservationist" who shortly appeared on the scene—the individual who cared little for aesthetic considerations and thought that any natural area was being wasted if it was not being utilized for timber, irrigation, grazing, or some other "practical" purpose. Grinnell's genius was his intellectual versatility, his ability continually to evoke working solutions for new problems, while remaining independent of those who sought to employ the same one-dimensional approach for every resource.

The one element common to all his approaches was the belief that *all* natural resources benefited from continuous, nonpolitical, systematic management. This idea was manifested both in his efforts to obtain a "government" for Yellowstone Park and in his attempts to have the Adirondacks scientifically exploited. Just because the first reservation was to remain outside the commercial sphere did not eliminate its need for continual fire patrol, wildlife protection, trail maintenance, etc. The same would be true for the national wildlife refuges and "wilderness areas" created in the twentieth century, despite the common belief that no management of these reserves is necessary.

Using the later antagonism between John Muir and Gifford Pinchot as their model, historians have tended to categorize every environmentalist as either a preservationist (like Muir) or a conservationist (like Pinchot). While this dichotomy applies in some cases, a true conservationist like Grinnell knew that natural resources must be conserved under a *variety* of administrative schemes. He would fight just as hard for the scientific exploitation of national forests as for the preservation of natural conditions in national parks. Thus, he championed the forestry work of Gifford Pinchot but joined John Muir in attacking the Hetch Hetchy dam project in Yosemite Park. And like another sportsman, Theodore Roosevelt, Grinnell would continue to love the chase while at the same time campaigning for the establishment of wildlife sanctuaries. Neither man felt any inconsistency in his position, because there was none. The "wise use of natural resources," a phrase the Roosevelt administration later popularized, meant that every unit in the conservation program—from national forests to national wildlife refuges—benefited from continuous, systematic management.

Nowhere was this need for administrative continuity based on firmly established principles more obvious than in the early mismanagement of Yellowstone National Park. Because Grinnell conceived of the reserve as a kind of nonprofit corporation run for the benefit of the public, the man obviously most responsible for its efficient administration was its manager, the Superintendent. *Forest and Stream*'s editor remained ever vigilant to see that this official was performing well, but in the early years of the park, Grinnell was often disappointed. During the spring of 1885, he became so disenchanted with Robert Carpenter, the man then occupying the post, that he led a campaign to oust him.[91] The latter was like so many of the political appointees whose inefficiency and dishonesty plagued the reserve for years. One historian of the national parks has labeled him "a devotee of private enterprise, who tried to wreck the park."[92] Grinnell exposed how he was spending much of his time in Washington, D.C., lobbying for the Improvement Company. Even more incredible, it was learned that he had filed claim on 1,400 acres of park land with the intention of mining for coal.[93] In late May the Superintendent was finally removed. With justice, Grinnell claimed that "Carpenter's removal is the direct result of the ventilation of his acts by . . . *Forest and Stream*."[94]

During the fight to have Carpenter ejected, Grinnell had expressed the hope that after his ouster the park would be put under a commission. It would consist of five men, to include the governors of Wyoming and Montana; the chief engineer in charge of road-building; a scientist, perhaps from the Geological Survey—he was probably thinking of Hague—and lastly, an intelligent, interested individual outside the agencies regularly concerned with the preserve.[95] A prime candidate for this last position was, of course, Grinnell himself. In the years ahead, commissions would become the dominant administrative forms for managing all natural resources.

By the summer of 1885, the guardians of the national park had still achieved almost nothing in the way of concrete results. Much of the problem lay in the fact that their struggle was taking place in an intellectual milieu shaped by the Romantic tradition. According to historian William H. Goetzmann, the establishment of Yellowstone Park—to protect its "mysteries" and "wonders"—was the culmination of the Romantic movement in America.[96] In a sense, those who had set the region aside might be compared to nineteenth-century reformers like the Greenbackers and Henry George's "single-taxers." For the supporters of these crusades, reform entailed a single panacea that, once accomplished, obviated the need for further action.[97] There was little or no realization of the need for continuity in handling problems. Those who had created the nation's first national park seemed to share this outlook. Laws had been enacted that proclaimed the curiosities of the Yellowstone officially preserved; nothing more was needed.

One who knew better was the editor of America's most-respected sportsmen's periodical, George Bird Grinnell. In an editorial in behalf of the reserve, he had exposed the sham by declaring: "This 'great and glorious government' has again stultified itself by enacting laws without supplying the means to enforce them."[98] In one of the earliest muckraking campaigns in American history, he sought to supply the missing means by exposing the inaction of the government and the greed of the would-be "monopolist." Where there was only a vacuum, Grinnell hoped to establish a *process,* an ongoing administration. Although he would have to struggle almost a decade longer to achieve this goal, his cause was becoming more popular.

One who found the message appealing was the young sportsman-naturalist, Theodore Roosevelt. Although he had already shown an interest in the future of the environment by supporting the creation of an Adirondack forest preserve, it was not until Roosevelt became involved in the battle over Yellowstone National Park that he initiated his career as an active conservationist. Grinnell was the man most responsible for bringing about this involvement, the genesis of which was a book review in *Forest and Stream.*

FIVE

The Boone and Crockett Club

W hen the twenty volumes of *The Works of Theodore Roosevelt* (1926) were being compiled by Scribner's, Roosevelt's widow asked that Grinnell write the Introduction to the first volume,[1] which included *Hunting Trips of a Ranchman* (1885) and *Ranch Life and the Hunting-Trail* (1888). The basis for her request is explained by Grinnell: "It was the writing of a review of 'Hunting Trips of a Ranchman' that brought me into intimate contact with Theodore Roosevelt. I had known him casually as a young man carrying on at Albany a fight for good politics, which commanded wide sympathy, and as interested in the cattle business in Dakota, in which, at the same time, I also was interested in another Territory [Wyoming]; but I had seen little of him until the appearance of this first book of his on hunting and Western life."[2]

The review appeared on July 2, 1885, in "New Publications," one of *Forest and Stream*'s regular sections. It began encouragingly: "Luxurious books upon the better class of field sports are certainly more highly appreciated now than they used to be. . . . Its author is Mr. Theodore Roosevelt, who is best known as an earnest and energetic politician of the best type. . . . The excellent work which he has accomplished at Albany shows him to be—if nothing more—a person of exceptionally well-balanced mind, and calm deliberate judgment, and these qualities cannot fail to make their impression in any pursuit to which their possessor may choose to turn his attention."[3]

Continuing, Grinnell took a new tack: "Mr. Roosevelt is not well known as a sportsman, and his experience of the Western country is quite limited, but this very fact in one way lends an added charm to his book. He has not become accustomed to all the various sights and sounds of the plains and the mountains, and for him all the difference which exists between the East and the West are still sharply defined." Conversely, "the old-timer who attempts to write of life in the Far West is almost sure to grow prosy. He takes too much for granted, and regards as commonplace a great many features of that life which are, in fact, extremely interesting to those before whom they are brought for the first time. Mr. Roosevelt's accounts of life on a ranch are delightful from their freshness." Despite the favorable elements in Grinnell's comments, it is unlikely that the proud Roosevelt was pleased with the notion that his volume was charming because of its naiveté.

As the review went on, the criticism became more specific: "Where Mr. Roosevelt details his own adventures he is accurate, and tells his story in a simple, pleasant fashion, which at once brings us into sympathy with him. We are sorry to see that a number of hunting myths are given as fact, but it was after all scarcely to be expected that with the author's limited experience he could sift the wheat from the chaff and distinguish the true from the false." In regard to the work's illustrations, Grinnell pronounced most of them "admirable." Nevertheless, he thought a few were very bad, and one, a sketch of a cow elk, he characterized as a "hydrocephalous dwarf."

Grinnell later justified the patronizing tone of his critique by reminding the reader that at the time it was written, "there were not many active writers who had seen so much of the West as I, and who in travelling through it had also given the same careful attention to the ways of the wild creatures."[4] His claim was valid. Whereas Roosevelt's experience was then limited to a two- or three-year period in what is now western North Dakota and eastern Montana, Grinnell's involvement with the Far West began fifteen years earlier, extended over much of its wilderness, and included close association with some of the region's most competent hunters and observers of nature, men like "Lonesome Charley" Reynolds and the North brothers, Frank and Luther.[5] His greater experience is best shown by the fact that he passed through the valley of the Little Missouri with Colonel George Armstrong Custer's 1874 expedition a decade before the young Roosevelt would begin a ranch there;[6] the same landmarks Grinnell had gazed at, and even helped to name, would be seen years later by an exuberant Roosevelt, who first came to the region to shoot a trophy buffalo.[7]

While Grinnell's criticism of *Hunting Trips* may have been justified, Roosevelt was piqued by the review. He called at the *Forest and Stream* office soon after it appeared to ask for an explanation. Grinnell remembered that "we talked freely about the book, and took up at length some of its statements." The editor must have made a strong case, for Roosevelt "at once saw my point of view."[8]

"After we had discussed the book and the habits of the animals he [Roosevelt] had described," Grinnell recalled, "we passed on to the broader subject of hunting in the West, which was still to some extent unexplored and unhunted, and to the habits of the animals as modified by their surroundings. I told him something about game destruction in Montana for the hides, which, so far as small game was concerned, had begun in the West only a few years before that, though the slaughter of the buffalo for their skins had been going on much longer and by this time . . . , the last of the big herds had disappeared."

Because of their deep mutual interests, "Roosevelt called often at my office to discuss the broad country that we both loved, and we came to know each other extremely well. Though chiefly interested in big game and its hunting, and telling interestingly of events that had occurred on his hunting trips, Roosevelt enjoyed hearing of the birds, the small mammals, the Indians, and the incidents of travel of early expeditions on which I had gone. He was always fond of natural history, having begun, as so many boys have done, with birds; but as he saw more and more of outdoor life his interest in the subject broadened and later it became a passion with him."[9] Grinnell's involvement with the natural world had proceeded along the same lines.[10]

The two had something else in common: "We were both familiar with life on a cow-ranch. . . ." After working in western Nebraska on a ranch belonging to William F. ("Buffalo Bill") Cody and the North brothers, Grinnell had decided to buy a spread of his own. In 1883 he purchased land in one of his old hunting grounds, the Shirley Basin of southeastern Wyoming Territory.[11] Like Roosevelt, who bought land in Dakota Territory the same year, he had been lured into ranching by the cattle boom of the early '80s. Both would suffer large losses when, during the winter of 1886–87, blizzards lashed the ranges of the northern Great Plains and wiped out cattle by the tens of thousands. With the coming of spring, many ranchers found that they were ruined. Only their wealth kept Grinnell and Roosevelt from being included.

As the two talked about their experiences in the West, Grinnell returned often to the subject of hide hunting and showed Roosevelt the published protest he made in the *Report* of the 1875 Ludlow expedition against the commercialization of big game.[12] This document, plus his verbal descriptions of the killing, "much impressed Roosevelt, and gave him his first direct and detailed information about this slaughter of elk, deer, antelope, and mountain sheep. No doubt it had some influence in making him the ardent game protector that he later became, just as my own experiences had started me along the same road [earlier]."[13] In Grinnell's usual self-effacing way[14] he suggested that he may have had some part in shaping the viewpoint of the future President; in fact, as this study will show, he was one of the two individuals who most influenced Roosevelt's conservation philosophy; the other, of course, was Gifford Pinchot.

During those first conversations, "we talked of these things [the commercialization of wildlife] at length, and in a vague way foresaw the dangers that already threatened big game in many parts of the West as soon as a point should be reached where their products could be turned into dollars." They perceived that the key factor was "available transportation, for as soon as the skins could be brought to a market the animals that yielded them would be killed. Destruction had already taken place near the railroads, but though we felt that in time it would follow everywhere, we did not comprehend its imminence and the impending completeness of the extermination." Significantly, he added: "Neither had we any comprehension of the attempts that would at once be made to turn into money all our natural things, whether big game, birds, or forests."[15]

Grinnell admitted that "Those who were concerned to protect native life were still uncertainly trying to find out what they could most effectively do, how they could do it, and what dangers it was necessary to fight first. We regretted the unnecessary destruction of game animals, but we did not know all it meant, nor had we the vision to look forward and imagine what it portended. So, though we discussed in a general way the preservation of game, it must be confessed—in the light of later events—that we were talking of things about which we knew very little."[16]

Even though Grinnell and Roosevelt underestimated the rapidity with which the wildlife of the country would be decimated, they agreed that the game should be preserved "chiefly with the idea that . . . there might still be good hunting which should last for generations."[17] Both men soon decided that some sort of organized effort in this direction should be started. Although hundreds of sportsmen's associations with a similar goal were already in existence, too many of them were concerned only with local wildlife conservation or spent more time talking about protecting game than in actually working for it. As he stated in an 1884 *Forest and Stream* editorial, Grinnell wanted "a live [national] association of men bound together by their interest in game and fish, to take active charge of all matters pertaining to the enactment and carrying out of the laws on the subject. There is abundant material for such a body. Why can it not be organized?"[18]

The establishment of the Boone and Crockett Club, named after two of America's most famous hunters, was the result of this thinking. After Grinnell became intimately associated with Roosevelt, he emphasized the need for an effective sportsmen's society, to do for the larger mammals what the Audubon Society—founded by Grinnell in 1886—was doing for birds. Roosevelt agreed.[19] Accordingly, in December, 1887, the latter invited a number of his sportsmen friends to a dinner party in Manhattan at which he suggested the formation of such an association.[20] The recommendation was accepted by those present who included, in addition to Roosevelt and Grinnell, Roosevelt's brother Elliott and his cousin, J. West Roosevelt, Archibald

Rogers, E. P. Rogers, J. Coleman Drayton, Thomas Paton, Colonel James E. Jones, John J. Pierrepont, and Rutherford Stuyvesant.[21] All were prominent, wellborn New Yorkers.

A little later, Grinnell, Roosevelt, and Archibald Rogers "formulated the purposes and objects of the organization."[22] There were five in number: (1) "To promote manly sport with the rifle." (2) "To promote travel and exploration in the wild and unknown, or but partially known, portions of the country." (3) "To work for the preservation of the large game of this country, and, so far as possible, to further legislation for that purpose, and to assist in enforcing the existing laws." (4) "To promote inquiry into, and to record observations on the habits and natural history of, the various wild animals." (5) "To bring about among the members the interchange of opinions and ideas on hunting, travel, and exploration; on the various kinds of hunting rifles; on the haunts of game animals, etc."[23]

Regular membership was limited to one hundred men, all of whom had to "have killed with the rifle in fair chase, by still-hunting or otherwise, at least one individual of three of the various kinds of American large game." In its constitution the club declared against "killing bear, wolf or cougar in traps"; "killing game from a boat while it is swimming in the water"; "fire-hunting" (shooting, at night, animals stunned by the light of a torch);[24] and "crusting" (destroying animals immobilized in deep snow). From the time of Frank Forester, American sportsmen had been campaigning against these methods, labeling them as violations of gentlemanly behavior.[25] The emphasis the club's constitution placed on "fair chase" meant that the reform potential in what the writer has called the "code of the sportsman" was at last going to be fully realized.

It was probably Grinnell who first pointed out that some provision should be made for those who were not big-game hunters but who had worked for wildlife preservation. Examples were his two friends, geologist Arnold Hague and Supreme Court lawyer William Hallett Phillips; the latter was also an enthusiastic angler.[26] Their service for Yellowstone Park entitled them to membership, even though neither man had killed any big game.[27] After some consideration, it was decided that nonhunters could be elected to associate or honorary membership.[28] This rule and article (3) of the constitution were indications that the society was to be more than a dining club of select outdoorsmen.[29] In time its members would include many of the most famous and respected men in America, individuals like Henry L. Stimson, Henry Cabot Lodge, Elihu Root, Owen Wister, Wade Hampton, Gifford Pinchot, and many others. As a result, the organization's influence would prove far in excess of any ordinary association of similar size. In fact, the Boone and Crockett Club—and *not* the Sierra Club—was the first private organization to deal effectively with conservation issues of national scope.

Virtually all the early regular members were from a somewhat similar social background. They had attended college, often at Ivy League schools; they possessed venerable family names; they were financially well-off if not wealthy; and all were from the East, particularly the New York area. They were part of what some historians have called the American patrician class.[30] The exclusive Union, Metropolitan, University, Cosmos, and Century Clubs were their usual social haunts. Until 1909, when the Boone and Crockett acquired its own center, most of the society's meetings were held in either the University Club in Manhattan or the Metropolitan Club in Washington, D.C.[31]

As is usually the case, the work of the organization was accomplished by only a small number of members, the rest being content merely to attend the annual dinner. Of these active members, Grinnell was the most influential. He formulated almost every idea the club came to stand for; he brought up most of the issues it became involved in; he did a great part of the work on the Boone and Crockett book series on hunting and conservation; and he effectively used *Forest and Stream* as the "natural mouthpiece of the club."[32] In 1896 George S. Anderson, then Superintendent of Yellowstone National Park and a regular member of the Boone and Crockett, expressed the belief that without Grinnell, the club could not continue to exist.[33] And in a letter to Grinnell a year later, Roosevelt acknowledged him as one of the two or three "leaders of our organization."[34] A subsequent director of the society, the noted explorer and naturalist of Alaska, Charles Sheldon, went so far as to declare: "The Boone and Crockett Club . . . has been *George Bird Grinnell* from its founding. All its books, its work, its soundness, have been due to his unflagging work and interest and knowledge."[35] Because the statement was substantially correct, its significance lies in the fact that some of the most important figures in the first conservation movement—including its two future leaders, Roosevelt and Pinchot—were members of the club. "When Theodore Roosevelt became President," Stewart Udall has pointed out, "the Boone and Crockett wildlife creed . . . became national policy."[36] Forests and water could be included in that "creed," for in time the club took as its basic approach Grinnell's idea that all renewable resources benefited from efficient administration.

This concept, taken from the ideology of the scientific and business worlds, was reinforced by the code of the sportsman, with its emphasis on the use, without waste, of all game killed. As shown by its constitution, one of the club's essential *raisons d'être* was to achieve the wider acceptance of this code. After a year of existence, Grinnell claimed in *Forest and Stream* that the Boone and Crockett had already obtained notable success in this endeavor among "the best classes of society." He observed that with the exception of market gunners, the greatest destroyers of Western wildlife in the past had been upper-class pseudosportsmen. He affirmed, however, that in the last year the members of the club had ceaselessly expressed "their views about the folly and the wrong of *wanton* butchery, and their opinions on sport are therefore spread among that very class which in the past has given most offense in this respect." As a result, "those who used to boast of their slaughter are now ashamed of it, and it is becoming a recognized fact that a man who *wastefully* destroys big game, whether for the market, or only for heads, has nothing of the true sportsman about him."[37]

The importance the club's leaders placed on the etiquette of sport is illustrated by their stance in regard to Adirondack deer "hounding" (the use of dogs to drive deer into water where they are shot or clubbed to death). As usual, Grinnell had led the way with an editorial in *Forest and Stream* published three years before the club was founded. In the issue of November 6, 1884, he asked rhetorically: "What is Adirondack deer hounding? . . . Is hounding a legitimate way to kill deer in the Adirondacks? . . . Ought it to be abolished? Can it be abolished? Will it be abolished?"[38] This was the beginning of a seven-month campaign to end the practice which he later described as "destructive, unsportsmanlike and brutal."[39] *Forest and*

Stream printed petitions against hounding and sent them all over the state.[40] After being returned with thousands of signatures, they were forwarded to the Assembly in Albany.[41]

Tangible results were achieved when, in late winter, 1885, a bill was introduced in the Assembly to prohibit the custom. *Forest and Stream* agitated for its passage,[42] and by May this had been accomplished—twice in fact[43]—but Governor David B. Hill hesitated to add his signature.[44] Adirondack hotel owners and guides, as well as wealthy visiting "sportsmen," were against the legislation. Nevertheless, the anti-hounders had their way, and the bill became law the next month.[45]

Although the statute quickly resulted in a greatly reduced slaughter of deer,[46] the more effective it became in eliminating hounding, the greater the agitation by hotel keepers, guides, and pseudosportsmen to have it repealed. By early 1886, this movement had become a groundswell.[47] Though *Forest and Stream* circulated petitions to retain the law,[48] the opposition was too great, and in May, 1886, the New York Assembly repealed the prohibition.[49]

Although hounding again became one of northern New York's favorite fall pastimes, *Forest and Stream* had succeeded in making this form of recreation suspect among many of the state's sportsmen. One was the Boone and Crockett Club's president, Theodore Roosevelt. Then on the Civil Service Commission in Washington, D.C., he wrote Grinnell on January 13, 1894: "Don't you think the executive committee plus Madison Grant[50] . . . might try this year to put a complete stop to hounding in the Adirondacks? Appear before the Legislature, I mean. I wish to see the Club do something."[51] Later in the same month, he again urged Grinnell to "meet Madison Grant and have a talk over whether the Club could not take some action . . . about hounding deer in the Adirondacks."[52]

This was the beginning of a Boone and Crockett effort that continued sporadically for several years. Finally, in May, 1897, New York's governor signed a bill prohibiting, for five years, both hounding and "jacklighting" (shooting, at night, wildlife stunned by the glare of an artificial light). Several members of the club—including Grinnell, who testified at the hearings—were responsible for the introduction of the legislation and its passage. Nevertheless, the lion's share of the credit belonged to Madison Grant, who carried on a series of face-to-face negotiations with various senators and assemblymen.[53]

By the time the five years expired, New York's deer hunters had decided that the use of dogs and lights was unsportsmanlike, and the prohibition became permanent. Other Eastern states quickly followed New York's example by forbidding these practices.

The club's interest in the preservation of big game naturally turned it toward Yellowstone National Park. When that book review brought Grinnell and Roosevelt together, *Forest and Stream* and Senator Vest had already spent several years in crusading for the reserve.

They had been joined in this effort by Samuel S. Cox. A graduate of Brown and an eminent member of the lower house of Congress, this New Yorker was the most faithful defender of the park in the House until his death in 1889.[54] Cox was also a dedicated angler—he once made what he called a "pilgrimage" to the tomb of Izaak Walton—and he worked diligently to preserve fishing opportunities in the Potomac.[55] Though historian Roderick Nash asserts that Cox's advocacy of the reserve was "in the tradition of the Transcendentalists and Frederick Law Olmsted [the landscape architect],"[56] it is more likely that his commitment was based on the code of the sportsman, a tradition far older than American Transcendentalism or even European Romanticism.

Another adherent to the code of the sportsman was Theodore Roosevelt.[57] Describing his early relationship with Roosevelt, Grinnell later recalled that "the original attempt by a certain group of men to secure for their own profit control of all the important attractions of the park had been defeated before I knew him well, but as soon as he understood about the conditions in Yellowstone Park, he gave time and thought to considering its protection."[58] It would not be long before he joined Grinnell, Vest, Phillips, and Hague in actively working to establish a "government" for the park.

Between the time Grinnell and Roosevelt got together and the beginning of Roosevelt's active participation in the crusade, *Forest and Stream* continued to supply the public with a never-ending barrage of information on the park, including the state of the Vest bills in Congress, the dangers to the preserve, exposés of ineptitude and corruption in its handling, and definitions of the reservation's meaning for the American people.[59] Besides his newspaper efforts, Grinnell also acted as a lobbyist for the Vest bills, despite the fact that his patrician contempt for political maneuvering made the work disgusting to him. In early 1887 he wrote the well-known plainsman, Luther North, that "lobbying is the meanest work I ever did. I would rather break bronchos for a living than talk to Congressmen about a bill. It makes me feel like a detested pickpocket to do it." And the worst part was that after enduring "this shame," the bill he had worked for failed to pass.[60] It was Grinnell's deep sense of public service that kept him from giving up. With the commitment of the true muckraker, he told a friend: "We failed at Washington as I supposed we would, but I feel that, after all, truth is mighty and will prevail, and it is a newspaper's duty to kick with as much regularity and vigor as possible."[61]

Forest and Stream continued to "kick." Its newest tatic was the publishing of a seven-part model petition containing Grinnell's justifications for protecting the park, which he asked all sportsmen's clubs to copy, endorse, and send to Congress.[62] Later, *Forest and Stream* began issuing its own petitions, which it distributed across the country. Each week the names of the signatories were printed in the weekly.[63]

The first public record of Roosevelt's participation in the crusade for the Yellowstone is found in the *Forest and Stream* issue of April 3, 1890. The paper reported that he; Phillips; Hague; Captain F. A. Boutelle, the Superintendent of the reservation; and a few other "friends of the park" had been present at a recent meeting of the House's Public Lands Committee.[64] Under consideration was the latest Vest bill. Although Hague and others spoke, Roosevelt remained silent; evidently, he was still only an interested observer.

Soon, however, he was actively involved. By the end of April, Grinnell was able to write Hart Lyman of the New York *Tribune* that Roosevelt could now be counted among the reserve's most enthusiastic defenders. Like Phillips, Hague, and the others of its guardians, Grinnell believed that Roosevelt had no other "motive in this matter, except the proper preservation of the Park."[65]

But exactly what that "preservation" entailed soon became a source of potential disunity among the group. The issue was over whether a railroad should be allowed in the park. Captain Boutelle thought that such an "addition" would reduce Western opposition to the reserve, while doing it no material harm. To obtain a better idea of its needs, Roosevelt visited the reservation in late 1890. When he returned, it appeared to Grinnell "that Boutelle had converted him to a belief that a [rail]road would be beneficial to the Park."[66] Grinnell was particularly upset about this development, both because of his friendship with Roosevelt and because it would remove one of the preserve's most influential allies.[67]

Despite these considerations, Grinnell's commitment to his principles was then, as always, more important than friendship. He asked Hague and Archibald Rogers, another member of the Boone and Crockett interested in the park,[68] to try and "win Roosevelt back to his allegiance on this matter." But if they could not, "of course, we must throw him overboard."[69] Luckily, such a drastic move proved unnecessary, as one or both of these men did manage to bring him back to his original position. On December 24, 1890, Grinnell wrote Rogers: "I am glad to hear that Roosevelt is going to stand back on the question of railways in the Park and not to work against us."[70]

With the arrival of 1891, the leaders of the Boone and Crockett galvanized themselves for a new effort in behalf of the Yellowstone. The club's annual dinner was going to be held on January 14 at the Metropolitan Club in Washington, D.C., and Roosevelt wanted to use the occasion to emphasize to government officials the need for action. At the time, Grinnell was so busy with *Forest and Stream* matters that he thought he would be unable to attend. He changed his mind only after receiving an urgent plea from Roosevelt.[71] The dinner was kept informal,[72] even though Roosevelt had invited a gallery of notables. As president of the Boone and Crockett, he presided over the table. On his left sat Secretary of War Redfield Proctor,[73] and on his right, Speaker of the House Thomas B. Reed. Grinnell sat opposite Roosevelt, with Secretary of the Interior John W. Noble on one side and Samuel Pierpont Langley, physicist and Secretary of the Smithsonian Institution, on the other. A number of Congressmen, including Henry Cabot Lodge, Arnold Hague, William Hallett Phillips, and a few others, also attended.[74]

At a business meeting beforehand, Grinnell and Roosevelt drew up a series of resolutions which were read at the dinner: "*Resolved,* That the Boone and Crockett Club, speaking for itself and hundreds of [sportsmen's] clubs and associations throughout the country, urges the immediate passage by the House of Representatives of the Senate bill for the protection and maintenance of the Yellowstone National Park. *Resolved,* That this club declares itself emphatically opposed to the granting of a right of way to the Montana Mineral Railroad or to any other railroad through the Yellowstone National Park."[75]

After Roosevelt and Phillips made short speeches on the requirements of the reservation, one of the Congressmen asked a number of questions which were answered by Hague and Roosevelt.[76] "We then got to the subject of . . . large game," Grinnell reported to Archibald Rogers, "and Langley, in response to a request from Roosevelt, said that he believed from what he had heard, that the large game of the Continent would be practically exterminated except in such preserves as the Yellowstone Park, within the life of the present generation of men." The Secretary had probably obtained this viewpoint from Grinnell. The two had been in communication on wildlife matters for some time, and Langley had already incorporated at least one of Grinnell's suggestions. This was his idea for having the National Zoological Park, which the Smithsonian controlled, acquire the Yellowstone reserve's surplus bears and other unwanted predators, rather than destroying them as formerly.[77]

After the Secretary had made his comment, "Roosevelt . . . asked me to say something of the way in which game had disappeared in my time," Grinnell continued in his letter to Rogers, "and I told them a few 'lies' about buffalo, elk, and other large game in the old days." Clearly, Grinnell's long and varied experience in the primitive West had entitled him to Roosevelt's esteem.[78] When he finished his description of "the old days," a general conversation followed until about eleven o'clock when the group broke up.[79]

Grinnell felt that the dinner had been a success, because "we excited a real interest," and he was now "more hopeful than . . . for two or three years."[80] Despite his optimism, the railroad lobby proved successful in keeping the House from considering the Senate bill before the end of the session.[81]

The future was not all black, however, as the issue was gaining a wider currency in the nation's periodicals. For some time, Grinnell had successfully used his position as the editor of *Forest and Stream* to foster unity of the press by encouraging fellow newspapermen to join his banner.[82] In view of the growing demand by the press that the park be protected, Robert Underwood Johnson of *Century Maga-*

zine asked Grinnell to head a "Defense Association" that he hoped to found for the purpose of fighting for the Yellowstone and the recently established Yosemite Park. Because Grinnell was the leader in the Yellowstone movement, Johnson thought he was the logical man for the job. But Grinnell declined, confidently asserting that the Boone and Crockett Club would be able to achieve, at least for the Yellowstone, the necessary legislation. He told Johnson that though the society appeared superficially to be only "a dining club of about 30 big game hunters," the "good social standing and more or less position and influence" of its members meant that the association had great potential.[83] Events would prove him right.

Johnson's offer did have one significant result, however; it encouraged the leaders of the club to expand their organization. On May 7, 1891, Grinnell wrote to Hague that "I am rather disposed to think with you that it is quite within the purview of the Boone and Crockett Club to care for these Parks, but in order to do that it will be necessary, as you say, to enlarge the scope of the club and to get in a great number of new members." The distribution of influence in the association is revealed by Grinnell's admonition that Hague consider the other side of the question: "You and I can now control the action of the Boone and Crockett in these matters, as you say, but if that club were ten or one hundred times as large, could we still do so?"[84]

By 1892, the park situation had changed little. The *Forest and Stream* office continued to act as a kind of clearinghouse for information received from Phillips, Roosevelt, and Hague in Washington, and from various Western informants, including the superintendents and Elwood ("Billy") Hofer, an experienced hunter and the reserve's principal guide and outfitter.[85] These intelligence reports were digested and incorporated into both editorials and pamphlets; the latter were distributed to the leading newspapers and every member of Congress.[86]

Forest and Stream's activity was matched by the park's Washington guardians. Roosevelt, Phillips, and Hague participated in hearings on the park held by the Public Lands Committee of the House early in 1892 and defended the reservation against the railroad lobby.[87] Later in the year, they sent Grinnell the endorsements he had requested[88] for his editorials. When *Forest and Stream* published "A Standing Menace" on December 8, which attacked the railroad interests, the paper followed it the next week with supporting letters from Phillips, Roosevelt, and George S. Anderson, a sportsman and the reserve's latest superintendent.[89]

By now, the railroad threat had taken a new form. Because those who were pushing for the right of way had been effectively blocked on the grounds that a line through the park would be an infringement on its "integrity," they reasoned that the perfect solution to the dilemma was to have the area in question cut off from the rest of the preserve and returned to the public domain. Legislation known as the "segregation bill" was introduced in Congress to accomplish this end. If passed, it would have removed 622 square miles from the northeastern portion of the park. This was the "Standing Menace" alluded to in Grinnell's editorial. Roosevelt's letter on the subject, dated December 5, 1892, is noteworthy:

> I have just read the article "A Standing Menace," printed in the *Forest and Stream,* in reference to the attempts made to destroy the National Park in the interests of Cooke City.[90] I heartily agree with this article. It is of the utmost importance that the Park shall be kept in its present form as a great forestry preserve and a National pleasure ground, the like of which is not to be found on any other continent than ours; and all public-spirited Americans should join with *Forest and Stream* in the effort to prevent the greed of a little group of speculators, careless of everything save their own selfish interests, from doing the damage they threaten to the whole people of the United States, by wrecking the Yellowstone National Park. So far from having this Park cut down it should be extended, and legislation adopted which would enable the military authorities who now have charge of it to administer it solely in the interests of the whole public, and to punish in the most vigorous way people who trespass upon it. The Yellowstone Park is a park for the people, and the representatives of the people should see that it is molested in no way.[91]

Obviously, Roosevelt had resolved his earlier indecision on the issue of railroads and the park. He now firmly believed that they represented a grave threat to the reservation, even in the form of "segregation." This is all the more significant, since he held this opinion in the face of "backsliding" by one of his Washington co-workers. Arnold Hague now favored segregation. He was weary of the seemingly endless crusade and wanted to finish his survey work, which was being held up by the controversy over the park's future. It is also possible that political pressure had been exerted on him through the Geological Survey to drop his opposition to the railroad interests.[92] This defection pained Grinnell. As he told Phillips, "I felt badly that he [Hague] should disagree with the rest of us. I must say that I am sick of this whole Park business, but it is one of the cases where you cannot very well stop fighting."[93]

Despite the desertion in his camp, Grinnell found the American public coming around to his position. The pamphlets *Forest and Stream* was continually printing and distributing were proving especially effective. The many thousands who saw the paper each week were met with the following appeal: "Every reader who appreciates the gravity of the situation, who would see the Park preserved, for his children and his children's children . . . is invited to assist in the Park defense movement by putting these circulars where they will best create public sentiment." And, he added, "the reprints will be sent in any desired numbers, post paid, to any address."[94] So many readers responded that the company most involved in trying to "develop" the Yellowstone was receiving such a volume of adverse mail that its publicity agent visited the *Forest and Stream* office to demand that its side also be printed.[95]

Even when the segregation bill passed the Senate in February, 1893, Grinnell successfully used his paper to keep it from passing the House. P. J. Barr, a paid lobbyist for the railroad interests, had sent a telegram to leading Democrats in Montana asking them to apply pressure on Charles F. Crisp, Speaker of the House, to have the legislation forced through. A copy of the telegram fell into Grinnell's hands and he printed it in *Forest and Stream,* accompanied by a sarcastic editorial entitled "Will Speaker Crisp be Deceived?" The Speaker may not have been deceived, but he was certainly embarrassed, and the hopes of the railroad lobby were crushed for that session of Congress.[96]

Although the reserve's guardians were making some progress in their efforts to involve the public in the future of the Yellowstone, they would not obtain final victory until they received the unwilling aid of a poacher. It all began when Superintendent Anderson assigned his chief scout, Felix Burgess, to watch the Pelican Creek area of the national park. In October, 1893, a buffalo herd had been sighted there, and Anderson knew that if the notorious poacher, Edgar Howell, were in the park, he would concentrate his activities in that vicinity. At the time, buffalo heads and robes were bringing large sums from taxidermists who hoped to stock up before the species became extinct.

A few months later the Superintendent's hunch paid off. It was a cold March day, and the snow was so deep that Burgess and his companion, a trooper named Troike, were using skis to make their reconnaissance. While scouting Astringent Creek in Pelican Valley, they happened on a man's trail. Following it, they found a cache of half a dozen fresh buffalo heads hanging in a tree and, farther on, a tepee. While the two were examining the lodge, six shots sounded close by. Moving to the top of a wooded slope, they looked down on a human figure busily skinning a fallen buffalo, while several others lay in the snow near him. Burgess recognized Edgar Howell. The situation was delicate, since Burgess and Troike had only a single .38-caliber revolver between them, while Howell, a man known for his savage temper, had a repeating rifle. Still, there was one chance. Because Howell needed both hands free to flay his kill, he had leaned his rifle against one carcass while working on another. Taking this opportunity, the scout drove his ski poles into the snow and raced down the slope. Howell was so intent on his work that by the time he looked up, it was too late. Burgess was standing only a few feet away, his gun pointed in the poacher's direction.[97]

What made this incident more than an isolated encounter in the wilderness was the presence in the park of a *Forest and Stream* reporter, Emerson Hough.[98] In addition to being a dedicated sportsman,[99] he achieved fame for his many historical romances, including *The Story of the Cowboy* (1897), *The Passing of the Frontier* (1918), and *The Covered Wagon* (1922). In later years, Hough demanded full credit for supposedly seizing on Howell's arrest as an opportunity for publicizing the needs of the park. In reality, he was at first "unwilling to take the responsibility of sending a telegram to *Forest and Stream*" and finally did so only after being argued into it by Anderson and Hofer.[100]

The story first appeared on March 24, 1894. In "A Premium on Crime" the weekly protested: "The occurrence calls public attention again and most forcibly to the criminal negligence of which Congress has been guilty for all these years in failing to provide any form of government for the Park, or to establish any process of law by which crimes against the public committed within its borders can be punished."[101] Succeeding issues continued to hammer away in the same vein.[102] In "Save the Park Buffalo" *Forest and Stream* asked "that every reader who is interested in the Park or in natural history, or in things pertaining to America, should write to his Senator and Representative in Congress asking them to take an active interest in the protection of the Park." Another editorial dramatically underscored its point with three photographs showing a buffalo hunter and his slain victims.[103]

The call was answered by the American people.[104] Eight years earlier, a railroad spokesman's rhetorical question—"Is it true that the . . . demands of commerce [meaning a right of way through the park] . . . are to yield to . . . a few sportsmen bent only on the protection of a few buffalo"[105]—went almost unchallenged. Now, these "few sportsmen" were joined by a significant percentage of the articulate public. After other papers followed *Forest and Stream*'s lead, the Howell capture "created an interest throughout the country. . . ."[106] Carefully prepared by the continuous teachings of Grinnell's weekly, the nation was at last beginning to realize that it owned Yellowstone National Park and its wildlife. The poaching incident revealed the speed with which its property was being eaten up by a greedy few. The resulting sense of loss was intensified by the sentimental attachment felt for the buffalo, the symbol of the virgin West, now that the animal and the life it represented seemed doomed. *Forest and Stream* had perpetuated the idea that the survival of the species depended on those in the park. As a consequence, what alarmed the public about the Howell case was that even though the poacher had destroyed only a few buffalo, he had killed "enough to show that, with a little more time, he would have exterminated the herd altogether."[107]

Only a week after *Forest and Stream* first reported the incident, Congressman John F. Lacey of Iowa, a member of the Boone and Crockett Club, introduced a bill in the House similar to the ones Vest had presented in the Senate so many times before. But now the legislation found little opposition. In early May it emerged from committee, passed both Houses, and was signed by President Cleveland on the 7th.[108]

The "Act to Protect the Birds and Animals in Yellowstone National Park" was the victory that Grinnell, and later the Boone and Crockett Club, had fought for so long. It incorporated the park within the United States judicial district of Wyoming, making the laws of that state applicable except where federal law took precedence. Killing animals, except to protect human life or property, was forbidden. All traffic in wildlife, alive or dead; removal of mineral deposits; and destruction of timber were also prohibited.

The emphasis in the act was on enforcement. A commissioner appointed by the United States Circuit Court would reside in the park to judge cases. He would be backed up by a force of United States marshals who could arrest, without process, anyone caught violating a regulation. Possession of dead wildlife was to be considered *prima-facie* evidence of guilt. The penalty for this or other infractions was a fine of up to $1,000 or a jail sentence of up to two years, or both. To house the lawbreakers, a jail would be constructed in the preserve.[109]

Despite the satisfaction the passage of this legislation brought the guardians of the park, they knew the law was not perfect. All believed, for example, that the clause allowing the killing of animals that endangered life or property would be misused in the future. Still, the act was as close to ideal as could be had. Although "the . . . bill is not perfect," Grinnell wrote Roosevelt, "with a good man at the head of the Interior Department, and a good superintendent, it will prove effective."[110] To ensure the proper enforcement of the regulations, Roosevelt and Phillips immediately took "steps to see that good men are appointed for deputy marshals."[111]

Historians agree that Grinnell and *Forest and Stream* deserve most of the credit for the passage of the Lacey bill.[112] But as we have seen, the publicity given the Howell case entailed an attack on the "criminal negligence" of Congress. In a manifestation of an attitude that would later produce the famous assault on the "muckrakers," Roosevelt complained that Grinnell's blanket condemnation of the national assembly had been uncalled for. Because Roosevelt was a latecomer to the

Yellowstone crusade, Grinnell may have been irritated by this somewhat presumptuous judgment of his tactics. Nevertheless, he politely
answered: "I am glad to have your suggestions and entirely agree
with you that as a rule it does not do much good to blackguard Congress as a whole. This has been done in a very moderate way in *Forest
and Stream,* and for a particular purpose, which purpose seems to
have been accomplished in just the way we wished to have it." Although he felt that William Hallett Phillips "has of late years done
more than anyone else for the Park," Grinnell fed Roosevelt's substantial ego by declaring: "You personally have done a great deal and
ought to be 'blown off' for your help." As was customary, he took
no credit for himself.[113]

In founding a policy and administration for the nation's first national park, Grinnell and his co-workers had established precedents
that would be followed in the handling of all later parks. As one
historian has observed, "the provisions of the Lacey Act . . . formed
the basis for the present law and policy under which the National
Park Service has administered the natural treasures of the United
States since 1916,"[114] the year that agency came into existence.

In *A Brief History of the Boone and Crockett Club* (1910), Grinnell
explains that "the attempt to exploit the Yellowstone National Park
for private gain in a way led up to the United States forest reserve
system as it stands to-day,"[115] because "as a natural sequence to the
work that they [the club's leaders] had been doing" in regard to Yellowstone Park "came the impulse to attempt to preserve western forests
generally."[116] Since their original concern had been the park, it might
seem odd that concrete results on the forestry question were obtained
three years before the passage of the Lacey bill. The reason for this
was simply that the battle over the park took place in a public arena
against determined Western opposition, while the results in forestry
were achieved by circumventing the popular forum. Nevertheless, the
interrelationship of the two issues is shown by the fact that the first
forest reserve President Harrison chose to set aside in 1891 was the
Yellowstone National Park Timberland Reserve adjacent to the national preserve. "In essence," says one observer, "the Yellowstone became the birthplace for both the national parks and national
forests."[117] He might have added that the systems for managing both
were created largely by members of the Boone and Crockett Club.

As in the case of Yellowstone National Park, Grinnell led the club on the forestry issue. The editorial effort he began in 1882 to transform the nation's orientation toward its woodlands continued unabated through the decade.[118] The central thrust of these sophisticated but simply stated expositions was that "the Federal government must husband its resources and place them under systematic management,"[119] the purpose of which was exploitation without waste. Grinnell emphasized, in fact, that not to use resources was in itself wasteful: "The proposal to lock up the forests and prevent all further utilization of their products is one that cannot be entertained."[120] The latter statement was made in 1888 and matches exactly the policy that would be established in future years by two other Boone and Crockett members, Gifford Pinchot and Theodore Roosevelt.

In the late '80s *Forest and Stream* repeatedly asserted that the concepts and techniques of scientific forestry could only be effectively adapted to American conditions "by entrusting the administration of the forests to a skilled executive." Until forestry schools could be established in the United States capable of producing such a man, Grinnell requested "the importation of a competent staff of European officers."[121] Given the situation then existing, with the forests being wastefully cut down and burned over and the government unwilling or unable to reverse the destruction, he urged that the timberlands be "absolutely closed and the laws against trespass rigidly enforced."[122] But it is plain that he thought this drastic move should only be a stopgap, to save the woods until a plan for their administration could be drawn up and put into effect.

In "Popular Forestry Instruction," *Forest and Stream*'s editorial for December 6, 1888, Grinnell included a brief history of the weekly's crusade for the introduction of forestry in the United States.[123] He claimed, and probably with justice, that it had been the paper's seven-year campaign that had stimulated so much interest in the subject throughout New York State that the Assembly was finally forced into action. "They drafted a bill admirable in every detail, and displayed a praiseworthy zeal in incorporating every good suggestion in it; they appointed a Forest Commission, whose duty it would be to undertake the economic and scientific administration of the State forests, restock denuded areas, bring the whole under a high system of conservancy, establish chairs of forestry in our universities and colleges, and above all, to diffuse among the people at large a mass of popular literature, designed to enlighten them as to the economic importance of properly conserved forests." Now, he complained, the public thought that no further action was necessary when, in reality, nothing substantial had been accomplished. The reason, he affirmed, was that the men filling the newly created offices had no professional training or expertise.[124]

With an attitude approaching resignation, Grinnell wrote: "And so there is nothing for us [to do] but to recur to the subject from time to time, and keep alive the public interest in the problem, the attempted solution of which will probably constitute the severest test of the capacity of a republican government to deal with great economic questions, which the Government of the United States has ever been exposed to."[125] How right he was became increasingly obvious as the democratic West tried to block every federal effort to bring about land stewardship—an effort initiated mainly by Eastern patricians.

While Grinnell was acting in his usual capacity as the instigator of public opinion, the Supreme Court lawyer, William Hallett Phillips, was busy in his customary role as a behind-the-scenes negotiator. Like others in the Boone and Crockett Club, he had arrived at his interest in forestry via his involvement in the crusade over the Yellowstone. "In 1887 Phillips . . . had succeeded in interesting Mr. [Lucius Q. C.] Lamar, Secretary of the Interior, and a number of Congressmen, in the forests, and gradually all these persons began to work together. At the close of the first Cleveland Administration, while no legislation had been secured looking toward forest protection, a number of men in Washington had come to feel an interest in the subject."[126]

In 1889 President Benjamin Harrison appointed John W. Noble of Missouri Secretary of the Interior. As in the case of his predecessors, Noble received the "treatment" from the directors of the Boone and Crockett as soon as he entered office. This consisted of personal visits from Phillips, Hague, and Roosevelt, and invitations to the club's dinners. But the one all-important difference was that Noble, unlike his forerunners, was highly receptive to the organization's expression of concern for the forests.

Why this should be true is not entirely clear. Although Noble was later an associate member of the Boone and Crockett Club, it is not known whether he ever hunted for recreation or accepted the environmental obligation inherent in the code of the sportsman. But it is known—as discussed in Chapter 1—that he believed field sports helped individuals who pursued them to make a success of their lives, and this, of course, is one of the basic themes of the sporting tradition.

Regardless of whether Noble was a sportsman himself, he seemed to enjoy the attentions of the prestigious Boone and Crockett Club, and he was in close touch with at least two of its members, Phillips and Grinnell, by 1889. In fact, the latter believed that it was Phillips, who was already a good friend of the Secretary of the Interior, who was most responsible for involving Noble in the effort to preserve Western forests.[127] It would seem that *Forest and Stream*'s editor knew what he was talking about, as he worked with both men in behalf of the same end.

Grinnell's relationship with Noble began in the spring of 1889. In addition to his conservation work, Grinnell was also a dedicated champion of the American aborigine.[128] After trying for months to oust an Indian agent who was exploiting the Blackfeet of northwestern Montana, he suddenly achieved success when the new Secretary of the Interior interceded personally in the affair after being alerted by Phillips.[129] From that time to the end of Noble's term in office, the Secretary and *Forest and Stream*'s editor were in frequent communication on conservation matters and Indian affairs.

Following the position advocated earlier by *Forest and Stream,* Noble came to agree that in order to save the timberlands, they would have to be withdrawn from the public domain.[130] The means for accomplishing this end were provided on March 3, 1891, when "An Act to Repeal Timber Culture Laws and for other Purposes. . . ." was signed by President Harrison. Pushed through at the close of the Fifty-First Congress, the legislation was an effort to revise the land laws of the United States. Those who worked hardest among the members of Congress to have the bill approved were Bernhard Fernow, Chief of the Division of Forestry, and to a lesser degree, Hague and Phillips.[131]

The granting of power to the President to set aside timberlands was not an obvious part of the act, but the last of twenty-four sections, being "inserted in [the] Conference Committee in the last hour of Congress by the insistence of Mr. Noble, that he would not allow the bill to be signed by the President unless the clause was added."[132] Grinnell later recalled that it "had little or nothing to do with the title, or indeed the purpose of the bill, and probably no one [in Congress] who read over the bill before it became law understood what the section meant."[133]

Soon after the passage of the bill, Hague "saw Secretary Noble and called his attention to the bill as it stood, suggesting the setting aside of the Yellowstone Park Forest Reserve adjoining the Park. . . ."[134] His aim, as Grinnell explained at the time, was "protection for the territory south and east of the Park, which it has so long been hoped might be added to the reservation."[135] Noble liked Hague's idea, but before acting, he wanted to be sure there were no hidden pitfalls of a legal nature. To resolve this question, Hague returned the next day with William Hallett Phillips, Noble's friend and adviser, and all three discussed the legal question. After dismissing all doubts, Noble carried the project to the President, who promised to give the order. The dimensions of the proposed tract were discussed in several conferences between Noble and Hague and, finally, on March 30, 1891, President Harrison issued the proclamation setting aside the first forest reserve. Calling the tract the Yellowstone National Park Timberland Reserve, Harrison defined its boundaries in exactly the same language Hague had used in his proposal to Noble.[100]

Though this land would be administered differently than the national park, it eventually obtained equivalent protection when the Forest Service eliminated uncontrolled fire and wasteful logging, the two factors which had previously threatened its existence. In a real sense, therefore, Harrison's proclamation was the culmination of the effort Grinnell had begun in 1882 to have Yellowstone Park extended on the east and south, an effort which Phillips and Hague had later taken up.

The Yellowstone reserve contained 1,239,040 acres, all in Wyoming, and was the inauguration of the national forest system totaling, as of July 1, 1967, 182.7 million acres in 154 national forests. Shortly after its announcement, Roosevelt, representing the Boone and Crockett Club, endorsed the action and commended Harrison and Noble.[137] Grinnell did the same in *Forest and Stream* and urged the public to accept the reserve and the policy it represented.[138] Some years later, Noble would gratefully acknowledge the aid Grinnell and "his very popular and influential paper" had given him, before and after the forest reserve system was initiated.[139]

From this discussion, it would appear that Yellowstone National Park was a focal point of the early dialogue on natural resources. After "conservation" gained currency, some of its supporters employed the word only in reference to resource "use"; those areas emphasizing the aesthetic were ordinarily excluded. As we have seen, when Grinnell was working out his ideas for the future of the Adirondacks, he may have shared this outlook. Soon, however, he came to regard the handling of all natural resources, including national parks, as being part of "conservation," since they all benefited from *continuous*, efficient management. This sense of the need for *process* was inherited by the directors of the Boone and Crockett Club, who, under Grinnell's leadership, became involved in the future of the national park. Their approach was his approach, the basis of which was the demand for a "government" for the reserve. By this, they meant an administration that would have the power and assured continuity to enforce effectively a series of regulations. This emphasis on the need for continuous, efficient enforcement is clearly evident in the 1894 act, and the application of its provisions to the national park was the first time a specific, publicly owned natural resource had received such systematic treatment.

The second reason the battle over the Yellowstone was a focal point of early conservation was because it was one of the first times a resource-related issue gained national popular support that included nonsportsmen as well as hunters and fishermen. Only the fish-culture movement (Chapter 2) attained a similar popularity, but it lacked the emotionalism attending the crusade to preserve the Yellowstone. The uproar caused by the Howell poaching incident shows that by 1894 there existed something approaching a mass concern for the park. While other issues like forestry and irrigation remained without public understanding or backing, a significant segment of "the people" clamored for the protection of "their" national park. Their involvement in the drive was based on sentimentality—the desire to see the buffalo saved—rather than on a deep scientific or aesthetic appreciation. Yet it was the beginning of an ever-greater willingness to

acknowledge the crisis in natural resources and accept the need for con-
certed national action.

In later years, both Roosevelt and Pinchot maintained that forestry
was the first issue to gain and keep mass support for conservation.[140]
Because of their central positions in the crusade, historians have un-
critically accepted this viewpoint.[141] It is likely, however, that the two
were reflecting their own, later concentration on forestry as the focus
of conservation, rather than their memory of how the movement actually began.[142] Long before the public had a comprehension of the
principles and practices of scientific forestry, or even an awareness
that the timber stocks were supposedly[143] in danger of being exhausted,
it knew that many kinds of mammals, birds, and fish were rapidly
disappearing. The public's attention was drawn first to wildlife because
the disastrous consequences of unregulated industrial growth were
most obvious in terms of this resource. As the most accessible, it was
depleted quickest; and as the most conspicuous, its loss was noticed
first. A man might not understand or care about forestry statistics,
but he felt regret at viewing an empty prairie that had been darkened
only a few years before by thousands of buffalo. The completeness
with which the supposedly countless bison were wiped out provided
the earliest, and the most dramatic, challenge to the nineteenth-century myth of the inexhaustibility of resources.[144]

One individual who eventually perceived the incompatibility between myth and reality was Theodore Roosevelt. Although he had
expressed an interest in 1884 in the movement to set aside an
Adirondack Preserve, his orientation toward the outdoors was still
as a sportsman-naturalist who had not fully accepted the environmental obligation intrinsic to the code of the sportsman. Except for two
ornithological studies published in the 1870s and one history work
in the early '80s, his first books dealt with hunting in the West. While
they reveal that Roosevelt possessed the code of the sportsman, these
volumes do not manifest the same commitment to the perpetuation
of natural resources so much a part of the later Boone and Crockett
book series created and edited by him and Grinnell. Under Grinnell's
tutelage, Roosevelt's love for big-game hunting soon developed into
a concern for the future of big game, as he became increasingly aware
of the speed with which it was disappearing. The belief that Yellow-

stone National Park was its last refuge was the origin of his involvement in the crusade for that preserve, which, in turn, was the beginning of his active career as a conservationist. It was only somewhat later that he became concerned, first, for the forests of the Yellowstone, and still later, for the Western forests generally.

The third reason for calling the campaign for the Yellowstone a focal point of early conservation was that it brought together for the first time several of the most important leaders of the national conservation movement. These included Arnold Hague, who would become Gifford Pinchot's assistant and co-worker in the forestry field, Roosevelt, and Pinchot himself. Although Pinchot was not actually involved in the Yellowstone fight, it was the extension of the Boone and Crockett Club's interest in the Yellowstone's forests to Western forests as a whole that made them want Pinchot for a member when they heard of his professional ability; he joined in 1897.

The fourth and last reason why the crusade for the Yellowstone represents a focal point of early conservation has already been given: The Yellowstone was not only the birthplace of the national parks and the policy for administering them—it was also the cradle of the forest reserves. These were the basis of the national forest system, the single most important element in the Roosevelt-Pinchot conservation program.

By the middle 1890s, the foundations of conservation had been laid, and the full flowering of the movement was just around the corner. Of those who had set the course for the future, none had been more important than George Bird Grinnell. For twenty years, he had been at the center of the evolution of conservation and was intimately involved in legitimizing the place of the sportsman in American society and consolidating his increasing dissatisfaction with disappearing game and habitat; in bringing about better enforcement of game statutes by changing the public's attitude toward lawbreakers; in fighting off the assaults on the nation's first and, for a long time, only national park; in achieving a clear-cut definition of the meaning of the park and establishing a policy for its administration; in cofounding and directing the Boone and Crockett Club, the first conservation organization in the United States to deal effectively with issues of national scope; in arousing an interest, first in New York State and later throughout the country, in the future of the nation's forests; and in planting in the public mind an incipient awareness of the fact that in order for natural resources to serve man, while lasting indefinitely,[145] they must be administered on a continuous basis.

Grinnell's impact had been great, but it would be greater still when a friend, whose conservation philosophy he had done much to form, became Governor of New York and then President of the United States. The friend, of course, was Theodore Roosevelt.

SIX

Establishment of a National Conservation Policy

W hen Roosevelt assumed the governorship of New York in early 1899, he discovered that all ideas for improving the handling of the state's natural resources had to be channeled through an already existing administrative body: the New York State Fisheries, Game, and Forest Commission. Although the agency was established some years before, it had accomplished little, as its members were customarily appointed solely on the basis of political influence. Grinnell had been editorializing since 1888 to have the administration of New York's resources separated from politics; efficient management of the state's natural assets would be obtained, he asserted, only if they were put into the hands of impartial experts.[1]

With the ascendancy of his friend to New York's highest political office, Grinnell's wish for a reconstituted commission might now be granted. As he observed in May, "the state of New York is fortunate at present in having a Governor who is not only deeply interested in all matters of game, fish and forest preservation, but [who] also has so clear an acquaintance with these subjects that he can always be depended upon to act on them for the public good." And, he added, even when Roosevelt's own great knowledge proved insufficient, he knew exactly which "expert advisers" to call on for aid.[2] Of these, Grinnell would continue to be the most important.

One of the manifestations of the commission's ineptitude was its total failure to enforce game laws. Inadequate law enforcement was a problem Grinnell had been publicizing for almost two decades, and one which Roosevelt had taken up when he joined the crusade for the Yellowstone. In a letter addressed to the commission, dated November 28 and printed in *Forest and Stream,* the Governor attacked the utter inefficiency of the state's game wardens and requested the commissioners to provide him with a full report on the wardens' capabilities, distribution, and numbers.[3]

In referring to the needs of New York's northern mountain region, Roosevelt foreshadowed his later emphasis on forestry as the focus of his national conservation program. He asked that the commissioners concentrate their efforts on the Adirondacks, "both from the standpoint of forestry and from the less important but still very important standpoint of game and fish protection."[4] Here, in capsule form, was the Roosevelt plan for the state's—and later the nation's—natural assets. Although wildlife and other resources would be a significant part of the plan, its major emphasis would be the woodlands.

It was probably for this reason that the Governor's first proposal for improving the efficiency of the commission was to eliminate four of its members, making it a single-headed agency.[5] The source of this idea was Gifford Pinchot, who had visited Roosevelt soon after he took office, and offered his suggestions for reforming the administration of New York's natural resources.[6] As in later years, Pinchot revealed a lack of interest in any resource except the forests, and in proposing an agency headed by a single commissioner, he expected that the official's time would be spent wholly in adapting the principles and practices of scientific forestry to the state's timberlands. Then, as later, Pinchot seemed to assume that if the forests were properly managed, all other resources would be automatically taken care of.

Grinnell could not agree. One man might be sufficiently versed in forestry to administer the woodlands properly, but it was highly unlikely that he would be equally knowledgeable about the other major resource categories. To ensure that the whole field was covered, the editor of *Forest and Stream* advocated splitting up the commission into sections and putting a commissioner at the head of each. The number of commissioners would then be reduced from five to three, and their departments would be forestry; game and fish protection; and fish culture and oyster farming. As in his earlier editorials on this subject, he emphasized that the only way to establish efficiency in the agency's functioning was to staff it with apolitical professionals.[7]

Grinnell's continuing influence on Roosevelt is shown by the fact that when the Governor announced his reconsidered plan for the makeup of the commission, he had discarded Pinchot's suggestion for a single commissioner and adopted Grinnell's proposal for a three-headed agency, differentiated into separate departments.[8] Evidently, Roosevelt had concluded that even though Pinchot's plan was simpler and had the advantage of stressing forestry, it inadequately provided for the administration of the other major resources.[9]

In the end, neither plan was adopted. Because the commission was a source of patronage, the state's politicians were unalterably opposed to any change in its basic character. Under the circumstances, Roosevelt's last hope for improving the agency lay in his right to nominate new members for the commission when the old one expired by limitation on April 25, 1900. If qualified men could be appointed, the fact that their terms would be five years long meant that much future good might be accomplished. Particularly important, of course, was the president of the commission. A competent individual in this position could affect for the better the whole tenor of the agency.

When Roosevelt announced his nominations, it was immediately apparent that he had picked such a man. The Governor's choice was W. Austin Wadsworth, sportsman and president of the Boone and Crockett Club. In his editorial of March 10 Grinnell applauded the Wadsworth nomination, but in regard to Roosevelt's other selections, he proved that once again his commitment to principle was more important than friendship. He expressed the hope that Wadsworth would be able to control the other members, for he was the only one "who appears not to have been selected without regard to politics." In brief biographical sketches Grinnell condemned in turn each of the other four nominations.[10]

Soon after the editorial appeared, Roosevelt wrote Grinnell in dismay: "Today I found . . . your paper . . . being actively circulated by the men who are here [in Albany] in the interest of the lumber . . . and cold storage lobby to defeat my nominees for the Forest,

Fish and Game Commission, the argument being that as the men interested in forest, fish and game preservation cared .so little for the new nominees, and as every political and financial interest was enlisted against them, there was no possible object in making the change." Ironically, those who desired the perpetuation of unregulated lumbering and game traffic had discovered an unexpected ally in one who had long been their worst enemy.

As the Governor's letter went on, it was obvious that he was more hurt than angry. Feeling that Grinnell had unfairly censured his nominees, he proceeded to give a detailed, self-justifying explanation of how and why each of them was selected. Roosevelt told Grinnell that he had no idea of the obstacles the Governor had to overcome when there was "no effective popular feeling one way or the other about the forest[s] or the preservation of fish and game," and when the lobbyists of the lumber and cold-storage interests and "every politician in the state" were working to have the old commission retained. In an implied slap at Grinnell's "armchair politics," Roosevelt asserted: "I chose the men the way I did because my business was to improve the Commission—not to issue a manifesto about them."[11]

In essence, Roosevelt's defense was valid. Although Grinnell was not a stranger to political maneuvering, having been a lobbyist many times, he was still somewhat naive about the difficulties a politician had to face and surmount before a reform measure could be implemented. While Roosevelt was in full agreement as to the value of Grinnell's goal, the Governor knew, as an experienced political tactician, that compromise was the key to success.

Roosevelt's letter points out another, more important, difference between the two men. When it came to reform, Roosevelt prided himself on being a "doer," a man of action. Grinnell, on the other hand, was a creator and amalgamator of ideas who, as the historian of the Boone and Crockett Club has observed, "was a pusher rather than a leader, working behind the scenes and quietly steering the energies of more active public officials into constructive channels."[12] Despite their occasional disagreements, this is precisely the relationship he had with Roosevelt.

Evidently, the Governor had adequately vindicated himself, for Grinnell wrote to him on March 17 that his additional information on the nominees put them in a different light. "A pretty strong point in their favor," Grinnell concluded, was "the fact that the wood pulp . . . and cold storage men are trying to prevent . . . their confirmation. . . ."[13]

Despite the opposition, the New York Senate confirmed the nominees on March 20. Four days later, Grinnell backed up his new view of the men by cautiously endorsing the Senate's action in *Forest and Stream*. He commented that because of Roosevelt's genuine interest in the work the commission was to undertake, it was inconceivable that he would have picked unqualified men. But, he added, "the work of the new commission will be watched with great interest."[14]

As if to obtain a more positive endorsement of his action, the Governor asked Grinnell to attend the preliminary meeting of the new commission at which Roosevelt was to give a talk outlining his expectations of the officials. The fact that Grinnell was still foremost among those whose opinions on natural resources Roosevelt trusted is shown by the Governor's question: "Can you suggest any first class men interested in forestry and fish and game whom it would be a good thing to have come here at the same time?"[15] Grinnell did attend, and he brought along a few of the "first class men" Roosevelt had asked for.[16] Afterwards, Grinnell told the Governor he was pleased with the speech to the commissioners and thought that it would achieve the desired result.[17]

Under President Wadsworth's leadership, the agency did accomplish much good. At the beginning of the administration of Governor Benjamin B. Odell, Roosevelt's successor, a sportsman's periodical, *The Gun,* stated that "in checking pollution of streams alone, its service has been of inestimable value. . . ."[18] Pollution had been a target of the commission ever since Governor Roosevelt's annual message of January, 1900. Besides sounding very much like Grinnell in emphasizing that what was needed in the field of natural resources was not more laws but better enforcement of existing statutes, the Governor also spoke out against pollution. Repeating arguments that had been appearing in sporting literature since before the Civil War, Roosevelt put particular stress on the contamination caused by pulp mills and its ruinous effects on fishing.[19]

Because the editor of *Forest and Stream* had been unsure at first of how conscientious the new conservation commission would prove, it may seem strange that its course was laid out largely according to ideas that he himself had formulated. This is not really surprising, however, when it is remembered that the agency's director was also president of the Boone and Crockett Club and very much under Grinnell's intellectual sway. Most of the recommendations made by the commission had been expressed earlier in *Forest and Stream* or at the meetings of the Boone and Crockett Club, and they had originated, invariably, in Grinnell's fertile mind. Examples were the proposed amendment to the state constitution that would permit the practice of "conservative forestry" in the Adirondack Preserve, the setting aside of state game refuges, and the abolition of spring waterfowl shooting.[20]

Roosevelt's tenure in the office of governor came to an end in late 1900. His major conservation accomplishments were the expansion of public concern for the state's natural resources and the vitalization of the agency responsible for administering them. The two-year term was really too short, however, to do more than begin the work required. When Roosevelt received, and accepted, the Vice-Presidential nomination in June, 1900, Grinnell was disappointed that he had not "held out" for the Presidency, believing that the lesser post might prove to be a dead end for his friend's political career.[21] Ironically, an assassin's bullet gave him the opportunity for implementing conservation that Grinnell thought was lost. When Theodore Roosevelt took the Presidential oath of office at 3:00 p.m. on September 14, 1901, a new era in the history of the American land began.

The conservation achievements of his administration were vast. The most important were the addition of 100 million acres to the forest reserves,[22] called "national forests" after 1907; the creation of a professional Forest Service that would efficiently manage the tracts according to the principles and practices of scientific forestry; the establishment of five national parks and seventeen national monuments; and the founding of an extensive system of wildlife refuges containing over fifty units.[23] Although Roosevelt's conservation program has been thoroughly examined by professional historians—who now consider it his most enduring accomplishment—they have overlooked the fact that the fundamentals of that program were foreshadowed in a series of books he co-edited years before. These were the three Boone and Crockett Club volumes on hunting and conservation that he and Grinnell compiled during the 1890s: *American Big-Game Hunting* (1893), *Hunting in Many Lands* (1895), and *Trail and Camp-Fire*

(1897). In one or more of these works can be found the demands that the federal government expand the national parks and forest reserves, establish a means for systematically administering them, and create a series of game refuges. As we have seen, all these proposals had been expressed earlier in *Forest and Stream.*

It was during the late 1880s that Roosevelt began acquiring the ideas he would later establish as national policy, and the fact that he repeatedly chose Grinnell to be his co-editor pinpoints the special advisory relationship the latter had to the future President. About 1891, the two men had first begun to talk of the desirability of publishing a book made up of contributions by club members on hunting and natural history, plus editorial material furnished by themselves. They seemed to feel that such a volume would help to consolidate the members and their ideas and increase the prestige of the club by making its reform efforts better known. The first book was such a success that they decided to initiate a series, and their literary partnership continued until Roosevelt became President.

Whenever there was a problem in interpretation, Roosevelt customarily acceded to Grinnell's greater experience and knowledge. When, for example, he wrote him about a paper submitted by a club member for the 1897 volume, Roosevelt told Grinnell: "Of course, whatever you wish to do . . . , I will gladly agree to."[24] Later, in discussing another matter pertaining to the same book, he replied to Grinnell: "All right—I am sure your judgment is correct. Early in July I will be able to send you my two articles."[25]

As the book neared completion, Grinnell—who, as usual, seemed to be doing most of the work— informed Roosevelt that he still had not received all the papers requested of the club members. Roosevelt replied: "I am sorry you should be so short of copy. . . . If there is any real difficulty about copy, I should suggest that you and I write a composite article (unless, which I believe, you could do it alone) on the past and present distribution of the big game animals of temperate North America, with a short description of each." As a bit of encouragement, he added: "Our first two volumes are really very good. I was looking over them the other day; and we must try to make this [one] up to the [same] level." If they were successful in this, he told Grinnell, and "the fellows don't come forward better in the future than in the past, we will simply stop publishing volumes until they do."[26]

When *Trail and Camp-Fire* appeared later that year, Roosevelt's expectations were fulfilled. In a letter to Grinnell, he judged it "the best volume we have put out yet." He was especially pleased with Grinnell's title choice, which he called "a particularly good one."[27] The critics seemed to share Roosevelt's enthusiasm; in a list of 4,332 volumes published during 1897–98, the New York State Librarian ranked it as one of the best fifty.[28]

From their close association as the leaders of the Boone and Crockett Club, Roosevelt received a thorough exposure to Grinnell's ideas for handling the nation's natural resources. There is little question that he was the original source of many of the concepts Roosevelt later established as national policy.

During the formative 1885–97 period, Roosevelt absorbed not only Grinnell's ideas, but also his point of view. In reviewing the evolution of Grinnell's thought on natural resources, three main themes can be delineated. The first was a product of his involvement with the more sophisticated, academic approach to Western exploration initiated by the Marsh expedition of 1870 (Chapter 3). Grinnell's field studies in paleontology and zoology made him aware of the changes the earth and its life forms had undergone and taught him that the land was vulnerable. This insight led to a concern for natural resources and a horror at how they were being abused—the spark of his commitment to reform.

The second theme in Grinnell's thinking is what I have termed the "code of the sportsman." Transmitted through the pages of *Forest and Stream,* it became a part of the value system of the outdoorsmen who composed the Boone and Crockett Club. The belief that there was only one correct way for a "gentleman" to pursue game, and that all other methods were crude or even immoral, lay behind much of the club's activities and all of its thinking. The single most important element in the code was the requirement of noncommercial use, without waste, of all game killed.

The third and last major theme in Grinnell's conservation thought was his application of the business community's ideology to the handling of natural resources, especially the idea that they could be "managed" like a firm. Whether forests or wildlife, if only the "interest" was used and sufficient "capital" left behind to produce the next generation, renewable resources could be exploited indefinitely without fear of shortages.

It can be seen that these three themes had certain elements in common. All, for example, tended toward an emphasis on the need to eliminate waste and produce efficiency. This was even true of the code of the sportsman, with its taboo against the wanton destruction or waste of game. The primary common factor, however, was a belief in the *perpetual* responsibility of the nation for its resources and a confidence that those natural assets could be enjoyed forever if only administered on a continuous, systematic basis.[29]

This is the "point of view," mentioned above, that Grinnell passed on to Roosevelt. When the latter became President, he too made the efficient administration of resources the keynote of his conservation policy. Because he appointed Gifford Pinchot as the chief administrator of his various programs, historians have focused on the forester. The literature on Pinchot is extensive and includes three biographies.[30] Scholars appear to assume that before Pinchot made his appearance, Roosevelt had little real interest in conservation reform. Even those who point to his record as New York's governor emphasize that it was at the beginning of Roosevelt's tenure in that office that Pinchot became his adviser. This portrait of the forester's indispensability is partly the result of Pinchot's own brush strokes, for in his autobiography he spares no efforts to prove that *he* was the conservation movement.[31]

The fact is that Pinchot originated few ideas. His great contribution to conservation lay in his talents as a manager, one who implemented concepts already familiar to Roosevelt.[32] In essence, he was the "trained professional" Grinnell had first called for in 1884, who would lead the nation in the "inauguration of a system of forest conservancy."[33]

In attempting to explain the origins of national conservation, historians have neglected the intellectual antecedents of Roosevelt's policy. This study has found that Grinnell, the originator and synthesizer of ideas, *prepared* Roosevelt for Pinchot, who executed those ideas. Although the latter two men had met as early as 1894, it was not until 1899, at the beginning of Roosevelt's tenure as governor, that they became well acquainted. But from the very first consultation,

Pinchot was impressed with the Governor's grasp of forestry and his enthusiasm for suggestions on how the timberlands could be perpetuated and exploited simultaneously.[34] Behind that receptivity was almost fifteen years of tutelage by George Bird Grinnell.

Historians may be oblivious to Grinnell's place in the evolution of conservation, but Roosevelt's contemporaries were not. After Roosevelt died, a group of his friends formed the Roosevelt Memorial Association and in 1923 created the Roosevelt Medal for Distinguished Service. When, in the spring of 1925, the presentations were made in the outdoor-conservation field, it was no accident that Grinnell and Pinchot were given medals at the same time and coupled as "pioneers"—the word President Coolidge used in the White House ceremony. Because there was only one award in each category, Pinchot appropriately received the medal for conservation, while Grinnell's prize was in the "promotion of outdoor life."[35] The important point is that in the minds of the Association's members, many of whom were Roosevelt's old friends and fellow naturalists, Grinnell, Pinchot, and the late President were inextricably linked.[36]

Only one scholar has perceived this relationship. James B. Trefethen, historian of the Boone and Crockett Club, delineated it in a letter to the author: "Grinnell . . . and Gifford Pinchot were the two strongest influences in shaping the conservation philosophy of Theodore Roosevelt, which is largely the basis of the modern conservation program in America."[37]

It is indeed ironic that the individuals who established that program were sportsmen, for if they lived today, they would find themselves being increasingly accused of insensitivity to nature and its wild things. But if an affinity for hunting and fishing—which often entails the taking of life—is a manifestation of insensitivity, then how does one explain the fact that American sportsmen were by far the single most important group in the making of conservation?

A
Picture Album
of Sport
and Conservation

"Frank Forester" (Henry William Herbert), English-born prophet of the American code of the sportsman. (Courtesy of the New York Public Library.)

John James Audubon as he looked *circa* 1841; a portrait painted by his sons, John Woodhouse and Victor Gifford Audubon. Like Louis Agassiz Fuertes, Lynn Bogue Hunt, and many later wildlife artists, the great ornithological artist loved to hunt the birds he painted. (Courtesy of the American Museum of Natural History.)

George Catlin, the first American—so far as we know—to suggest the national park idea. While painting and studying the Western aborigines, he hunted buffalo for sport. From an 1849 oil painting by William Fisk. (Courtesy of the National Portrait Gallery, Smithsonian Institution.)

An illustration from [Thomas] Mayne Reid's *Boy Hunters* (1852). His romantic tales of the frontier endeared him to multitudes of youthful readers. Among those who believed that Reid's books sparked their first interest in the "Wild West" were George Bird Grinnell and Theodore Roosevelt.

FACING PAGE, TOP   Like many sportsmen's clubs, the Currituck Club on
Currituck Sound, North Carolina, preserved wildlife habitat that might otherwise
have been lost to human encroachment. Hunting was regulated by club rules
which preceded state laws. The Currituck Club was one of the earliest such
associations, founded in 1857 by a group of Yankees. Its "grounds" included
3,100 acres of marsh. This is a photograph of the "new" clubhouse, built in
1879 about 75 yards from the original one. It had 21 rooms, one for each member. From Eugene V. Connett, ed., *Duck Shooting Along the Atlantic Tidewater*
(1947). (Courtesy of William Morrow and Company.)

FACING PAGE, BOTTOM   An 1867 Currier and Ives lithograph entitled "Home
From the Woods. The Successful Sportsmen." (Courtesy of the Library of
Congress.)

ABOVE   A "heart-pound net" in Lake Michigan. Variations of the pound net,
used on both coastal and inland waters, were despised by sport and commercial
hook-and-line fishermen. Opposition to these contrivances on the part of New
England's coastal inhabitants was the major factor in the organization in 1871
of the U.S. Fish Commission, first federal agency to deal with conservation of
a specific natural resource. In the illustration the "leader" is the net fence
extending out from the shore to guide fish into the middle section, or "heart."
Fish mill around the heart until they pass through the "tunnel" into the "pot,"
also called the "bowl" or "crib." From the U.S. Fish Commission's *Report on
the Condition of the Sea Fisheries of the South Coast of New England in 1871
and 1872* (1873).

ABOVE One of the basic themes of the sporting tradition is that the disciples of hunting and fishing benefit physically and mentally from these avocations. This illustration from *Harper's New Monthly Magazine* (August, 1870) shows a city man before and after a trip to the Adirondacks.

BELOW "Seth Green Taking Spawn from a Salmon Trout [lake trout]. The Proper Position." Green, a dedicated angler, was the pre-eminent non-governmental fish culturist of his day. From Robert Barnwell Roosevelt and Seth Green, *Fish Hatching, and Fish Catching* (1879).

An interior view of the New York State hatching house at Caledonia, as it looked in 1875. Several years later, two of the nation's leading fish culturists reported that "in it have been hatched in one season two million and a half of whitefish, two million salmon trout [lake trout], and one million and a half of brook trout together with several hundred thousand [Atlantic] salmon, these figures . . . being taken by . . . actual count." The 1870s witnessed the rise of the "fish culture movement," a crusade spearheaded by sportsmen-naturalists. Despite what virtually all historians claim, wide-scale conservation efforts in regard to wildlife preceded those in behalf of forests. From Robert Barnwell Roosevelt and Seth Green, *Fish Hatching, and Fish Catching* (1879).

George Perkins Marsh, whose book *Man and Nature* (1864) has been called the "fountainhead of the conservation movement." An enthusiastic angler in youth, he was a proponent of fish culture as early as the 1850s.

"Lonesome Charley" Reynolds, expert hunter and "generally ranked as the greatest of the Western scouts" (*Concise Dictionary of American Biography*). Close association with such authentic frontiersmen was a mark of pride for Easterners like Theodore Roosevelt and George Bird Grinnell.

Robert Barnwell Roosevelt, believer in the code of the sportsman, well-known hunting and fishing author, political reformer, and pioneer of environmental concern. He undoubtedly played a part in formulating the outdoor interests of his nephew, Theodore Roosevelt. From Charles Hallock, *An Angler's Reminiscences* (1913).

ABOVE   Thaddeus Norris. Like every other pioneer in the science of fish culture, he was first an angler. From Fred Mather, *My Angling Friends* (1901).

FACING PAGE, TOP   "Englishmen in Colorado: Fishing for Breakfast," an illustration from the London *Graphic,* August 17, 1872. Well-born foreign sportsmen were attracted to America, and some of them contributed to the early conservation movement. (Courtesy of the Western History Department, Denver Public Library.)

FACING PAGE, BOTTOM   With a "jacklight" in the bow to stun the birds, boatmen quietly row down on ducks massed on the water and will fire when the greatest number can be killed. The caption accompanying this illustration— "The Nefarious Pot-Hunter"—indicated what sportsmen thought of such activities. From *Scribner's Monthly,* November, 1877.

ABOVE Carp—pride and joy of government fish culturists, led by Spencer Fullerton Baird. The carp was introduced throughout the United States, disrupting ecosystems wherever established, a classic example of the tragic consequences often attending the introduction of alien organisms. Photograph by Donald W. Pfitzer. (Courtesy of the Bureau of Sport Fisheries & Wildlife.)

BELOW Because every true sportsman was expected to have an interest in natural history, glass cabinets containing mounted specimens of animals and birds bagged on outings were very much in vogue. Taxidermy flourished, and the practice of this art encouraged more systematic studies. Entitled "Room in a Taxidermist's Shop," the illustration is from *Century Magazine,* December, 1882.

"Summer Life at North Mountain
House." Located "in the centre
of an unbroken primeval forest of
25,000 acres" in northeastern
Pennsylvania, this resort had "fishing
for those who like it, and hunting
in the woods. . . ." From John
B. Bachelder, *Popular Resorts,
and How to Reach Them* (1874).

Charles Hallock, founder of *Forest
and Stream,* in 1896. From Fred
Mather, *My Angling Friends* (1901).

The front page of the first issue of *Forest and Stream,* August 14, 1873.

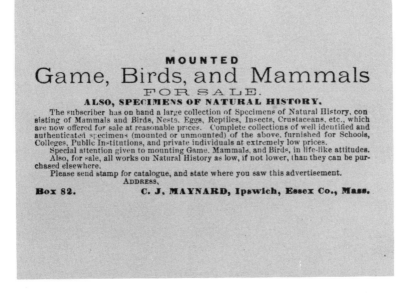

ABOVE   This ad is typical of those that appeared frequently in sportsmen's newspapers and books in the last quarter of the nineteenth century and is an example of the interrelationship between sport and natural history. From Charles Hallock's *Camp Life in Florida: A Handbook for Sportsmen and Settlers* (1876).

BELOW   James Henry Moser's well-known painting of "The Still Hunt" (1888). A market hunter, using a Sharps rifle, has already killed more than a dozen buffalo. (Courtesy of the National Park Service Collection, Yellowstone National Park.)

ABOVE Skinning a buffalo on the northern Great Plains in the last years of
commercial buffalo slaughter. (Courtesy of Huffman Pictures, Miles City,
Montana.)

BELOW Because of the growing demands of tanneries and fertilizer plants, the
commercial destruction of the buffalo became a year-round industry. This
woodcut, *circa* 1874, shows the curing of hides and bones in the West. Raw
hides were pegged out to dry before being pressed (to the right) and baled
for shipment to the East. In the background are heaps of buffalo bones that
will also be sent East to be ground into fertilizer. (Courtesy of the Bettmann
Archive.)

ABOVE Guns and shooting were an integral part of the lives of most males in nineteenth-century rural America. Entitled "The Turkey Shoot," this 1879 oil painting by John W. Ehninger shows a match taking place near Saratoga, New York. Using a percussion arm, a contestant is firing from a rack. The man on the left has proven his marksmanship by winning a turkey. (Courtesy of the Museum of Fine Arts, Boston.)

BELOW Unlike sportsmen—who usually did not depend on the natural world for a livelihood—farmers of the nineteenth century manifested little appreciation of nature. Quite naturally any living thing that seemed to be a "competitor" was killed. Here, Iowa farmers are shooting passenger pigeons flying over their newly sown grain field. From *Leslie's Illustrated Newspaper,* September 21, 1867.

"Martha," the last passenger pigeon. She died in the Cincinnati Zoo on September 1, 1914, when she was 26 years old. Her species, once perhaps the most abundant avian form ever to have lived on the planet, became extinct mainly because of habitat changes and systematic destruction by commercial hunters. (Courtesy of the Zoological Society of Cincinnati.)

ABOVE Angler Cornelius Hedges, whose idea for "a great National Park" in the Yellowstone region was the beginning of the effort that eventually led to the establishment of America's first such reserve. The illustration shows him as he looked when he graduated from Yale in 1853. (Courtesy of the Montana Historical Society.)

LEFT Commercial pigeon netters at work. When the passenger pigeons in the dead trees all drop to the ground, a trigger mechanism will be released by the men in the blind and a net will be thrown over the whole flock. To attract passing flocks, the pigeoners often baited the area with buckwheat or some other food, then tethered live decoy pigeons on small platforms called "stools" (hence the term "stool pigeon"). When these were raised and lowered, the captive birds fluttered as if alighting and thus lured flying pigeons. From *Leslie's Illustrated Newspaper,* September 21, 1867.

The Lower Falls of the Yellowstone, taken by hunter and pioneer photographer William Henry Jackson. His photographs played a major part in the passage of the bill creating Yellowstone National Park. (Courtesy of the Library of the State Historical Society of Colorado.)

ABOVE The Fulton Meat Market in Durango, Colorado, in the 1880s. The mounted elk indicated that game was for sale. Elk carcasses hang on the right. Commercialization of wildlife threatened many species, and sportsmen were the only significant group that opposed the market gunner. (Courtesy of the Western History Department, Denver Public Library.)

LEFT In the 1840s surf fishing with rod and reel began to replace the traditional hand line, and by the post-bellum period it was a popular sport for gentlemen anglers in the Northeast. Entitled "Playing a [Striped] Bass in the Surf," the illustration is from Genio C. Scott, *Fishing in American Waters* (1875); first published in 1869.

FACING PAGE, TOP The chase inspired many of the nineteenth century's leading artists, among them Albert Bierstadt, Frederic Remington, and Winslow Homer. All three of these men were sportsmen, as was Arthur B. Frost, who "by 1900 . . . was probably the country's most popular illustrator" [*Concise Dictionary of American Biography*]. This lithograph is entitled "Quail—A Dead Stand." From Frost, *Shooting Pictures* (1895–96).

FACING PAGE, BOTTOM An Arthur B. Frost lithograph entitled "Rail Shooting." In the stern a "pusher" propels his clinker-built double-ender with a 12-foot pole, while the gunner in the bow fires at a sora rail. Once a popular sport along tidal rivers in the East, rail shooting (for several species) has vanished in many areas, a casualty of industrial pollution and development. From Frost, *Shooting Pictures* (1895–96).

ABOVE Expert hunter Galen Clark, who, in the words of historian Shirley Sargent, "did more than anyone else to preserve and protect the Yosemite Grant [1864], now Yosemite National Park." Although the wide publicity given to John Muir's much later efforts have overshadowed Clark's importance, Clark deserves the title of "father of Yosemite Park." Photograph by George Fiske, showing Clark in Yosemite Valley. (Courtesy of the California State Library.)

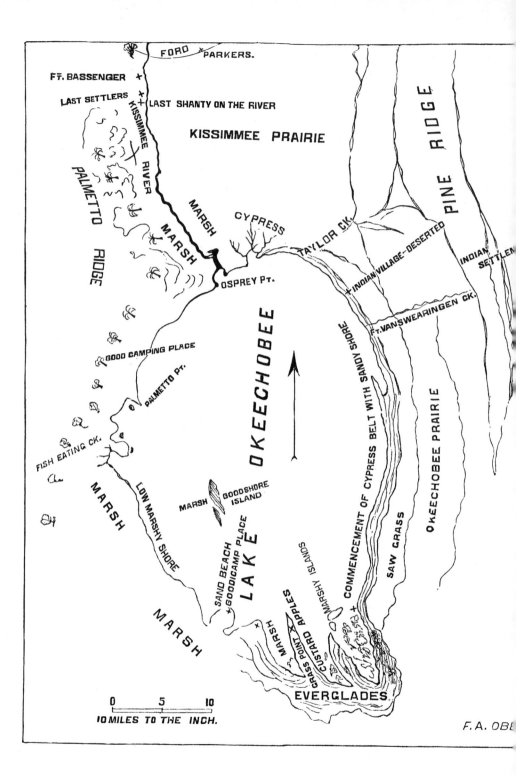

FORD PARKERS.

FT. BASSENGER +

LAST SETTLERS +
+ LAST SHANTY ON THE RIVER

KISSIMMEE PRAIRIE

PALMETTO RIDGE

KISSIMMEE RIVER

MARSH

MARSH

CYPRESS

PINE RIDGE

TAYLOR CK.

+ INDIAN VILLAGE-DESERTED

INDIAN SETTLEM

OSPREY PT.

FT. VANSWEARINGEN CK.

OKEECHOBEE

GOOD CAMPING PLACE

PALMETTO PT.

FISH EATING CK.

LAKE

MARSH

LOW MARSHY SHORE

MARSH GOODSHORE ISLAND

COMMENCEMENT OF CYPRESS BELT WITH SANDY SHORE

OKEECHOBEE PRAIRIE

SAND BEACH
GOODCAMP PLACE +

SAW GRASS

MARSH

MARSH

GRASS POINT APPLES

CUSTARD

MARSHY ISLANDS

EVERGLADES

0   5   10

10 MILES TO THE INCH.

F.A. OBE

FACING PAGE One of the little-known facts of sporting history is that outdoorsmen played an important role in "opening up" wild regions by sponsoring scientific expeditions. Less was known about the interior of southern Florida in the early 1870s than almost any part of the "Wild West." This is perhaps the first good map ever made of Lake Okeechobee, compiled on an 1873 expedition sponsored by *Forest and Stream*. From *Forest and Stream*, April 16, 1874.

ABOVE Commercial elk and deer hunters and their kill (which also includes a bighorn sheep and mountain lion) in Colorado in 1885. Men like these were despised by sportsmen. (Courtesy of the Western History Department, Denver Public Library.)

ABOVE   George Bird Grinnell, crusading editor
of *Forest and Stream* from 1880 to 1911
(natural history editor from 1876 to 1880).
Pioneer in the preservation and management of
wildlife, forests, and scenic areas; influential
adviser to Theodore Roosevelt; and author of the
effort that resulted in the creation of Glacier
National Park, he played a leading role
in the conservation movement of the nineteenth
century. When he died in 1938, the New York
Times noted that Grinnell had often been
referred to as "the father of American
conservation."

BELOW Using "a dozen flat painted strawboard decoys" in wheat stubble, two goose hunters pursue their sport on the "prairie shooting grounds" of Minnesota. By Charles A. Zimmerman, the sketch is from the *Chicago Field* (later name of *Field and Stream*), October 12, 1878.

BELOW   Before 1885—when commercial fishermen and "progress" began to move in—catches of eight or nine brook trout averaging over four pounds were common along the south shore of Lake Superior on Michigan's Upper Peninsula. The photograph shows a sportswoman landing a four-pounder in 1886. Photograph by George Shiras, 3d. From his *Hunting Wild Life With Camera and Flashlight* (1936), I; first published in 1935. (Courtesy of the National Geographic Society.)

ABOVE Weathered stumps are the sole
evidence that a forest once covered
this barren area on Mt. Rose near
Virginia City, Nevada. The timber went
to the Comstock Lode in the 1870s
for mining purposes. Photograph taken
on July 3, 1938, by R. C. Wilson.
(Courtesy of the U.S. Forest Service.)

FACING PAGE, TOP   The Hudson River above Lake Sanford in New York's Adirondacks. The region was the scene of the first large-scale campaign to save American forests, and the movement was spearheaded by sportsmen. An 1888 photograph taken by S. R. Stoddard. (Courtesy of the Adirondack Museum, Blue Mountain Lake, New York.)

FACING PAGE, BOTTOM   A big-game hunter in his younger days and an avid angler his whole life, Gifford Pinchot once said that his original interest in becoming a forester was sparked by a boyhood fishing trip to the Adirondacks. Entitled "In the Spring the Angler's Fancy Lightly Turns to Thoughts of Trout," the photograph is from Pinchot, *Just Fishing Talk* (1936).

BELOW   Looking out at the Great Smoky Mountains from a terrace of the Biltmore Mansion near Asheville, North Carolina. Once part of George Vanderbilt's 120,000-acre Biltmore Estate and now part of the Pisgah National Forest, this area was the home of one of the first efforts at systematic forestry in the United States. Photograph by Daniel O. Todd, July, 1961. (Courtesy of the U.S. Forest Service.)

ABOVE A swivel "big gun" mounted on a skiff, used by market hunters to fire huge quantities of shot into waterfowl massed on the water. Scores of ducks and geese might be killed or crippled at one blast. (Courtesy of the Shelburne Museum, Shelburne, Vermont.)

BELOW Angler, fish merchant, ichthyologist, and New York State Fish Commissioner, Eugene G. Blackford (in top hat in center) did much to popularize the study of fishes. In New York City's famous Fulton Market for several days every spring—beginning on opening day of trout season—he exhibited a large collection of live and dead specimens of numerous species. Because he specialized in the rare and exotic, both the sporting and scientific communities awaited Blackford's openings with keen anticipation. The illustration is from the *Chicago Field,* April 12, 1879.

FACING PAGE, TOP August prairie-chicken shooting in the West. From *Scribner's Monthly,* August, 1877.

FACING PAGE, BOTTOM Several members of a sportsmen's club chatting in front of the evening fire. Entitled "Telling Fish Stories," the illustration appeared in *Scribner's Monthly,* February, 1877.

ABOVE Fly-casting contest of the second Anglers' Tournament of the National Rod and Reel Association in 1883, at Harlem Mere, Central Park, New York City. In the lower right-hand corner a judge is weighing the contestants' fly rods. From Herbert Manchester, *Four Centuries of Sport in America, 1490-1890* (1968); first published in 1931. (Courtesy of Benjamin Blom, Inc.)

ABOVE Grover Cleveland fishing for bass in Duncan Lake, Ossipee, New Hampshire. Photographed by John H. Finley. From Charles Eliot Goodspeed, *Angling in America* (1939). (Courtesy of George T. Goodspeed and the Houghton Mifflin Company.)

FACING PAGE Chester A. Arthur fighting (?) a salmon on the Cascapédia River of Quebec's Gaspé Peninsula. Copied from a photograph by Carl Beckstead. From Charles Eliot Goodspeed, *Angling in America* (1939). (Courtesy of George T. Goodspeed and the Houghton Mifflin Company.)

Bernhard E. Fernow, German-born sportsman and leading pioneer in forestry. He personifies the tremendous debt Americans owe to Old World conservationists and their ideas. (Courtesy of the Library of Congress.)

William C. Harris, editor of *American Angler*. From Charles Hallock, *An Angler's Reminiscences* (1913).

VOLUME 7, No. 19.

MAY 9, 1885.

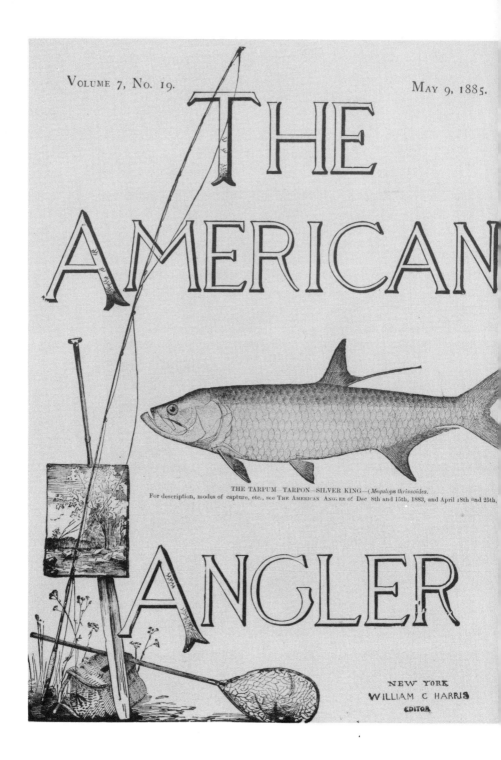

THE AMERICAN ANGLER

THE TARPUM—TARPON—SILVER KING—(*Megalops thrissoides*.
For description, modes of capture, etc., see THE AMERICAN ANGLER of Dec 8th and 15th, 1883, and April 18th and 25th,

NEW YORK
WILLIAM C HARRIS
EDITOR

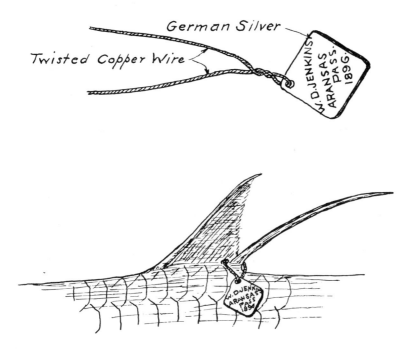

German Silver

Twisted Copper Wire

W.D.JENKINS
ARANSAS
PASS.
1896.

ABOVE Many believe that the technique of tagging fish to trace their migration
patterns is a relatively recent development. Actually, the practice goes back
to the last century. The picture shows a tag devised by angler W. D. Jenkins
of Texas. Made of "German silver," it was attached to the dorsal fin of a tarpon
by means of a twisted copper wire. From *American Angler,* October-November,
1896.

FACING PAGE Because they had to know their quarry in order to hunt or fish
successfully, nineteenth-century sportsmen added much to the knowledge of
wildlife habits. For example, almost nothing was known about the life histories
of grayling and tarpon before anglers began to seek them out. In the 1880s
the latter species became the new "glamour fish," and anglers flocked to Florida
to see if they could conquer the "silver king." Almost unheard-of a few years
before, the fish was so well known by the spring of 1885 that it rated a front-page
illustration in *American Angler,* the leading periodical on sport fishing.

William Hallett Phillips, a Supreme Court lawyer and dedicated angler who wielded a powerful, behind-the-scenes influence in the efforts to preserve Yellowstone National Park and set aside forest reserves. (Courtesy of the Haynes Foundation, Bozeman, Montana.)

Attempting to look like the frontiersmen he admired, a buckskin-clad Theodore Roosevelt poses with his rifle in a studio in 1884. He later said that he would never have become President if it had not been for his Western ranching experience, which began with a desire to shoot a trophy buffalo. From Hermann Hagedorn, *Roosevelt in the Bad Lands* (1921). (Courtesy of the Houghton Mifflin Company.)

ABOVE Sleeping black-duck decoy, carved from one piece of sugar pine in New England, *circa* 1900. Some believe that the wooden decoy, created to lure game birds, was the highest expression of American folk art. That it reached its greatest development here cannot be denied, but it was not unique to North America. Apparently without realizing the importance of his discovery, a Swedish author, Gunnar Brusewitz, in his book *Hunting* (translated into English and published in New York in 1969), shows that painted wooden decoys were in wide use in Scandinavia by the first quarter of the nineteenth century. (Courtesy of the Shelburne Museum, Shelburne, Vermont.)

FACING PAGE, TOP The White House dining room during Theodore Roosevelt's Presidency, showing the trophy heads of elk, bison, bear, and moose (partially visible). From Roosevelt's *Outdoor Pastimes of an American Hunter* (1905). (Courtesy of the Theodore Roosevelt Collection, Harvard College Library.)

FACING PAGE, BOTTOM The first wildlife sanctuaries in America were established by gentlemen sportsmen who adapted an Old World precedent to New World conditions. The photograph shows the entrance gate to the Adirondack game, fish, and forest preserve of banker John Pierpont Morgan. 1899 photograph by S. R. Stoddard. (Courtesy of the Adirondack Museum, Blue Mountain Lake, New York.)

ABOVE President Benjamin Harrison (on right) in his blind on the property of the Bengies Ducking Club near Baltimore. On his left is William Joyce Sewell, powerful Republican politician from New Jersey. The man on the right is unidentified. From his crouching position and the concentration of the retriever, it appears that ducks are at that moment coming to the decoys which are barely discernible in the distance in the original photograph. This picture was taken in March, 1891, the same month Harrison set aside the first forest reserve. (Courtesy of the Indiana Historical Society Library.)

FACING PAGE President Harrison after the hunt. With his double-barreled shotgun and bag of ducks, he stands on the steps of the Bengies Ducking Club. (Courtesy of the Indiana Historical Society Library.)

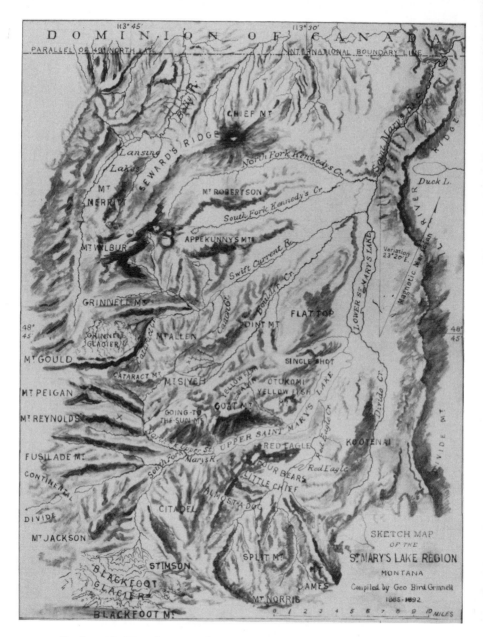

By the mid-1880s, there were few regions of the United States outside of Alaska that had not been explored thoroughly. One exception was the St. Mary's Lake country in the northwestern corner of Montana. This is a "sketch map" of the region compiled by George Bird Grinnell between 1885 and 1892. By the latter year, he had already begun his campaign to have this magnificent area preserved as a national park. Largely through his efforts, Glacier National Park became a reality in 1910. (Courtesy of the National Park Service.)

ABOVE The Woodmont Rod and Gun Club, established in western Maryland in 1880. Its official motto was "Protect and Enjoy," and one of its prominent members was George Graham Vest. From *American Angler,* October 21, 1882.

BELOW The published works of ornithologists like William Brewster, Elliott Coues, Daniel G. Elliot, and Frank M. Chapman reveal that a prerequisite for knowing birds was to have a knowledge of how to hunt them. Like so many other naturalists of the nineteenth century, the Curator of Chicago's Field Museum, Charles B. Cory, began his "faunal studies" with a gun and never lost his love for the chase. Entitled "Brant Shooting. 'Get Ready,' " the illustration shows two hunters in a pit blind using both wooden and live decoys. From Cory, *How to Know the Ducks, Geese, and Swans of North America* (1897).

ABOVE New York City's American Museum of Natural History in 1889. As in the case of the National Museum in Washington, D.C., and the Field Museum in Chicago, sportsmen-naturalists like George Bird Grinnell, Charles B. Cory, and William T. Hornaday played an important role in building up this institution's early collections of mammals and birds. (Courtesy of the American Museum of Natural History.)

BELOW *"Ovis stonei,"* once believed to be a new form of mountain sheep, on exhibit in the American Museum of Natural History. It was discovered and "collected" by an expedition sent out under the auspices of George Oliver Shields' *Recreation,* a popular sportsmen's magazine founded in 1894. "Stone's Sheep" is now generally regarded as simply a blackish color phase of the Dall's, or white, sheep (*Ovis dalli*). From *Recreation,* June, 1897.

A water color by Edmund H. Osthaus, *circa* 1904, called "Just Look at Them!"
Gazing out of a window of their clubhouse at flights of waterfowl, the hunters
and their dog—perhaps an American water spaniel—are eager to be off.
(Courtesy of the Eleutherian Mills Historical Library, Greenville, Delaware.)

LEFT While variations of the term "game hog" had been in use for some time (e.g., "trout hog," "grouse hog," etc.), sportsman George Oliver Shields gave it a far wider circulation when he established the magazine *Recreation* in 1894. Subscribers sent in information regarding those who had violated a basic component of the code of the sportsman by killing game in excess, and Shields "roasted" them in *Recreation*, using names, addresses, photographs, and humorous commentary to embarrass these pseudo-sportsmen. Another technique was the satirical cartoon, as shown here. Entitled "A Distinguished Member of the Herd," it appeared in the April, 1898, issue.

FACING PAGE, TOP   For sportsmen-naturalists like Theodore Roosevelt—who had hunted wilderness bears uncorrupted by man—"the effect of protection upon bear life in the Yellowstone [Park] has been one of the phenomena of natural history." By the 1890s, incidents between bears and ignorant tourists were common, but the feeding of "tame" bears at the park dumps has only recently been discontinued. From George Bird Grinnell, ed., *American Big Game in Its Haunts* (1904).

BELOW   Joseph T. Rothrock, pioneer in forestry at the state level and a dedicated sportsman. (Courtesy of the University of Pennsylvania Archives.)

ABOVE Madison Grant. A founder of the New York Zoological Society (which established the "Bronx Zoo"), the Save-the-Redwoods League, and other organizations, he was one of the Boone and Crockett Club's most active members. This leading representative of the New York patrician class typifies the all-important role of upper-class individuals in the making of conservation. (Courtesy of the American Museum of Natural History.)

FACING PAGE "The Hunter's Cabin" at the World's Columbian Exposition, held at Chicago from May to November, 1893. Symbolizing the central role of the wilderness hunter in the making of American history, the cabin "is the headquarters of the Boone and Crockett club, an organization of prominent sportsmen throughout the United States, whose object is to preserve the large game of the country, especially that of the Yellowstone or National park. The structure is built of rough logs, and within, over the rude fireplace, is the skull of a grizzly bear." Standing out front is Elwood Hofer, hunter, guide, and packer, who was brought from Yellowstone Park by the Boone and Crockett Club to act as the exhibit's interpreter. Photograph and quoted passage from Hubert Howe Bancroft, *The Book of the Fair* . . . (1894). (Courtesy of Crown Publishers.)

After George Bird Grinnell, *Forest and Stream*'s editor, launched his crusade
to define the meaning of Yellowstone National Park and establish for it an
effective administration, he succeeded in interesting other editors in the issue.
This cartoon from *Harper's Weekly* (January 20, 1883) shows what will happen
if the "Yellowstone Park Improvement Company" is allowed to exploit the
reserve for private gain—a visitor is set upon by profiteers at the park entrance.
Note that the tourist brings a cased gun with him, for hunting was an accepted
activity in the park for many years. Not until 1894, when sportsmen obtained
passage of the "Act to Protect the Birds and Animals in Yellowstone National
Park," was hunting entirely stopped.

An avid sportsman and a Republican Congressman who represented Iowa almost
continuously from 1889 to 1907, John F. Lacey was responsible for drafting
much of the key legislation of early conservation, including the 1894 act to
protect Yellowstone Park, which established the definition of a "national
park"; the "Lacey Act" of 1900, which stopped market hunting and interstate
shipment of wildlife or wildlife products in violation of state law; and the
original transfer act for forest reserves, which set the stage for the establishment
of the U.S. Forest Service. As he suggested in a speech favoring passage of
the Lacey Act, the genesis of his commitment was the responsibility for the *total*
environment inherent in the code of the sportsman. (Courtesy of the Iowa State
Department of History and Archives, Des Moines.)

BELOW During his active career, angler-ichthyologist
George Brown Goode was United States Fish
Commissioner, Assistant Secretary of the
Smithsonian Institution, and chief administrator
of the National Museum. (Courtesy of the
Smithsonian Institution.)

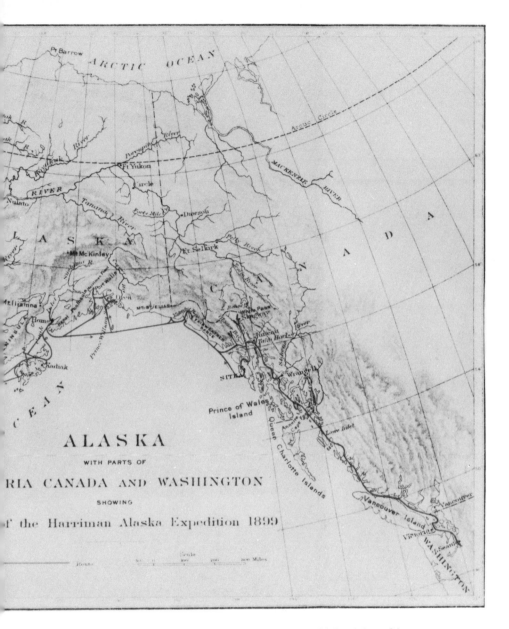

ABOVE Route of the 1899 Harriman Alaska Expedition, which originated in the desire of railroad executive Edward H. Harriman to shoot a trophy Kodiak bear. Using a luxurious steam yacht provided by him, a group of the country's leading naturalists—including C. Hart Merriam, George Bird Grinnell, John Burroughs, and John Muir—explored and studied the wild coasts of Canada, Alaska, and Siberia, journeying as far north as the Bering Strait. Despite the fact that Muir accepted Harriman's hospitality, he condemned him for shooting the bear he had come for. From Harriman Alaska Expedition, *Alaska* (1901), I.

ABOVE   The Catalina Tuna Club at Avalon on Santa Catalina Island, California. Founded in the 1890s by angler-ichthyologist Charles Frederick Holder, the organization was confined to "gentleman anglers" and pioneered in the study and conservation of marine game fishes. From Holder's *Game Fishes of the World* (1913).

FACING PAGE, TOP   The dividing line between scientific "collecting" and recreational "hunting" was often indistinct or nonexistent. This is a National Museum exhibit of lions "bagged" ("collected") by sportsman-naturalist Theodore Roosevelt on the Smithsonian-Roosevelt African Expedition of 1909. (Courtesy of the Smithsonian Institution.)

ABOVE   While his greatest contribution to conservation was the realization that
the federal government—and not the states—had jurisdiction over migratory
birds, sportsman George Shiras, 3d, also contributed through the medium of
photography. He increased the public's appreciation of wildlife by pioneering
a number of photographic techniques, one of which was the use of the
pot-hunter's "jacklight" to obtain stunning pictures of animals on their nocturnal
rounds. Taken in the 1890s on his hunting grounds in Michigan's Upper
Peninsula, this picture is entitled "A Midnight Reflection" and is one of a series
that won the highest awards at the World Exposition in Paris in 1900 and
the Louisiana Purchase Exposition in St. Louis in 1904. From George Shiras,
3d, *Hunting Wild Life with Camera and Flashlight* (1936), I; first published
in 1935. (Courtesy of the National Geographic Society.)

FACING PAGE, TOP Hunting for science—usually called "collecting"—was as much fun as hunting for sport. Here is William Brewster on a houseboat on Florida's Suwannee River in 1890 holding the now extinct, or nearly extinct, ivory-billed woodpecker, stalked and shot by Frank M. Chapman. The other men in the photograph are unidentified, but one is holding the main collecting tool: a double-barreled shotgun. (Courtesy of the Library of the Museum of Comparative Zoology, Harvard University.)

FACING PAGE, BOTTOM In the nineteenth century well-meaning sportsmen as well as some anti-hunter, self-proclaimed "animal lovers" believed that the killing of "vermin" like cougars and wolves was beneficial because it resulted in greater numbers of "good" animals like deer and elk. Tragically, they were right. By the early part of this century, herbivores were so numerous in some places that they were destroying their habitats and beginning to starve. In the photograph a deer stands on its hind legs, reaching for forage. Having already destroyed the ground cover and lower branches, the deer has to stretch for the upper branches. When they are consumed, the animal will starve, and the quality of the whole herd may be impaired. In such a situation only man—assuming his natural role as a predator—can restore the balance and save both the deer and its habitat. Photograph by Charles McDonald. (Courtesy of the U.S. Forest Service.)

ABOVE "Trouting," from Henry Van Dyke's *Little Rivers* (1895). Van Dyke was a popular writer who was revered for conveying the beauty, even the spirituality, of sport fishing. Like most influential outdoor writers of his time, he was more interested in the pursuit of his quarry—and in the esthetics of its surroundings—than in capturing it.

ABOVE A commercial gunner of Elliott Island, Maryland, holding a shotgun with which he killed—so he claimed—35,000 ducks over an eight-year period in the first quarter of the present century. Shooting for sport had a minor impact on waterfowl populations, but havoc was wreaked by market hunters. From Harry M. Walsh, *The Outlaw Gunner* (1971). (Courtesy of Tidewater Publishers, Cambridge, Maryland.)

LEFT Sportsmen-naturalists perpetuated the code of the sportsman by inculcating it in the youth of America. From left to right, the photograph shows Ernest Thompson Seton, Lord Baden-Powell, and Daniel Carter Beard, the founders of the Boy Scout movement. All three were dedicated sportsmen. (Courtesy of the Boy Scouts of America, New York, N.Y.)

Because of a penchant for self-flattery, William T. Hornaday has been accepted
by literal-minded historians as one of the greatest wildlife conservationists. As
the first Director of the New York Zoological Park and a crusader for the
bison, Hornaday deserves a place in the history of conservation—but not the
place he has chosen for himself. Far more important conservationists like George
Bird Grinnell and Charles Sheldon believed that Hornaday actually did more
harm than good by splitting the ranks of environmentalists through his bitter
attacks on anyone who did not agree precisely with "Mr. Hornaday," as he
often called himself. In recent years anti-sportsmen historians have quoted him
for his assaults on hunters, failing to understand that he was against those hunters
who, in his opinion, abused the sport but he certainly was not against hunting.
Hornaday believed that only he and a small minority of gunners who agreed
with his often erroneous notions of wildlife management were the true adherents
to the code of the sportsman. This photograph, taken by naturalist John M.
Phillips, shows Hornaday clutching the hide of a mountain goat he has just
shot in British Columbia, and the caption he chose for the picture was " 'The
Moment of Triumph'—Caught Unawares [by the Camera]." From Hornaday,
Camp-Fires in the Canadian Rockies . . . (1916); first published in 1906.

ABOVE The New York Zoological Park ("Bronx Zoo"), one of the world's great zoos and a pioneer in the creation of natural "habitats" for its collections, was established by the Boone and Crockett Club in the 1890s to preserve wildlife from extinction, particularly big-game animals. As an institution closely linked with hunters, it included among its exhibits a museum containing the trophy heads of various big-game animals collected by sportsmen-naturalists. The photograph shows this "Heads and Horns Museum Building," opened in 1922. (Courtesy of the New York Zoological Society.)

BELOW Aldo Leopold, "father of the American land ethic," examining what appears to be a woodcock; note the shotguns on top of the car's fender. His land ethic represents the highest development of the environmental responsibility inherent in the code of the sportsman. (Courtesy of the University of Wisconsin Archives.)

NOTES

Introduction

1. Bureau of Outdoor Recreation, *1970 Survey of Outdoor Recreation Activities—Preliminary Report* (Washington, D.C., 1972), 52. The figure given as of 1970 was 20,887,000 and is now probably considerably larger. In 1970 this represented over 12 percent of the American population.

It is interesting to note that the same survey found that 49,435,000 Americans—or more than 29 percent of the population—were sport fisherman or "fisherwomen"; see page 34.

2. This idea is suggested by Aldo Leopold. See his *Sand County Almanac* (New York, 1966), 6; this work was first published in 1949.

3. The first volume of his classic work, *Democracy in America,* appeared in 1835 and the second in 1840.

4. Woodward, *American Attitudes Toward History* (Oxford, England, 1955), 5.

5. *Ibid.*

6. *Ibid.*, 19.

7. *Ibid.*

8. *Ibid.*

9. *Ibid.*

10. John F. Reiger, ed., *The Passing of the Great West: Selected Papers of George Bird Grinnell* (New York, 1972), 120–21; Hine's comments on Grinnell's supposed hypocrisy are in a review of the above work in the *Pacific Historical Review,* XLII (February, 1973), 115.

11. Holway R. Jones, *John Muir and the Sierra Club: The Battle for Yosemite* (San Francisco, 1965), 4.

12. Shankland, *Steve Mather of the National Parks* (New York, 1951), 270.

13. *Ibid.,* 268. The early history of the first organization is discussed in detail in the present work; for its subsequent history, and the composition of the latter two groups, see James B. Trefethen, *Crusade for Wildlife: Highlights in Conservation Progress* (Harrisburg, Pennsylvania, 1961).

14. I am speaking here of adult wildlife; weather (rain, flooding, etc.) is often the biggest factor in determining mortality rates for the young of wildlife, particularly birds. It should also be emphasized that I am speaking of wildlife unaffected by man's activities, such as automobile traffic, the use of pesticides, etc.

15. In case some reader might think I am seriously attacking fishing, let me note that I am an avid angler.

16. Of course, this includes insects and plants as well.

17. George Reiger, "First the Whales . . . Now the Porpoises?" *National Wildlife,* XII (February–March, 1974), 18–20.

18. A few extremists have recently gone so far as to bemoan even the destruction of plants for food, because they are alive and "feel."

19. In the broadest sense, this also includes insects and vegetation.

20. Under the leadership of Jay N. ("Ding") Darling and other sportsmen-conservationists, the Migratory Bird Hunting Stamp Act was passed in 1934. It obligates waterfowl hunters to purchase a stamp before they can shoot, and the money brought in is used to preserve waterfowl habitat. This device and the actions of private sportsmen's groups such as Ducks Unlimited have reserved huge areas in the United States and Canada that would otherwise have been lost to agricultural and industrial development.

21. Shaw, "The Hunting Controversy: Attitudes and Arguments," *Big Sky,* II (Spring, 1974), 4. This article, which has the same title as his dissertation, is a summary of his findings.

22. See the 1973 edition of *Threatened Wildlife of the United States,* published by the Bureau of Sport Fisheries and Wildlife. In the section on "Extinct or Presumed Extinct Wildlife," "overhunting" is *sometimes* listed as contributing to extinction, but the compilers are *not* referring to sport hunting—like the students in Shaw's study—but rather to killing for commerce, food, or crop protection; examples of species wiped out mainly, or partly, because of these factors are the passenger pigeon, great auk, and Carolina parakeet.

23. For example, see *National Wildlife,* XI (February–March, 1973), 24A.

24. Shaw, "The Hunting Controversy," 5.

25. *Ibid.,* 2.

26. *Ibid.*

27. Vance Bourjaily, in his book *The Unnatural Enemy* (New York, 1963), has some things to say on this subject; see, for instance, 166–68.

28. Ernest Hemingway, for example, suggests this idea in *Death in the Afternoon* (New York, 1932), 5.

29. Shaw, "The Hunting Controversy," 3.

30. *Ibid.*

31. David Sumner and Carolyn Johnson, "700,000,000,000 Barrels of Soot," *Sierra Club Bulletin*, LIX (April, 1974), 28. This statement appears in a section separated from the main body of the article, is signed "R.R.O." (?), and accompanies photographs of big-game animals.

32. I am using this term simply to mean those historians who have concentrated on the study of man's relationship to the natural world.

33. Robert Detweiler, Jon N. Sutherland, and Michael S. Werthman, eds., *Environmental Decay in Its Historical Context* (Glenview, Illinois, 1973), second page (unnumbered) of Preface.

34. Lawrence Rakestraw, "Conservation Historiography: An Assessment," *Pacific Historical Review*, XLI (August, 1972), 288.

35. The last two books were published posthumously; Leopold died in 1948.

36. In a review of Robert McHenry, ed., *A Documentary History of Conservation in America* (New York, 1972), Richard A. Bartlett states: "For anyone involved with the conservation movement, or, to use a more modern word, ecology, it will provide sources for countless arguments and speeches." See *History: Reviews of New Books*, I (November–December, 1972), 32.

37. Herbert C. Hanson, *Dictionary of Ecology* (New York, 1962), 121. Of course, "ecology" is not only the study of those interrelationships, but it is the interrelationships themselves.

38. In his autobiography, *Breaking New Ground* (New York, 1947), Pinchot says he discovered this concept while horseback riding one evening in Rock Creek Park near Washington, D.C. See 322–26.

39. I am using this term to mean the history of the writing of history.

40. The best example of this thesis is J. Leonard Bates, "Fulfilling American Democracy: The Conservation Movement, 1907 to 1921," *Mississippi Valley Historical Review*, XLIV (June, 1957), 29–57.

41. See Peter G. Filene, "An Obituary for 'The Progressive Movement,'" *American Quarterly*, XXII (Spring, 1970), 20–34.

42. Except for *Forest and Stream,* the names of these newspapers changed frequently. These changes are traced in my "Selected Bibliography." The *Field and Stream* discussed in this study is *not* the magazine of the same name in existence today.

43. This phrase was suggested to me by Stewart L. Udall's term: "Myth of Superabundance." See his *Quiet Crisis* (New York, 1967), 66. Udall's book was first published in 1963.

44. John W. Noble to George Bird Grinnell, March 15, 1910, Grinnell File. (The latter is the name I have given to a huge mass of uncatalogued, miscellaneous material pertaining to pioneer conservationist George Bird Grinnell located in a metal filing cabinet in the library of the Birdcraft Museum of the Connecticut Audubon Society in Fairfield.)

45. For the view that even the natural sciences "are a fashion of the time,"

see J. Samuel Bois, *The Art of Awareness* (Dubuque, Iowa, 1973), 215; the book was first published in 1966.

CHAPTER ONE: *American Sportsmen and Their Code*

1. Earlier, articles on hunting and fishing had frequently appeared in periodicals like *American Farmer, Porter's Spirit of the Times, Wilkes' Spirit of the Times, Leslie's Weekly,* and *Harper's New Monthly Magazine,* but these journals were not devoted *primarily* to hunting and fishing. The so-called "sporting" papers already in existence were concerned mainly with horse racing.

2. *Forest and Stream,* July 2, 1885, XXIV, 451.

3. Interestingly, under the various definitions of the word "nature," the *American Heritage Dictionary of the English Language* states that "against nature" means something "profoundly wrong or unnatural: *'the taking [of] fish in spawning-time may be said to be against nature'* (Walton)."

4. "Will Wildwood" [Frederick E. Pond], ed., *Frank Forester's Sporting Scenes and Characters* (Philadelphia, 1881), I, 27.

5. Francis J. Grund, *The Americans in their Moral, Social, and Political Relations* (London, 1837), II, 263–64. Grund emigrated to Boston from his native Austria about 1827.

6. The life expectancy of Americans is now 71.2 years; see *The 1974 World Almanac and Book of Facts* (New York, 1973), 1019.

7. While these complaints were continually being made by the 1850s, they were not uncommon even in earlier decades—particularly in regard to diminishing fish stocks. For two examples from the early 1830s, see Charles Eliot Goodspeed, *Angling in America: Its Early History and Literature* (Boston, 1939), 113; and Jerome V. C. Smith, *Natural History of the Fishes of Massachusetts, Embracing a Practical Essay on Angling* (Boston, 1833), 345–46. The latter author laments not only commercial fishing, but dams and water pollution!

8. *Sports Afield,* II (January 17, 1889), 5; Dwight W. Huntington, *Our Big Game: A Book for Sportsmen and Nature Lovers* (New York, 1904), 29.

9. In almost all cases, the editorials appearing in the sporting periodicals were unsigned, but I am assuming that they were written by the editor. That assumption will be followed throughout this work. In this instance, the paper was theoretically conducted by the "Parker *Brothers*"—as noted in the masthead—but Wilbur seems to have been responsible for the editorial matter. The Parker family name is best remembered today for the making of fine shotguns.

10. Volume II, 24.

11. *Ibid.*

12. *Ibid.*

13. December, 1872, II, 40; October 11, 1873, III, 26; November 22, 1873, III, 120; November 29, 1873, III, 139; April 18, 1874, IV, 40.

14. George Bird Grinnell to Charles Sheldon, March 6, 1922, Letter Book, 206. Grinnell's Letter Books may be found in the library of the Birdcraft Museum of the Connecticut Audubon Society in Fairfield, Connecticut. Arranged chronologically, most volumes have approximately 1,000 pages of copied letters. Thirty-eight books in all, they extend, with few gaps, from August 2, 1886, to October 17, 1929.

15. *Forest and Stream,* September 11, 1873, I, 73; *Ibid.,* April 29, 1875, IV, 186; "Fishculture" was a regular column of the weekly; *Forest and Stream,* March 18, 1875, IV, 88; Grinnell to C. A. Hazen, September 20, 1916, Letter Book, 402.

16. I am indebted to George M. Fredrickson for suggesting this possibility.

17. "A New Gospel of Aesthetics," *Forest and Stream,* August 24, 1876, VII, 40.

18. *Ibid.*

19. *Ibid.,* August 14, 1873, I, 8.

20. *Ibid.*

21. Grinnell to Charles Sheldon, March 4, 1925, Grinnell File; Memoirs, 86–87. A typewritten autobiography written between November 26, 1915, and December 4, 1915, and covering Grinnell's life up to about 1883, the "Memoirs" abruptly end in the middle of a sentence on page 97. The manuscript is in the Grinnell File, but when citing this source, I will simply refer to it as the Memoirs.

22. His early life (1849–83) is traced in Reiger, ed., *The Passing of the Great West.* Grinnell is best known today for his writings on the American Indian.

23. "A Ten Years' Review," *Forest and Stream,* January 1, 1880, XIII, 950.

24. "A Much Abused Title," *Ibid.,* August 10, 1882, XIX, 21–22.

25. " 'Pot-Hunters,' " *Ibid.,* April 20, 1882, XVIII, 223; "The Order of Trout Hogs," *Ibid.,* June 16, 1881, XVI, 379.

26. *Ibid.,* February 12, 1880, XIV, 31.

27. *Ibid.*

28. *Ibid.*

29. See his *Age of Reform: From Bryan to F.D.R.* (New York, 1955), 135–66.

30. This term comes from a novel of the same name written by Mark Twain and Charles Dudley Warner and published in 1873. Their book castigated the vulgarity of the time, and its title has been used by historians to characterize the years from about 1877 to about 1896.

31. *The Inner Civil War: Northern Intellectuals and the Crisis of the Union* (New York, 1968), 221.

32. Grinnell to Frank G. Page, September 15, 1926, Letter Book, 421–22; *Forest and Stream,* December 24, 1891, XXXVII, 445; Memoirs, 44.

33. Reiger, ed., *The Passing of the Great West,* 57–58 and 78–80.

34. *The Inner Civil War,* 266.

35. Of these businesses, the Bosworth Machine Company of Milford, Connecticut, was the largest. It made sewing machines for heavy industrial uses.

36. This is precisely the idea expressed by Aldo Leopold. See his *Sand County*

Almanac (New York, 1966), 213; this edition is an enlarged version of the book published in 1949, combining essays that first appeared in *Round River* (1953).

37. For a suggestion of this concept, see Robert Henry Welker, *Birds and Men: American Birds in Science, Art, Literature, and Conservation, 1800–1900* (New York, 1966), 119; Welker's book was first published in 1955.

38. For the idea that hunting involves one *intimately* with his quarry and the natural world, see the edition of Leopold's *Sand County Almanac* cited above and José Ortega y Gasset's *Meditations on Hunting* (New York, 1972); the latter was originally published in 1943. The idea is scattered throughout both works. For merely one example of the same belief in the period under discussion, see "Science and Field Sports," *American Field* (later name of *Field and Stream*), August 7, 1886, XXVI, 121.

39. Welker, *Birds and Men*, 119.

40. Of course, some Romantics probably thought these areas appealing because they were "mysterious," but they rarely actually entered them—unlike the hunter.

41. See note no. 20 of my Introduction, above.

42. Elliott, *Carolina Sports, By Land and Water.* . . . (Charleston, 1846), 166–67. In the quoted sections, paragraphing and extraneous commas have been eliminated.

Elliott goes on to attack commercial deer hunters specifically, because they were killing what animals were left, and Americans generally, because they were unwilling to give the slightest protection to wildlife, seeing any such move as aristocratic and a threat to the "rights" of the people.

43. Brown, *The American Angler's Guide; or, Complete Fisher's Manual, For the United States: Containing the Opinions and Practices of Experienced Anglers of Both Hemispheres.* . . . (New York, 1857), 231–32. The enlarged edition of Brown's work, containing the section quoted here, first appeared in 1849.

44. Roosevelt, *Superior Fishing; or, the Striped Bass, Trout, and Black Bass of the Northern States.* . . . (New York, 1865), 184–85.

45. Because of its almost universal use, I sometimes employ the term "buffalo," even though "bison" is the only technically correct name for the wild cattle of North America.

A later member of the Boone and Crockett Club, Parkman "ran" buffalo on this trip for pleasure, not simple necessity: "My chase was more protracted, but at length I ran close to the bull and killed him with my pistols. Cutting off the tails of the victims by way of [a] trophy, we rejoined the party. . . ." See page 360.

46. Parkman, *The Oregon Trail: Sketches of Prairie and Rocky-Mountain Life* (Boston, 1872), ix–x.

47. Issue of February 20, 1875, V, 328.

48. For a recent appraisal of Murray's impact, see the 1970 edition of his famous book, edited by William K. Verner and with an Introduction of over

sixty pages by Warder H. Cadbury; published in Syracuse, New York, by Syracuse University Press.

49. *Rod and Gun and American Sportsman* (same paper but with a new title), October 7, 1876, IX, 5.

50. Actually, this is the last of several titles; *Field and Stream* changed its name to *The Field, Chicago Field,* and finally *American Field.*

51. "Long Island As It Was.—The Lesson It Teaches," *American Field,* July 1, 1882, XVIII, 8. Paragraphing eliminated.

52. For the history of what was perhaps the first club, the Schuylkill Fishing Company founded in 1732, see *Rod and Gun* (formerly *American Sportsman*), December 4, 1875, VII, 150; Robert Adams, Jr., "The Oldest Club in America," *Century Magazine,* XXVI (August, 1883), 544–50; and Goodspeed, "The Schuylkill Fishing Company," *Angling in America,* 29–54.

53. Exceptions to this statement were the duck-hunting clubs, already common by the antebellum period in some waterfowl regions.

54. Burnham, "The Old Era—and the New," *Bulletin of the American Game Protective [and Propagation] Association,* XIV (January, 1925), 13.

55. This group was originally called the American Fish Culturists' Association; since 1884 it has been known as the American Fisheries Society.

56. Pages 61–68. I have left out a number of clubs formed by Americans in Canada. Hallock's book was published in New York.

57. Hallock does not specifically state this, but it was a common practice of the day to name clubs after famous outdoorsmen and their leading periodicals.

58. *American Club List and Sportsman's Glossary,* 33–37 and 43. I have also left out four fox-hunting clubs in Canada.

59. There are many sources of documentation for the fact that most wildlife legislation originated with sportsmen and that their efforts go back to the beginning of American history. By the 1870s they had forced the passage of a huge number of laws in every part of the country—the main problem was enforcement.

For merely a sample of the literature pertaining to this subject, see T. S. Palmer, *Chronology and Index of the More Important Events in American Game Protection, 1776–1911* (Washington, D.C., 1912); Ralph M. Van Brocklin, "The Movement for the Conservation of Natural Resources in the United States Before 1901" (Ph.D. dissertation, University of Michigan, 1952); John Henry Reeves, Jr., "The History and Development of Wildlife Conservation in Virginia: A Critical Review" (Ph.D. dissertation, Virginia Polytechnic Institute, 1960); Eugene T. Petersen, "The History of Wild Life Conservation in Michigan, 1859–1921" (Ph.D. dissertation, University of Michigan, 1953); and Marvin W. Kranz, "Pioneering in Conservation: A History of the Conservation Movement in New York State, 1865–1903" (Ph.D. dissertation, Syracuse University, 1961). Kranz, for example, states that "most of the laws restricting shooting appeared to be, and in fact were, designed by wealthy sportsmen" (p. 102).

As an illustration of how strong this movement had become by the 1870s, *Forest and Stream* reported in 1874 that 30,000 petitioners were backing up an effort by some Ohio legislators to pass new game laws; see the issue of April 16, 1874, II, 153.

60. Volume III, 53.

61. *American Sportsman,* December 20, 1873, III, 188. As in most cases of this kind, the correspondent included the names of the elected officers.

62. This, of course, is untrue.

63. *American Sportsman,* June 13, 1874, IV, 168. Paragraphing has been eliminated.

64. *Ibid.,* August 29, 1874, IV, 344.

65. David Lowenthal, *George Perkins Marsh: Versatile Vermonter* (New York, 1958), 185. The appointment of Marsh was probably mainly due to the influence of his relative and close friend, George Franklin Edmunds, then Speaker of the Vermont legislature and an avid angler. See Dean C. Allard, Jr., "Spencer Fullerton Baird and the U.S. Fish Commission: A Study in the History of American Science" (Ph.D. dissertation, George Washington University, 1967), 65 and 114.

66. Marsh, *Report, Made Under Authority of the Legislature of Vermont, on the Artificial Propagation of Fish* (Burlington, 1857), 8–9. On the latter page he even goes so far as to claim that England was a great nation partly because of its emphasis on field sports.

In youth Marsh was an enthusiastic angler, and in later years he "collected" (killing in the name of science) all sorts of animals and birds—and he did so with great joy. See Lowenthal, *George Perkins Marsh,* 185 and 139–40.

67. Lewis Mumford, *The Brown Decades: A Study of the Arts in America, 1865–1895* (New York, 1931), 78.

68. Marsh, *Report, Made Under Authority of the Legislature of Vermont,* 10–15.

69. Because of indifference on the part of the general public, Marsh's *Report* had no immediate result; Lowenthal, *George Perkins Marsh,* 186.

70. Noble, "General Benjamin Harrison," *The Independent,* LIII (March 21, 1901), 646.

71. The great majority of these individuals have publications written by them, or pertaining to them, in my "Selected Bibliography" that document their hunting or fishing. There are some, however, whose experience in these activities cannot be readily ascertained by consulting the titles in that compilation: Ainsworth was a wealthy angler who pioneered in fish culture (Thaddeus Norris dedicated his early work on that subject to Ainsworth and cites him as an angler); Anderson was a hunter (George Bird Grinnell to Anderson, September 7, 1892, Letter Book, 371); Arthur, Clinton, Greeley, Harrison, and Webster were anglers (see Goodspeed, *Angling in America*); Baird's youthful angling and hunting are mentioned in Dall's biography, while his later angling interests are cited in George Reiger, *Profiles in Saltwater Angling;* Bierstadt and Grant were regular members of the Boone and Crockett Club and both hunters; the fact

that Cox, Vest, and Moran were sportsmen will be documented later in this study; Dutcher was a hunter (see John B. Burnham's article, "Conservation's Debt to Sportsmen"); Edmunds was an angler (see Dean C. Allard, Jr., "Spencer Fullerton Baird and the U.S. Fish Commission. . . ."); Harris, Parker, and Rowe were editors of leading sporting periodicals and well-known sportsmen; Ludlow was a hunter (see photograph of grizzly bear he helped to "bag" on Custer's 1874 Black Hills expedition in Reiger, ed., *The Passing of the Great West*); and Merriam was a hunter and a member of the League of American Sportsmen. All the works mentioned above are in my "Selected Bibliography."

CHAPTER TWO : *Conservation Begins with Wildlife*

1. Their statement of this position can be found in their memoirs. See Roosevelt, *Theodore Roosevelt: An Autobiography* (New York, 1913); and Pinchot, *Breaking New Ground,* already cited.

2. Following in the tradition of Samuel P. Hays, most historians have stressed the utilitarian objectives of Roosevelt and Pinchot and ignored the aesthetic side of their personalities. This is particularly true in regard to Pinchot.

Recently, however, one scholar has attempted to set the record straight. See Lawrence Rakestraw's book review of Frank Graham, Jr., *Man's Dominion: The Story of Conservation in America* (New York, 1971), in *Forest History,* XVI (April, 1972), 31–32; his article, "Conservation Historiography: An Assessment," particularly 278–81; and his book review of Henry Clepper's *Professional Forestry in the United States* (Baltimore, 1971), in the *Pacific Historical Review,* XLII (February, 1973), 118. In the latter piece Rakestraw cites Pinchot's " 'Forest Reserve Order No. 19' which ordered classification and special protection for areas of 'popular, historic or scientific interest.' . . ."

Dedicated national-park defender, George Bird Grinnell—who began his continuous editorial effort to preserve the Yellowstone *years before* John Muir initiated a similar drive in regard to Yosemite Valley—had the greatest admiration for the utilitarian Pinchot and worked closely with him on matters pertaining to both wildlife and forest conservation; proof for this statement may be found in correspondence in Grinnell's Letter Books and in his editorials in *Forest and Stream.* See, for example, Grinnell to Pinchot, June 11, 1901, Letter Book, 712–13; Grinnell to Pinchot, September 30, 1901, *Ibid.,* 895–96; Grinnell to Pinchot, October 5, 1901, *Ibid.,* 918; Grinnell to Pinchot, December 4, 1901, *Ibid.,* 959–60; Grinnell to Alden Sampson, December 23, 1901, *Ibid.,* 12; Grinnell to Pinchot, January 28, 1904, *Ibid.,* 509; Grinnell to Rosewell B. Lawrence, June 4, 1906, *Ibid.,* 415–16; Grinnell to Pinchot, June 3, 1907, *Ibid.,* 953; Grinnell to John J. White, Jr., February 5, 1908, *Ibid.,* 344; Grinnell to Madison Grant, March 6, 1908, *Ibid.,* 392; Grinnell to Pinchot, March 25, 1908, *Ibid.,* 444; "The Biltmore Forest," *Forest and Stream,* January 6, 1894, XLII, 1; "Yale School of Forestry," *Ibid.,* March 24, 1900, LIV, 221; *Ibid.,* January 30, 1904, LXII, 81; "Transfer of Forest Reserves," *Ibid.,* February 11, 1905, LXIV,

109; "The Forest Service," *Ibid.*, January 26, 1907, LXVIII, 127; and "Gifford Pinchot," *Ibid.*, January 15, 1910, LXXIV, 87.

After Roosevelt left office, Grinnell and Pinchot would find themselves on opposite sides of the fence in the controversy over whether a portion of Yosemite National Park should be destroyed to create a reservoir, but this was *one* issue and did not mean that they had split over their general approach to conservation.

Pinchot's stand in favor of the reservoir has been treated frequently by historians; for Grinnell's position, see "The Hetch-Hetchy Project," *Forest and Stream,* February 6, 1909, LXXII, 207; "Hetch-Hetchy Valley," *Ibid.*, March 5, 1910, LXXIV, 367; "Hetch Hetchy Next Year," *Ibid.*, June 18, 1910, LXXIV, 967; Grinnell to H. L. Myers, September 23, 1913, Letter Book, 486–87; Grinnell to R. U. Johnson, September 25, 1913, *Ibid.*, 515; and Grinnell to James A. O'Gorman, October 7, 1913, *Ibid.*, 548.

This unity in regard to basic goals was shared by most of the leaders of the aesthetically oriented Boone and Crockett Club during Roosevelt's administration, as shown by papers in the Boone and Crockett Club File. This "File" is the designation I have given to the large mass of uncatalogued material pertaining to the Boone and Crockett Club and its members located at the Theodore Roosevelt Birthplace National Historic Site in New York City. See Pinchot to Roosevelt, November 11, 1901; George B. Cortelyou to Pinchot, November 30, 1901; Pinchot to Alden Sampson, November 15, 1901; "Report of Committee on Game Refuges Submitted to Executive Committee at Players' Club, New York on January 7, 1902"; Pinchot to Sampson, January 13, 1902; Pinchot to Sampson, January 15, 1902; Pinchot to Sampson, March 6, 1902; Pinchot to Sampson, April 2, 1902; John F. Lacey to Madison Grant, June 12, 1902; Pinchot to Grant, January 31, 1903; Sampson to Grant, October 28, 1903; and Grinnell to Grant, March 6, 1907.

Contrary to Samuel Hays's interpretation, Pinchot's "boss," Theodore Roosevelt, had a highly developed aesthetic consciousness, which is manifested repeatedly in his writings on hunting and natural history. For example, he wrote to ornithologist Frank M. Chapman in 1899: " 'How immensely it would add to our forests if the great Logcock [ivory-billed woodpecker] were still found among them! The destruction of the Wild Pigeon and the Carolina Paroquet [parakeet] has meant a loss as severe as if the Catskills or the Palisades were taken away. When I hear of the destruction of a species I feel just as if the works of some great writer had perished; as if we had lost all instead of only part of Polybius or Livy.' " [Frank M. Chapman, *Autobiography of a Bird-Lover* (New York, 1935), 181; paragraphing eliminated.] Chapman's book was first published in 1933. Also see Willard B. Gatewood, "Theodore Roosevelt: Champion of 'Governmental Aesthetics,' " *Georgia Review,* XXI (1967), 172–83. Finally, in speaking of the need to preserve the giant sequoias of California, Roosevelt stated in 1903 that " 'there is nothing more practical in the end than the preservation of beauty, than the preservation of anything that appeals to the higher emotions of mankind.' " See John Ise, *Our National Park Policy: A Critical History* (Baltimore, 1961), 109.

For the idea that Roosevelt continually stressed the utilitarian objectives of his conservation program because of political necessity rather than from a lack of aesthetic appreciation, see Pinchot to Sampson, November, 15, 1901, Boone and Crockett Club File; Roosevelt to Roger S. Baldwin, October 13, 1903, in Elting E. Morison and John M. Blum, eds., *Letters of Theodore Roosevelt* (Cambridge, Massachusetts, 1951–54), III, 329–30; Grinnell, "Theodore Roosevelt," in Grinnell, ed., *American Big Game in Its Haunts* (New York, 1904), 15–16; and Roosevelt to Robert Underwood Johnson, January 17, 1905, in Morison and Blum, eds., *Letters of Theodore Roosevelt,* IV, 1104–05.

3. As a big-game hunter, Pinchot seems to have held the same view. In 1901 he wrote to Roosevelt that nothing should be done to arouse public opposition to the extension of the forest-reserve system, "which is the prime necessity for the preservation alike of forests, streams, and game." See Pinchot to Roosevelt, November 11, 1901, Boone and Crockett Club File.

4. Bernhard E. Fernow, *A Brief History of Forestry in Europe, the United States and Other Countries* (Toronto, Canada, 1907), 413; Van Brocklin, "The Movement for the Conservation of Natural Resources . . . Before 1901," 32; Kranz, "Pioneering in Conservation," 138.

5. Forester, *Frank Forester's Fish and Fishing of the United States, and British Provinces of North America* (London, 1849), 84–89, 256, and 293–96.

For another call for the adoption of a wide-scale fish-culture program as early as the '40s, see Brown, *American Angler's Guide,* 264–66. On the latter page, he even suggests the possibility of establishing striped bass in fresh water!

6. Roosevelt, *Game Fish of the Northern States of America.* . . . (New York, 1862), 52–53, 89, 95, 230–35; Roosevelt, *Superior Fishing,* 185–95; Norris, *American Angler's Book.* . . . (Philadelphia, no date—first published in 1864), 32, 459–60, 599–600; Norris, *American Fish-Culture.* . . . (Philadelphia, 1868), 20–21, 143–44; Scott, *Fishing in American Waters* (New York, 1875), 151–54, 365–66, 379, 407–18; Scott's book was first published in 1869.

For merely a sample of the large number of attacks on these evils found in the sporting periodicals, see "Fishways in Streams," *American Sportsman,* February, 1872, I, 7; "The Pollution of Rivers and Streams," *Ibid.,* May 2, 1874, IV, 72; "Dirty Water," *Ibid.,* December 5, 1874, V, 152; "The Pollution of Rivers," *Forest and Stream,* March 18, 1875, IV, 88; "Pollution of Streams," *The Rod and the Gun* (later name of *American Sportsman*), August 14, 1875, VI, 296; Seth Green, "Destruction of Fish by Paper Mills," *American Angler,* November 19, 1881, I, 28; "Destruction of Food Fishes" and "The Poisoned Schuylkill," both in *Forest and Stream,* July 13, 1882, XVIII, 463; "The Sawmill and the Trout," *American Angler,* September 23, 1882, II, 199; *American Field* (later name of *Field and Stream*), July 14, 1883, XX, 25; "The Pollution of the Schuylkill River, Pa.," *American Angler,* August 22, 1885, VIII, 118; "Polluting New York Harbor," *Forest and Stream,* June 10, 1886, XXVI, 387; *American Angler,* January 1, 1887, XI, 8; "Fertilizers Destructive to Fish Life," *Ibid.,* January 8, 1887, XI, 30; "Fish Slaughter and Stream Pollution," *Ibid.,* August 13, 1887, XII, 97; Seth Green, "Can Stream Pollution be Stopped?"

Ibid., August 13, 1887, XII, 107; and "River Pollution in Ohio," *Forest and Stream,* December 22, 1887, XVIIII, 421.

7. Because it is not a game fish in any sense of the word, sportsmen tended to be against the carp from the beginning, but "scientist" Spencer Fullerton Baird, head of the United States Fish Commission, praised it to the heavens. Proud of his ability to extract appropriations from a niggardly Congress, he always stressed the practical in his scientific endeavors. The carp was to be a major new protein source for the masses, but instead, most Americans have ignored it as food, while this living pollution has ruined wildlife habitat all over the nation.

8. Brown, *American Angler's Guide,* 265; Charles Hallock, *The Sportsman's Gazetteer and General Guide. . . .* (New York, 1879), Part I, 284 and 382. This important work was first published in 1877, and for the fact that it was actually written by George Bird Grinnell and others—while Hallock took the credit—see Reiger, ed., *The Passing of the Great West,* 167.

9. Marsh, *Report, Made Under Authority of the Legislature of Vermont,* 16–17.

10. By this term, I mean those who fished mainly for food or commerce, rather than sport.

11. Although the controversy went back at least to 1856, when a petition was sent to the Rhode Island legislature, it did not pick up steam until 1866, when the commissioners of fisheries of the New England states (virtually all of whom were anglers) met in Boston to develop methods "for restoring salmon and increasing the number of shad in the different rivers of the States." See United States Commission of Fish and Fisheries, *Report on the Condition of the Sea Fisheries of the South Coast of New England in 1871 and 1872* (Washington, D.C., 1873), IX and 197; hereinafter, this source will be referred to as the *U.S. Fish Commission Report.*

12. Allard, "Spencer Fullerton Baird and the U.S. Fish Commission," 73.

13. *Ibid.,* 76–90. Theodore Lyman, James W. Milner, and Senator George F. Edmunds were well-known anglers who had a part in bringing about federal intervention.

Because "the alleged diminution of the fisheries was in tidal and navigable waters of the United States, and over which the Federal Government exercises jurisdiction in other matters, it was maintained by many that the State governments had no control, and that any enactments on the subject must be made by Congress; especially as, if left to the States, it would be impossible to secure that harmony and concurrence of action necessary for a successful result." *U.S. Fish Commission Report,* X.

14. Allard, "Spencer Fullerton Baird and the U.S. Fish Commission," 93; *U.S. Fish Commission Report,* XXXIV–XXXVI.

15. *Ibid.,* 97–101 and 164–65.

16. Genio C. Scott, "Spring Birds and Fishes," *The Rod and the Gun* (later name of *American Sportsman*), April 17, 1875, VI, 34; Fred Mather, "Stall Fed vs. Wild Trout," *Ibid.,* May 1, 1875, VI, 72.

17. Allard, "Spencer Fullerton Baird and the U.S. Fish Commission," 111–63, 284, 293–94, and 352; Theodore W. Cart, "The Struggle for Wildlife Protection in the United States, 1870–1900: Attitudes and Events Leading to the Lacey Act" (Ph.D. dissertation, University of North Carolina, 1971), 159.

18. Seth Green, "Fish Culture in New York," *American Field* (later name of *Field and Stream*), July 1, 1882, XVIII, 2. Because Green fails to say exactly when the "frost fish" were produced, I am assuming that it was during the same period as the other species cited.

19. Spencer Fullerton Baird was the leading government culturist, and he was also an angler. See my "Notes" to Chapter I, above.

In addition, it should be mentioned that sportsmen like Robert Barnwell Roosevelt and George Franklin Edmunds played key roles in getting the federal government involved in fish culture. See Allard, "Spencer Fullerton Baird and the U.S. Fish Commission," 126–31.

20. This fact is documented in the books by, or about, these individuals listed in my "Selected Bibliography."

21. *Forest and Stream,* February 19, 1874, II, 26.

22. For merely one example, see Baird's letter in *Ibid.,* January 1, 1874, I, 330.

23. Interestingly, suggestions for stocking the Great Lakes with "salmon"—meaning Atlantic salmon—can be found in the sporting literature as early as 1849. See Forester, *Frank Forester's Fish and Fishing,* 86; for a later recommendation of the same idea, see "Third Annual Convention of the American Fish Culturists [*sic*] Association," *American Sportsman,* February 14, 1874, III, 308.

24. T. S. Palmer, *Private Game Preserves and their Future in the United States* (Washington, D.C., 1910), 2–3.

25. *Ibid.,* 3. Also, see *American Sportsman,* December 20, 1873, III, 187, for Caton's own description of the animals in his preserve.

26. Palmer, *Private Game Preserves and Their Future in the United States,* 3 and 4. The purpose of the protected deer park was to provide a continual supply of game to the surrounding area, and wardens were employed to ensure that no poaching took place.

27. "Fall Sport at Blooming Grove Park," *American Sportsman,* November 8, 1873, III, 85. Though modified from earlier years, Blooming Grove still exists.

28. Charles Hallock, *The Fishing Tourist: Angler's Guide and Reference Book* (New York, 1873), 225–26.

29. *Ibid.,* 227. The timber-management program was under the direction of "Grand Forester" F. W. Jones; see *American Sportsman,* December 27, 1873, III, 201.

30. Henry Clepper, "Pinchot, Gifford" in Clepper, ed., *Leaders of American Conservation* (New York, 1971), 259; for a similar statement, see Harold T. Pinkett, *Gifford Pinchot: Private and Public Forester* (Urbana, Illinois, 1970), 22.

31. Cart, "The Struggle for Wildlife Protection in the United States," 92.

32. H. J. Cookingham, "The Bisby Club and the Adirondacks," *American Field* (later name of *Field and Stream*), March 10, 1883, XVIII, 172.

33. *Ibid.*

34. *Ibid.*, 173; "The Bisby Club," *Ibid.*, April 22, 1882, XVII, 272. Also, see "Wonderful Trout Growth at Bisby Park," *American Angler,* June 6, 1885, VII, 359, for a discussion of the results of planting hybrid brook-rainbow trout in the waters of Bisby Park.

35. S. R. Stoddard, *The Adirondacks* [Glens Falls, New York, 1893 (?)], 215–16; this is the 24th (1894) edition of his guide and has a copyright date of 1893.

36. *Ibid.*, 216.

37. *Ibid.*

38. Andrew D. Rodgers III, *Bernhard E. Fernow: A Story of North American Forestry* (New York, 1968), 253; this work was first published in 1951.

39. See Lynn White, Jr., "The Historical Roots of Our Ecological Crisis," *Science,* CLV (March 10, 1967), 1203–07.

40. Peter Matthiessen, *Wildlife in America* (New York, 1964), 57; this work was first published in 1959.

41. The exception was the predatory mammal or bird, which was regarded as "evil" because it killed "innocent" species. The common, but erroneous, belief was that the diminution of predators would result in an absolute, *permanent* increase in almost every other species. While temporary increases did occur, the long-run results were overpopulation, habitat destruction, and staggering losses to disease, crippling, etc.

42. "Uniform Game Laws," *Forest and Stream,* February 21, 1884, XXII, 61; also, see *Ibid.*, February 19, 1874, II, 24; and *Ibid.*, April 29, 1875, IV, 186, for Hallock's earlier statements of this position.

43. "A Proposition to Gentlemen Sportsmen," XV, 319.

44. *Ibid.*, March 24, 1881, XVI, 139.

45. "New Facts on Game Protection," *Ibid.*

46. *Ibid.*

47. *Ibid.*, January 26, 1882, XVII, 503.

48. *Ibid.*

49. "Should the Gun be Taxed?" *Ibid.*, January 22, 1880, XIII, 1010.

50. *Ibid.*

51. *Ibid.*

52. *Ibid.*, July 23, 1885, XXIV, 505.

53. "A Bad Example," *American Field,* April 10, 1886, XXV, 337.

54. With tragic irony, the Cincinnati Zoo also has the distinction of having been the home of the last Carolina parakeet; the latter died on February 21, 1918, in the same building that housed the last passenger pigeon.

55. Graham, *Man's Dominion,* 50.

56. One historian states that "by the turn of the century the prices paid for

egret plumes had risen to $32 an ounce (four herons contributed an ounce), or twice the price of gold"; *Ibid.*, 48.

57. Even a casual reading of the leading sportsmen's papers already cited in this study—with the exception of *American Angler*—will reveal that during the commercial buffalo slaughter of the 1870s and early '80s, they frequently attacked the market hunters.

For a sample of these papers' protests against the commercial pigeon hunters, see William B. Mershon [comp.], *The Passenger Pigeon* (New York, 1907), 77, 93, and 223–25. The latter citation refers to a *Forest and Stream* editorial of July 14, 1881, attacking the "sport" of using live passenger pigeons in trapshooting contests; it condemned the shooters directly and the commercial netters indirectly—for supplying the living targets.

Sportsmen's efforts in behalf of nongame birds went back at least to the 1850s: "Henry Herbert ['Frank Forester'] worked continually for better legislation and drafted New York State's first game law to include protection for insectivorous birds less than two months before he took his life in 1858"; Cart, "The Struggle for Wildlife Protection in the United States," 87.

For merely an indication of the sporting press's attitudes concerning the destruction of nongame birds, see "Spare the Small Birds," *American Sportsman,* October 4, 1873, III, 9; "Game Laws and the Protection of Birds," *Ibid.,* January 24, 1874, III, 260; *Ibid.,* August 29, 1874, IV, 344; "Killing Insectivorous Birds," *The Rod and the Gun* (later name of *American Sportsman*), July 10, 1875, VI, 232; *The Field* (later name of *Field and Stream*), August 21, 1875, IV, 8; "Protect the Birds," *Chicago Field* (later name of *Field and Stream*), September 21, 1878, X, 81–82, *Forest and Stream,* April 22, 1880, XIV, 230; "Destruction of Song Birds," *Ibid.,* March 23, 1882, XVIII, 143; "The Destruction of Small Birds," *Ibid.,* March 30, 1882, XVIII, 163; "A Spring Plague," *Ibid.,* April 27, 1882, XVIII, 244; "The Destruction of Insectivorous and Song Birds," *American Field* (later name of *Field and Stream*), January 5, 1884, XXI, 1; "The Sacrifice of Song Birds" and "The Destruction of Small Birds," both in *Forest and Stream*, August 7, 1884, XXIII, 21 and 24; "Birds, Bonnets and Butchers," *Ibid.,* September 25, 1884, XXIII, 161; "Bird Destruction," *Ibid.,* January 14, 1886, XXV, 482; "Fashion and the Birds," *American Field,* March 20, 1886, XXV, 265; "Save the Birds," *Ibid.,* April 17, 1886, XXV, 361; "Unsportsmanlike Destruction," *Ibid.,* May 29, 1886, XXV, 505; "Birds of Plumage," *Ibid.,* June 12, 1886, XXV, 553; "The Audubon Society," *American Angler,* September 25, 1886, X, 201; and "The Audubon Society," *Ibid.,* December 25, 1886, X, 410.

58. Lacey stated: " 'I have always been a lover of the birds; and I have always been a hunter as well; for to-day there is no friend that the birds have like the true sportsman—the man who enjoys legitimate sport. He protects them out of season; he kills them in moderation in season.' " In addition, he attacked the " 'game hog' " and said that his bill was " 'directed against the pot hunter.' "

See "Let Us Save the Birds: Speech of Hon. John F. Lacey, in the House of Representatives," *Recreation,* XIII (July, 1900), 33.

59. See Cart, "The Struggle for Wildlife Protection in the United States," already cited in my "Notes." He summarizes his arguments in a recent article: "The Lacey Act: America's First Nationwide Wildlife Statute," *Forest History,* XVII (October, 1973), 4–13.

60. Charles F. Batchelder, a member of the club and its historian, later stated: "It should not be forgotten that in those days a hunting dog was very apt to be found a member of the household of any active ornithologist, for there seldom was much of a dividing line between ornithologists and sportsmen. Few were the ornithologists who, in season, did not turn keenly to the pursuit of game-birds, and it was only the dullest-witted sportsmen whose eyes and guns were not directed instinctively toward any strange bird that appeared on the horizon." See his *Account of the Nuttall Ornithological Club, 1873 to 1919. Memoirs of the Nuttall Ornithological Club,* No. VIII (Cambridge, Massachusetts, 1937), 13–14.

61. Matthiessen, *Wildlife in America,* 165; Graham, *Man's Dominion,* 29 and 32. On the latter page Graham claims that the "results" of the first meeting of the American Ornithologists' Union "were the wellspring from which flowed a large part of the modern conservation movement."

62. One example is Frank M. Chapman's description of his "capture" in 1890 of the now extinct, or nearly extinct, ivory-billed woodpecker on a collecting expedition down Florida's Suwannee River: "It was my good fortune to encounter the one Ivory-billed Woodpecker seen on the voyage. I knew its voice the moment its loud *yap-yap* fell on my ears. Then followed memorable moments as I stalked it through the cypress trees, until, unbelievable glory, it was actually in my hands"; Chapman, *Autobiography of a Bird-Lover,* 93.

63. George Bird Grinnell and Theodore Roosevelt are two examples of sportsmen who made important collections for the leading museums.

64. See statement of George Brown Goode concerning *Forest and Stream* as a "medium of communication between field-naturalists": *Forest and Stream,* October 23, 1873, I, 174; also Elliott Coues' letter to *Forest and Stream* praising the quality of its ornithological contents: *Forest and Stream,* April 6, 1882, XVIII, 187; and his "Sketch of North American Ornithology in 1879," *American Naturalist,* XIV (January, 1880), 21, where he states that much of the "ornithological matter" in *Forest and Stream* and *The Field* (the later name of *Field and Stream*) is "precisely of the character of the shorter notes in the *Nuttall Bulletin,* or in Harting's *Zoölogist.*" In addition, see the statement of another ornithologist, Frank M. Chapman, to the effect that the first time he appeared in print was in an 1883 issue of *Forest and Stream* and that "*Forest and Stream* was [then] . . . not only the leading journal for sportsmen but its high standing made it a recognized means of communication between naturalists"; Chapman, *Autobiography of a Bird-Lover,* 32.

In the early 1930s the well-known bibliophile and sportsman-naturalist, John C. Phillips, observed that "years ago almost the whole field of conservation,

sport and ornithology could be followed in the pages of one or two journals";
see his "Naturalists, Nature Lovers, and Sportsmen," *1582 to 1925 Auk,*
XLVIII (January, 1931), 40. And after compiling his monumental *American
Game Mammals and Birds: A Catalogue of Books* (Boston, 1930), Phillips noted
that it was sometimes difficult to separate sporting and scientific journals (pp.
9–10).

The following is a random selection of leading "naturalists" and "scientists,"
in all fields, whose contributions I have found in one or more of the "big four"
sportsmen's periodicals: Spencer Fullerton Baird, William Brewster, Elliott
Coues, Joel A. Allen, Albert K. Fisher, C. Hart Merriam, Frank M. Chapman,
Robert Ridgway, Joseph T. Rothrock, Livingston Stone, Seth Green, Fred
Mather, Thomas M. Brewer, George Brown Goode, David Starr Jordan, Othniel
C. Marsh, John Burroughs, Theodore N. Gill, Joseph Bassett Holder, Charles
Frederick Holder, Theodatus Garlick, Henry W. Henshaw, and Edward Drinker
Cope.

65. See Cart's dissertation and article, already cited, for a full discussion of
the importance of the Lacey Act.

66. Perhaps this is a misprint—the original being a reference to the now
abandoned order of "Raptores," consisting of those species loosely called "birds
of prey": hawks, eagles, owls, and vultures; the latter, of course, feed only
on dead or dying animals and do not catch their own prey.

67. Grinnell was a prominent member of the Committee.

68. Volume XXVI, 41. In three cases minor errors in punctuation have been
corrected.

69. See *Forest and Stream,* February 25, 1886, XXVI, 83; and *Ibid.,* March
4, 1886, XXVI, 104, for pledges of support from Henry Ward Beecher, John
Burroughs, and others.

70. T. Gilbert Pearson, *Fifty Years of Bird Protection in the United States*
(New York, 1933), 201.

71. *Ibid.* Also see Grinnell to C. Hart Merriam, December 20, 1887, Letter
Book, 238; Grinnell to Frank M. Chapman, November 10, 1898, *Ibid.,* 949;
and Grinnell to Minnie K. Anderson, March 13, 1900, *Ibid.,* 792–93.

72. Pearson, *Fifty Years of Bird Protection,* 201. On the same page Pearson
notes that "as President of the Massachusetts State Sportsmen's Association,
[Brewster] had [already] been actively working for wild life preservation. . . ."

The Pennsylvania Audubon Society was organized in the fall of 1886, model-
ing itself after Grinnell's original society, "but it became dormant"; *Ibid.*

73. Grinnell to William Dutcher, November 3, 1906, Letter Book, 666.

Although a loose federation—the National Committee of Audubon Societies—was organized in 1901, it was not until 1905 that the National Association
of Audubon Societies was incorporated.

74. Not only was Grinnell an avid bird hunter, but so were Brewster and
William Dutcher, who was mainly responsible for organizing the national association. The fact that all of these men were sportsmen has already been documented in my "Notes."

75. Grinnell to Charles B. Reynolds, March 1, 1918, Letter Book, 418. In fact, Grinnell gives Reynolds credit for originating the proposition.

76. Volume XLII, 89.

77. See Trefethen, *Crusade for Wildlife,* particularly 160–78.

CHAPTER THREE : *The Early Fight for the Forests*

1. Many of these men were what might be called "literary conservationists," in the sense that their calls for woodland preservation usually came through the vehicle of literature rather than newspaper editorials, political action, etc. Discussion of Cooper, Irving, Audubon, Bryant, Greeley, Thoreau, and Lanman can be found in Roderick Nash, *Wilderness and the American Mind* (New Haven, 1973); this is a revised edition of a work first published in 1967.

For Adams, see Udall, *Quiet Crisis,* 86; Forester's works contain many attacks on what was later called "progress," which, indirectly at least, were calls for forest preservation—see, for example, *Frank Forester's Fish and Fishing,* page 86, for the comment: "modern improvements—heavens! how I loathe that word!" For Lewis, see his *American Sportsman: Containing Hints to Sportsmen, Notes on Shooting, and the Habits of the Game Birds and Wild Fowl of America* (Philadelphia, 1863), 129, for at least an indirect attack on forest destruction; this book was originally published, under a different title, in 1851. Clinton, Elliott, and Hammond are discussed elsewhere in the present study.

2. See my Chapter I, above, and its Notes.

3. See David M. Emmons, "Theories of Increased Rainfall and the Timber Culture Act of 1873," *Forest History,* XV (October, 1971), 6–14.

4. *Ibid.,* 12; Henry Clepper, "Morton, Julius Sterling," in Clepper, ed., *Leaders of American Conservation,* 230.

5. The German-born pioneer of forestry, Bernhard E. Fernow, later commented that "it is to be noted as characteristic of much American legislation . . . that this . . . was secured only as a 'rider' to an appropriation for the distribution of seed"; Fernow, *A Brief History of Forestry,* 408.

6. Henry Clepper, "Hough, Franklin Benjamin," in Clepper, ed., *Leaders of American Conservation,* 173.

7. *Ibid.*

8. Page 456. The *Concise Dictionary of American Biography* (New York, 1964) is merely a one-volume abridgment of the multivolume, supposedly authoritative, *Dictionary of American Biography.*

9. Schurz, "Reminiscences of a Long Life," *McClure's Magazine,* XXVI (November, 1905), 6 and 14; and *Ibid.,* XXVI (December, 1905), 170–71.

10. Udall, *The Quiet Crisis,* 99.

11. Olson, *The Depletion Myth: A History of Railroad Use of Timber* (Cambridge, Massachusetts, 1971), 40, 75, and 192.

12. Donald Worster, ed., *American Environmentalism: The Formative Period, 1860–1915* (New York, 1973), 73; editor speaking. In looking back on his early efforts, Fernow wrote in 1907 that he had had "the disadvantage of being a foreigner who had first to learn the limitations of democratic government"; Fernow, *A Brief History of Forestry,* 416.

13. James Penick, Jr., is one of the few to understand this idea. In his review of Harold Pinkett's *Gifford Pinchot,* he states that forestry was an example of patrician reform that depended on the backing of upper-class conservationists; *Pacific Northwest Quarterly,* LXII (October, 1971), 141.

For a good discussion of the *noblesse oblige* orientation of the Roosevelt conservation program, see G. Edward White, *The Eastern Establishment and the Western Experience: The West of Frederic Remington, Theodore Roosevelt, and Owen Wister* (New Haven, 1968), 171–83. Although he does not discuss conservation specifically, another scholar presents a wealth of insights regarding the patrician class, including Roosevelt, that can be applied directly to the latter's conservation program; see Michael D. Clark, "American Patricians as Social Critics, 1865–1914" (Ph.D. dissertation, University of North Carolina, 1965). The same is true of Walter E. Burdick, Jr., "Elite in Transition: From Alienation to Manipulation" (Ph.D. dissertation, Northern Illinois University, 1969).

14. Fernow later recalled: "'I have in years gone by carried my gun and cast my line occasionally, and taken pleasure in it. Indeed my profession as a forester in my native country where I studied and practiced it includes both, in the theoretical teaching and in the practice, the art of sportsmanship hunting and of conservative fishing, and I can assure you, there is a high standard of sportsmanlike behavior kept up by the foresters. . . .'" See Rodgers, *Bernhard E. Fernow,* 28.

15. Fernow's membership in an Adirondack sportsmen's association is discussed above. For Schenck's hunting, see his *Biltmore Story: Recollections of the Beginnings of Forestry in the United States* (St. Paul, Minnesota, 1955), 36 and 60. Schenck's book is edited by Ovid A. Butler.

16. *Ibid.,* 20.

17. *Ibid.,* 36.

18. Scattered references to this fact can be found in Francis P. Farquhar, ed., *Up and Down California in 1860–1864: The Journal of William H. Brewer* (New Haven, 1930).

19. The interest shown in this subject by *American Sportsman, Forest and Stream,* and *American Angler* will be documented shortly. For *Field and Stream,* see, for example, "Game—Its Extinction; The Cause, and the Remedy," *Chicago Field* (later name of *Field and Stream*), August 3, 1878, IX, 392; "Why the Prairies are Treeless," *Ibid.,* January 29, 1881, XIV, 394; "Tree Planting," *American Field* (later name of *Field and Stream*), July 21, 1883, XX, 49; "A Public Park," *Ibid.,* December 22, 1883, XX, 577; "State School of Forestry," *Ibid.,* July 16, 1884, XXII, 49; and "Nurseries for Game," *Ibid.,* October 24, 1885, XXIV, 385.

20. *American Angler,* May 17, 1884, V, 310; *Ibid.,* May 24, 1884, V, 328; *Ibid.,* December 20, 1884, VI, 386; "Destruction of the Trout and Trout Streams of Central New York," *Ibid.,* January 1, 1887, XI, 8–9; "How Shall We Preserve Our Water Supply?" *Ibid.,* March 5, 1887, XI, 145–46.

21. "Forest Legislation," *American Sportsman,* October 25, 1873, III, 56; "Foreign Sporting Notes," *Ibid.,* March 7, 1874, III, 361; "Wood and Forest," *Ibid.,* November 21, 1874, V, 120; *Ibid.,* March 13, 1875, V, 377; "Our Trees," *Ibid.,* March 20, 1875, V, 392; "Forest Preservation in Europe," *The Rod and the Gun* (later name of *American Sportsman*), July 10, 1875, VI, 231; A. S. Collins, "Decrease of Brook Trout in the United States," *Ibid.,* August 7, 1875, VI, 280; "Waste Land and Forest Culture," *Ibid.,* March 18, 1876, VII, 390; "Are we Drying Up?" *Ibid.,* January 20, 1877, IX, 246.

22. The very first issue of the paper (August 14, 1873) stated: "For the preservation of our rapidly diminishing forests we shall continually do battle. Our great interests are in jeopardy . . . from the depletion of our timber lands by fire and axe."

For some other examples of Hallock's interest in the subject, see: "Woodman Spare that Tree," *Forest and Stream,* August 21, 1873, I, 26; "The Preservation of Our Forests," *Ibid.,* September 4, 1873, I, 56; "The Adirondack Park," *Ibid.,* September 11, 1873, I, 73; "What the Germans Say About Wood Cutting," *Ibid.,* September 18, 1873, I, 89; *Ibid.,* September 25, 1873, I, 101; "The Waste of Timber," October 2, 1873, I, 121; "The State Park," *Ibid.,* October 9, 1873, I, 136–37; *Ibid.,* October 16, 1873, I, 149; *Ibid.,* November 27, 1873, I, 244; "The Forests and their Effects on Man," *Ibid.,* December 25, 1873, I, 321; "Adirondack Park and the Preservation of Our Forests," *Ibid.,* March 19, 1874, II, 88.

23. Grinnell became natural history editor in 1876; for a detailed discussion of his early career, see Reiger, ed., *The Passing of the Great West.*

24. *Forest and Stream,* April 13, 1882, XVIII, 204.

25. *Ibid.*

26. *Ibid.*

27. *Forest and Stream,* July 19, 1883, XX, 481.

28. *Ibid.*

29. *Ibid.*

30. *Ibid.*

31. "Forest Wealth," *Ibid.,* January 31, 1884, XXII, 2.

32. *Ibid.*

33. *Ibid.*

34. "Unheeded Lessons," *Ibid.,* March 27, 1884, XXII, 161.

35. *Ibid.*

36. *Ibid.,* May 15, 1884, XXII, 301.

37. *Ibid.*

38. "Forests and Forestry V," *Ibid.,* January 22, 1885, XXIII, 502.

39. *Ibid.*

40. "Forests and Forestry III," *Ibid.,* January 8, 1885, XXIII, 461–62; *Ibid.,* January 15, 1885, XXIII, 482.

41. Nash, *Wilderness and the American Mind,* 104–05.

42. Marsh, *Man and Nature,* 35, quoted in Nash, *Wilderness and the American Mind,* 104–05.

43. Marsh, *Man and Nature,* 234–36, cited in *Ibid.,* 105.

44. *Forest and Stream,* September 4, 1873, I, 56.

45. "The Adirondack Park," *Ibid.,* September 11, 1873, I, 73, cited in Nash, *Wilderness and the American Mind,* 118.

46. *Forest and Stream,* December 13, 1883, XXI, 381.

47. *Ibid.,* March 13, 1884, XXII, 121.

48. *Ibid.,* 121–22.

49. As early as 1873, Hallock had cited the possibility of using European methods of timber-cutting in the Adirondacks: see *Ibid.,* October 9, 1873, I, 136–37. Yet he made no effort to follow up this idea, and his later editorials reverted to the watershed justification.

50. *Ibid.,* XXI, 489.

51. This, of course, applies only to wildlife, forests, ranges, and water. But even nonrenewable resources like minerals and oil can be administered according to what Roosevelt later called "wise use," so as to make them last as long as possible.

52. "The Adirondack Forests," *Forest and Stream,* January 29, 1885, XXIV, 2.

53. *Ibid.*

54. Nash, *Wilderness and the American Mind,* 119.

55. *New York Laws,* 1885, Chap. 238, p. 482, cited in *Ibid.*

56. *Ibid.*

57. G. Wallace Chessman, *Governor Theodore Roosevelt: The Albany Apprenticeship, 1898–1900* (Cambridge, Massachusetts, 1965), 250. The author claims that when Pinchot presented his idea for scientific forestry in the Adirondacks to Theodore Roosevelt in 1900, Roosevelt "was most impressed"—suggesting that this was the first time he had heard such a proposal! In reality, Roosevelt had been reading all about how the Adirondack timberlands should be systematically managed in New York's leading outdoor periodical years before he had ever heard of Gifford Pinchot. As we will see later, Roosevelt would soon begin to hear the same ideas from George Bird Grinnell personally, when they began their close friendship in 1885; although he had briefly met Pinchot in 1894, Roosevelt did not become well acquainted with him until 1899.

58. *Forest and Stream,* April 17, 1884, XXII, 221.

59. "Who are the Skinners?" *Ibid.,* June 11, 1885, XXIV, 385.

60. For one example, see U.S. Congress, House, *Message from the President of the United States Transmitting a Message on Conservation and Water Management* (90th Cong., 2d Sess., House, Doc. 273), 1; in this message of March 8, 1968, President Johnson quotes Roosevelt.

61. *Forest and Stream,* January 15, 1885, XXIII, 482.

62. Gurth Whipple, *Fifty Years of Conservation in New York State, 1885–1935*

(Syracuse, 1935), 16; Van Brocklin, "The Movement for the Conservation of Natural Resources in the United States Before 1901," 12–13. For Clinton as an angler, see my earlier "Notes."

63. Hammond, *Wild Northern Scenes; or, Sporting Adventures with the Rifle and the Rod* (New York, 1857), 83.

Interestingly, Hammond was a dedicated believer in what I have called the code of the sportsman: see *Ibid.,* x–xi, 23, 43, 48, 81–82, and 341.

In an earlier work Hammond made a similar recommendation for an Adirondack preserve, but without specifying its size: Hammond, *Hunting Adventures in the Northern Wilds; or, A Tramp in the Chateaugay Woods, Over Hills, Lakes, and Forest Streams* (New York, 1856), 168; originally published in 1854 under the title, *Hills, Lakes and Forest Streams.* As in the later volume, this work contains many examples of his commitment to the code of the sportsman.

64. Quoted in Harold C. Anderson, "The Unknown Genesis of the Wilderness Idea," *Living Wilderness,* V (1940), 15; cited by Nash, *Wilderness and the American Mind,* 117.

65. For merely two examples, see "Forest Wardens," *Rod and Gun and American Sportsmen* (later name of *American Sportsman*), September 30, 1876, VIII, 424; and "An Adirondack Preserve," *Forest and Stream,* January 26, 1882, XVII, 511.

For the importance of this idea, see Eugene J. O'Neill, "Parks and Forest Conservation in New York, 1850–1920" (Ed.D. dissertation, Columbia University, 1963), 4, 10, 51, 183–84, 187, and 201.

"The use of forests to serve the function of recreation is as old as the Middle Ages. Indeed, the very word 'forest' meant an area reserved for the king's private pleasure. Only in the modern age did the word come to signify any tract of land covered with trees and underbrush"; *Ibid.,* 4.

Actually the idea probably goes back much earlier than the Middle Ages. As Carleton S. Coon points out, "the [ancient] Persians gave us the word *paradise,* which originally meant simply a hunting preserve"; *The Story of Man: From the First Human to Primitive Culture and Beyond* (New York, 1962), 112; this is a revised edition of a work first published in 1954.

66. For example, *American Field* (later name of *Field and Stream*) reported that the Fox Lake Club, an association established in 1879 near Chicago, "is a regular stock company, the members holding the shares, each being entitled to all the rights and privileges of the club. The initiation fee is $215; the year[ly] dues are $10." See issue of June 9, 1883, IX, 463.

67. Thoreau, *The Maine Woods* (New York, 1950), 321; this is Dudley C. Lunt's edition of a book first published in 1864. In the same passage Thoreau says that the kings "were impelled by a true instinct" in setting aside these hunting areas.

68. Thoreau, *The Concord and the Merrimack* (New York, 1954), 33–39; this is Dudley C. Lunt's edition of a book first published in 1849.

69. Thoreau, *The Maine Woods,* 65.

70. Thoreau, *The Concord and the Merrimack,* 6, 8, 24–27, 48–49; and

Thoreau, *Cape Cod* (New York, 1951), 178; this is Dudley C. Lunt's edition of a book first published in 1865.

71. For example: Thoreau, *The Maine Woods,* 24 and 86.

72. In the early 1870s *Forest and Stream* sent into the Lake Okeechobee-Everglades region two expeditions that uncovered much new information concerning its topography and fauna; in the 1880s George Bird Grinnell explored and mapped the still-wild country in what became—largely through his efforts—Glacier National Park; the famous Harriman Expedition of 1899, that studied the coast of Alaska, began with the desire of sportsman Edward H. Harriman to shoot an Alaskan brown bear; and sportsman-naturalist Charles Sheldon explored the Mt. McKinley region in the early years of this century and spearheaded the effort to make it a national park.

73. This is a well-established fact of Adirondack history; for merely one indication of its truth, see Goodspeed, *Angling in America,* 187, for the 1856 statement of a Herkimer County historian.

74. *Ibid.*

75. Their interest in forest preservation has been documented in my earlier "Notes"; a number of the editorials cited, particularly those of *Forest and Stream,* refer to the need for establishing a wilderness park in the Adirondacks.

76. For O'Neill's conclusions, see his "Parks and Forest Conservation in New York, 1850–1920"; Hays's thesis is discussed in the Introduction of the present work.

77. Nash, *Wilderness and the American Mind,* 119; while he does not cite Hays, Nash's discussion of this issue comes to the same conclusion.

78. *Forest and Stream,* September 11, 1873, I, 73. In later editorials Hallock and Grinnell continually fought for Adirondack preservation on the basis of "practical," economic arguments, despite the fact that they were always *most* interested in wildlife conservation.

79. This idea is discussed in my Chapter II, above.

80. See Kranz, "Pioneering in Conservation: A History of the Conservation Movement in New York State, 1865–1903," 43, 46–47, 50–51, 142, 150, 156–57, 161–62, 174, 178–79, 181–84, and 261–63.

Colvin, Cleveland, and Fernow have already been identified as sportsmen. For Hewitt as a sportsman, see *American Angler,* June 19, 1886, IX, 391; for Husted, see *Ibid.,* July 4, 1885, VIII, 8; and for Hill, see *Ibid.,* August 15, 1885, VIII, 106. Whitehead was a well-known sporting author of the period.

CHAPTER FOUR: *Development of the National Park Concept*

1. Catlin, *North American Indians: Being Letters and Notes on their Manners, Customs, and Conditions, Written During Eight Years' Travel Amongst the Wildest Tribes of Indians in North America, 1832–1839* (Philadelphia, 1913), I,

27–29. On the latter page, in describing a chase after buffalo, he says: "I went not for 'meat,' but for a trophy; I wanted his head and horns."
This two-volume work, originally published in London in 1841, was a collection of articles Catlin had written in the previous decade.

2. *Ibid.,* I, 294–95.

3. The context of their statements reveals that both Catlin and Thoreau were just as concerned over the future of large game as they were about the fate of the red man.

4. Catlin, *North American Indians,* I, 295.

5. For example, visitors to Alaska's Mt. McKinley National Park must use shuttle buses provided by the National Park Service, instead of taking their own cars anywhere they please. Special areas in other national parks have also been designated for restricted use.

6. Arkansas Hot Springs (1832) and Yosemite Valley (1864). For the fact that neither was really a national park, see Ise, *Our National Park Policy,* 13.

7. Hiram Martin Chittenden, *The Yellowstone National Park* (Cincinnati, 1905), 44–51. This book was first published in 1895.

8. *Ibid.,* 60.

9. Nathaniel P. Langford, *The Discovery of Yellowstone Park: Journal of the Washburn Expedition to the Yellowstone and Firehole Rivers in the Year 1870* (Lincoln, Nebraska, 1972), 117–18; this is a recent edition—with a Foreword by historian Aubrey L. Haines—of a work first published in 1905.

10. *Ibid.,* xix–xx.

11. Nash, *Wilderness and the American Mind,* 110.

12. U.S. Bureau of the Census, *Historical Statistics of the United States: Colonial Times to 1957* (Washington, D.C., 1960), 207; this figure includes public and nonpublic schools and refers to the percentage of 17-year-old Americans who had graduated from secondary school in 1870. It might also be noted that 20 percent of the population ten years old and over were illiterate in 1870; *Ibid.,* 214.

13. Langford, *The Discovery of Yellowstone Park,* xi.

14. Hedges, "Journal of Judge Cornelius Hedges," *Contributions to the Historical Society of Montana. . . . ,* V (1904), 370–94: scattered fishing throughout.

15. Nash, *Wilderness and the American Mind,* 110–11.

16. See William H. Jackson and Howard R. Driggs, *The Pioneer Photographer: Rocky Mountain Adventures with a Camera* (Yonkers-on-Hudson, New York, 1929), 300–02, for Jackson's own account of shooting the bear, including his pains to preserve its hide as a trophy.

17. *Ibid.,* 104–05 and 109; and Lewis W. Selmeier, "First Camera on the Yellowstone—A Century Ago. . . ." *Montana the Magazine of Western History,* XXII (Summer, 1972), 49.

18. Goodspeed, *Angling in America,* 207–08.

19. Nash, *Wilderness and the American Mind,* 111.

20. *Ibid.*

21. An important exception was Senator George Franklin Edmunds of Vermont—"one of the earliest conservationists in Congress"—who spoke in favor of the park bill. See Ise, *Our National Park Policy,* 16. For the fact that Edmunds was a devoted angler and key figure in the early fish-culture movement at both state and federal levels, see Allard, "Spencer Fullerton Baird and the U.S. Fish Commission," 65, 84, 114, 123–24, 129–30, and 157.

22. Ise, *Our National Park Policy,* 16.

23. Nash, *Wilderness and the American Mind,* 112.

24. For a discussion of this mentality, see Alfred Runte, " 'Worthless' Lands—Our National Parks," *American West,* X (May, 1973), 5–11; also see "Alaska: Preserving the Public Domain," *Sierra Club Bulletin,* LIX (February, 1974), 17, for the same attitude in regard to national wildlife refuges.

25. Nash, *Wilderness and the American Mind,* 111–12; and Selmeier, "First Camera on the Yellowstone," 52.

26. The first of these did not appear until shortly after the park bill was passed; *Ibid.*

27. Clarence P. Hornung, "A Gallery of Western Art," in Jay Monaghan, ed., *The Book of the American West* (New York, 1963), 579.

28. Ise, *Our National Park Policy,* 17–18.

29. Galen Clark, a key figure in the early history of what became Yosemite National Park, was a hunter. See Shirley Sargent, "Galen Clark—Mr. Yosemite," in Yosemite Natural History Association, *Yosemite: Saga of a Century, 1864–1964* (Oakhurst, California, 1964), 19–20; and Introduction by W. W. Foote in Galen Clark, *Indians of the Yosemite Valley: Their History, Customs and Traditions* (Yosemite Valley, 1904), xiii–xv. For the crucial part played by two sportsmen, Theodore Roosevelt and E. H. Harriman, in later getting Yosemite Valley added to Yosemite National Park, see Udall, *The Quiet Crisis,* 130.

The "fathers" of Glacier and Mount McKinley National Parks were George Bird Grinnell and Charles Sheldon, respectively; see Madison Grant, "The Beginnings of Glacier National Park" and "The Establishment of Mt. McKinley National Park," in George Bird Grinnell and Charles Sheldon, eds., *Hunting and Conservation* (New Haven, 1925), 438–70. Sheldon was a member of the Boone and Crockett Club and a well-known author on hunting and natural history.

Lassen Volcanic and Grand Canyon National Parks were first set aside as National Monuments by Theodore Roosevelt, and the legislation allowing him to take this action was passed mainly through the efforts of another sportsman, John F. Lacey; see Ise, *Our National Park Policy,* 151–52 and 156–57.

For the fact that the original proposals for a national park in the southern Appalachians came from sportsmen, see Charles D. Smith, "The Appalachian National Park Movement, 1885–1901," *North Carolina Historical Review,* XXXVII (January, 1960), 38, 41–42, and 65. Also, see Trefethen, *Crusade for Wildlife,* 285, for the impact of Charles Sheldon.

One of the main groups backing the effort that led to the creation of Isle Royale National Park was the Izaak Walton League, an organization of sport anglers; see Ise, *Our National Park Policy,* 333.

Among the very first to draw public attention to the need for preserving the Everglades were sportsmen A. W. Dimock, Frank M. Chapman, and William Dutcher. See Charleton W. Tebeau, *Man in the Everglades: 2000 Years of Human History in the Everglades National Park* (Miami, 1968), 168–69. This is the second, revised edition of a book originally published in 1964 under a different title. Chapman and Dutcher have already been identified as sportsmen, and Dimock wrote the angling classic: *The Book of the Tarpon* (New York, 1911). Also, see John C. Phillips, "Conservation of Our Mammals and Birds," in Grinnell and Sheldon, eds., *Hunting and Conservation,* 64.

30. Nash, *Wilderness and the American Mind,* 108–13.

31. *Ibid.,* 112.

32. "The Yellowstone National Park," *Scribner's Monthly,* IV (May, 1872), 121, cited in Nash, 113.

33. Ise, *Our National Park Policy,* 18.

34. *Ibid.*

35. *Memoirs,* 94.

36. Ise, *Our National Park Policy,* 21–22.

37. See "Notes" to Chapter I, above.

38. Reiger, ed., *The Passing of the Great West,* 117–19.

39. For Grinnell's buffalo hunting, see *Ibid.,* 58–72; also, see Grinnell's "Last of the Buffalo," *Scribner's Magazine,* XII (September, 1892), 267–86, for his poetic tribute to the vanished multitudes. The weathered skulls of the bull and cow bison he describes picking up on the prairie, "to keep as mementoes of the past," are on exhibit in the Birdcraft Museum of the Connecticut Audubon Society, Fairfield.

40. Roosevelt first went West to shoot a trophy buffalo; see Trefethen, *Crusade for Wildlife,* 2.

41. Catlin's desire to preserve the bison has already been discussed; for Audubon, see Francis Hobart Herrick, *Audubon the Naturalist: A History of His Life and Times* (New York, 1917), II, 255–56.

42. See Volume VIII (February, 1874), 65–79; on page 78 he implies that he is an angler.

43. Pages 34–35.

44. *Forest and Stream,* February 19, 1880, XIV, 51.

45. "Where Some Game Goes To," *Ibid.,* March 17, 1881, XVI, 119.

46. *Ibid.,* May 11, 1882, XVIII, 283.

47. "The President Speaks," *Ibid.,* June 29, 1882, XVIII, 423.

48. *Ibid.,* XIX, 382.

49. *Ibid.,* 382–83.

50. *Memoirs,* 95.

51. *Forest and Stream,* XIX, 382–83.

52. William Ludlow, *Report of a Reconnaissance from Carroll, Montana Territory, on the Upper Missouri, to the Yellowstone National Park, and Return, Made in the Summer of 1875* (Washington, D.C., 1876), 61.

53. Ludlow stated his belief that if the government would only assume its obligation to the park, "The day will come . . . when this most interesting region, crowded with marvels and adorned with the most superb scenery, will be rendered accessible to all; then, thronged with visitors from all over the world, it will be what nature and Congress, for once working together in union, have declared it should be, a National Park"; *Ibid.*, 37.

54. *Forest and Stream,* December 14, 1882, XIX, 383.

55. *Ibid.,* XIX, 441.

56. *Ibid.*

57. "The Woodmont Rod and Gun Club," *American Angler,* October 21, 1882, II, 259.

58. Ise, *Our National Park Policy,* 36.

59. *Ibid.*

60. Memoirs, 94; "The Park Monopolists," *Forest and Stream,* January 11, 1883, XIX, 461–62.

61. *Ibid.*

62. *Ibid.,* XIX, 481.

63. *Ibid.;* "Game in the Yellowstone Park," *Ibid.,* February 18, 1886, XXVI, 62.

64. Roosevelt, "Introduction," in Allen G. Wallihan, *Camera Shots at Big Game* (New York, 1901), 7; Roosevelt *et al., The Deer Family* (New York, 1902), 23; and "Forest Reserves as Game Refuges," *Forest and Stream,* February 8, 1902, LVIII, 101. In the latter item Grinnell is quoting Roosevelt.

65. *Ibid.,* XIX, 481.

66. Edwin J. Stanley, *Rambles in Wonderland* (New York, 1880), 63, quoted in Nash, *Wilderness and the American Mind,* 113.

67. *Forest and Stream,* March 8, 1883, XX, 107.

68. Nathan Cole, *The Royal Parks and Gardens of London, Their History and Mode of Embellishment. . . .* (London, 1877), 19–20. Also, see Michael Brander, *Hunting and Shooting: From Earliest Times to the Present Day* (New York, 1971), 74, for the fact that Regent's Park was originally "Mariebone Park," a royal hunting ground.

69. For examples of the importance of the Old World influence on the development of city parks in America and the idea that their origins can be traced back to the hunting preserves of royalty, see Grinnell to G. A. Parkson, March 2, 1921, Letter Book, 216; O'Neill, "Parks and Forest Conservation in New York, 1850–1920," 51 and 183–84; Jon A. Peterson, "The Origins of the Comprehensive City Planning Ideal in the United States, 1840–1911" (Ph.D. dissertation, Harvard University, 1967), 74–75, 77–78, and 102; and John B. Jackson, *American Space—The Centennial Years: 1865–1876* (New York, 1972), 217–18.

70. For the spread of the national-park idea to other countries, see Ise, *Our National Park Policy,* 658–69.

71. *Forest and Stream,* January 25, 1883, XIX, 501.

72. "The Yellowstone National Park," *American Field* (later name of *Field and Stream*), January 13, 1883, XIX, 21–22; "Congress Proposes to Check the Yellowstone National Park Grab," *Ibid.,* January 20, 1883, XIX, 41; *Ibid.,* February 3, 1883, XIX, 83; "The Yellowstone Park," *Ibid.,* March 3, 1883, XIX, 145; "The Syndicate Rules," *Ibid.,* March 10, 1883, XIX, 165; "The Yellowstone Park," *Harper's Weekly,* January 20, 1883, XXVII, 46–47; "Grabbing a Great Park," New York *Times,* January 20, 1883, XXXII, 1; *Ibid.,* 4; "Yellowstone Park Leases," New York *Herald,* January 21, 1883, 10.

73. "Park Protection," *Forest and Stream,* February 15, 1883, XX, 41.

74. "Mr. Vest's Victory," *Ibid.,* March 8, 1883, XX, 101.

75. *Ibid.,* 107.

76. *Ibid.,* March 22, 1883, XX, 141.

77. Troops were not stationed in the park until August, 1886. One historian claims that the Army "saved" Yellowstone and later national parks by protecting them from vandals, poachers, forest fires, etc. But the question might well be asked: Who deserves more credit—the soldiers who followed orders or the civilians like Grinnell who got them into the parks in the first place? See H. Duane Hampton, *How the U.S. Cavalry Saved Our National Parks* (Bloomington, Indiana, 1971).

78. "Congress and the Large Game," *Forest and Stream,* November 15, 1883, XXI, 301.

79. "The Yellowstone Park," *Ibid.,* December 20, 1883, XXI, 401–02.

80. "Yellowstone Park Matters," *Ibid.,* January 17, 1884, XXI, 494.

81. *Ibid.,* 489.

82. *Ibid.*

83. "Yellowstone Park Bill," *Ibid.,* February 7, 1884, XXII, 21.

84. *Ibid.*

85. *Ibid.;* "Yellowstone Park Matters," March 13, 1884, XXII, 121.

86. *Ibid.*

87. Grinnell to T. E. Hofer, May 15, 1917, Letter Book, 642; Grinnell to W. H. Phillips, November 7, 1889, *Ibid.,* 453–54.

88. "Diary, Through Two-Ocean Pass, Aug. 1884" [item no. 301 of Grinnell Collection checklist], entry of August 29, 1884; George Bird Grinnell Collection of Journals, Field Notes and other Materials on the Plains Indians, 1870–1930; Southwest Museum Library, Los Angeles. Hereinafter, this source is cited as the Grinnell Collection.

89. Hague to Senator Charles F. Manderson, February 4, 1886, *Forest and Stream,* February 25, 1886, XXVI, 83; Hague, "The Yellowstone Park as a Forest Reservation," *The Nation,* XLVI (January 5, 1888), 9–10.

90. "The Care of the National Park," XXIV, 1.

91. "Remove the Superintendent," *Ibid.,* April 9, 1885, XXIV, 201; "A Change Needed," *Ibid.,* April 23, 1885, XXIV, 245; "The Park Needs a Superintendent," *Ibid.,* May 14, 1885, XXIV, 305.

92. Ise, *Our National Park Policy*, 41.

93. *Forest and Stream*, April 9, 1885, XXIV, 201.

94. "A New Park Superintendent," *Ibid.*, May 28, 1885, XXIV, 345.

95. "Needs of the Park," *Ibid.*, May 7, 1885, XXIV, 287–88.

96. William H. Goetzmann, *Exploration and Empire: The Explorer and the Scientist in the Winning of the West* (New York, 1966), 330.

97. For an exposition of this thesis, see Robert H. Wiebe, *The Search for Order, 1877–1920* (New York, 1967), especially 62–75.

98. "Their Last Refuge," *Forest and Stream,* December 14, 1882, XIX, 382–83.

CHAPTER FIVE : *The Boone and Crockett Club*

1. Representative—signature is illegible—of the Roosevelt Memorial Association to Grinnell, January 23, 1923, Grinnell File.

2. Grinnell, "Introduction," *The Works of Theodore Roosevelt* (National Edition, New York, 1926), I, xiv.

3. *Forest and Stream,* XXIV, 451.

4. Grinnell, "Introduction," *The Works of Theodore Roosevelt* (National Edition), I, xiv.

5. Grinnell's friendship with these men is treated in Reiger, ed., *The Passing of the Great West*. The Reynolds cited here is no relation to Charles B. Reynolds, mentioned in Chapter II of the present work.

6. Grinnell's experiences on Custer's 1874 Black Hills expedition are described in *Ibid.*, 78–107.

7. Trefethen, *Crusade for Wildlife*, 2.

8. Grinnell, "Introduction," *The Works of Theodore Roosevelt* (National Edition), I, xv.

9. *Ibid.,* xv–xvi.

10. Parenthetically, it might also be noted that their fascination with the untamed West seems to have been sparked in youth by reading the same Romantic novels of Thomas Mayne Reid; see Roosevelt, *Theodore Roosevelt: An Autobiography;* and Reiger, ed., *The Passing of the Great West*.

11. Memoirs, 96.

12. See "Notes" to Chapter IV, above.

13. Grinnell, "Introduction," *The Works of Theodore Roosevelt* (National Edition), I, xvi.

14. Grinnell's gentlemanly desire to remain in the shadows, giving others the credit for actions he had initiated, is one major reason why his true importance in the conservation movement has so long been obscured. For example, he made no effort to publish an autobiography and gave the bulk of his invaluable papers—other than those that dealt mainly with ethnography—to a personal friend rather than a public archive.

As he wrote a friend in 1897, "Of course, I would rather keep in the background in this matter so far as the public is concerned. . . ." (Grinnell to Capt. Stouch, November 26, 1897, Letter Book, 186.) For other examples of this compulsion to remain anonymous, even when it meant bending the truth, see Madison Grant to Grinnell, May 26, 1910, Boone and Crockett Club File; Grinnell to Grant, May 26, 1910, Letter Book, 217; Grinnell to W. Austin Wadsworth, June 10, 1910, *Ibid.,* 269; and John B. Burnham to Grinnell, June 7, 1920, Grinnell File.

15. Grinnell, "Introduction," *The Works of Theodore Roosevelt* (National Edition), xvi–xvii. This statement is typical of Grinnell's self-effacement, for his editorials in *Forest and Stream* prove that he was not as naive as he suggests.

16. *Ibid.,* xvii.

17. *Ibid.*

18. *Forest and Stream,* May 15, 1884, XX, 301.

19. Grinnell to T. E. Hofer, January 15, 1919, Letter Book, 269.

20. *Forest and Stream,* February 16, 1888, XXX, 61.

21. Grinnell to Arnold Hague, February 22, 1888, Letter Book, 297.

22. Grinnell to Cromwell Childe, March 24, 1899, *Ibid.,* 215.

23. "The Boone and Crockett Club," *Forest and Stream,* March 8, 1888, XXX, 124.

24. Also called "jacklighting" or simply "jacking."

25. For a typical editorial attack on "fire-hunting," also known as "jacklighting," and "floating" (killing deer in the water), see "Jack Bluff and Bluster," *Forest and Stream,* August 20, 1885, XXV, 61.

26. Grinnell to W. H. Phillips, June 5, 1889, Letter Book, 354.

27. Grinnell to Arnold Hague, February 22, 1888, *Ibid.,* 297. Hague, however, applauded the "healthy, manly sport" of hunting and relished eating the game others killed! See Hague, "The Yellowstone Park as a Game Reservation," in Theodore Roosevelt and George Bird Grinnell, eds., *American Big-Game Hunting* (New York, 1901), 257; and Joseph P. Iddings, "Memorial of Arnold Hague," *Bulletin of the Geological Society of America,* XXIX (1918), 45. The former work first appeared in 1893.

Phillips was "a resident of Washington [D.C.], a Supreme Court lawyer, with a large acquaintance there." Because of this position, and the fact that he was a member of "one of the oldest and best-known Washington families," he was "tuned in" to all the latest legislative and political developments; *Forest and Stream,* May 15, 1897, XLVIII, 381; and Grinnell to N. P. Langford, July 25, 1905, Letter Book, 742–43. Besides being Grinnell's close friend, he was also his lawyer; Grinnell to W. H. Phillips, September 3, 1888, *Ibid.,* 476–77.

28. Because of Grinnell's influence, Hague and Phillips in fact became *regular* members, but they seem to have been the only nonhunters to receive that honor. And despite the rule that nonsportsmen could become associate or honorary members, almost all of those who joined under those classifications were—or had been—hunters.

29. Another such indication was the fact that when the suggestion was made for organizing the association, those present at the dinner "agreed that such a club could do some good"; Grinnell to Arnold Hague, February 22, 1888, *Ibid.*, 297. As soon as the society was formed, Grinnell made every effort to publicize it, hoping thereby to spur the members to action; see *Forest and Stream,* February 16, 1888, XXX, 61, for the announcement of the club: "It would seem that an organization of this description, composed of men of intelligence and education, might wield a great influence for good in matters relating to game protection." And the weekly promised that "the public will be kept advised"; "The Boone and Crockett Club," *Ibid.*, March 8, 1888, XXX, 124.

30. Edward N. Saveth, "The American Patrician Class: A Field for Research," *American Quarterly* (Summer, 1963), XV, Pt. 2, 235–52.

31. Trefethen, *Crusade for Wildlife,* 21.

32. Grinnell, ed., *A Brief History of the Boone and Crockett Club With Officers, Constitution and List of Members for the Year 1910* (New York, 1910), 20. After talking with Grinnell's co-workers in the Boone and Crockett, a later member believed: "His [Grinnell's] sane judgment guided the [Boone and Crockett] Executive Committee" and "in facing every problem that confronted the Club throughout its entire life, the court of last resort always seemed to rest within the mind of this one man. No course of action was determined until his judgment had been sought and no conclusions reached until his opinion had been given"; John P. Holman, "A Tribute to George Bird Grinnell," in "Boone and Crockett Club Officers, By-Laws, Treasurer's Report and List of Members for the Years 1938–1939" (July, 1939), 29–30, Boone and Crockett Club File.

33. Anderson to Grinnell, January 29, 1896, Boone and Crockett Club File.

34. Roosevelt to Grinnell, November 30, 1897, Theodore Roosevelt Papers, Library of Congress, Series 2. Also, see Roosevelt to William Austin Wadsworth, February 4, 1898, in Morison and Blum, eds., *The Letters of Theodore Roosevelt,* I, 768.

35. Sheldon to W. Redmond Cross, May 3, 1926, Boone and Crockett Club File. Emphasis in the original.

36. Udall, *The Quiet Crisis,* 161.

37. *Forest and Stream,* January 17, 1889, XXXI, 513. Italics mine.

38. "Adirondack Deer Hounding," *Ibid.,* XXIII, 281.

39. "Adirondack Deer Hounding," *Ibid.,* January 15, 1885, XXIII, 481.

40. *Ibid.*

41. "The Deer Bill," *Ibid.,* February 26, 1885, XXIV, 81.

42. "The Deer Hounding Bill," *Ibid.,* February 19, 1885, XXIV, 62; "The Deer Bill," *Ibid.,* February 26, 1885, XXIV, 81; "The Adirondack Deer Law," *Ibid.,* March 5, 1885, XXIV, 101; "Pass the Deer Hounding Bill," *Ibid.,* March 26, 1885, XXIV, 161.

43. *Ibid.,* May 14, 1885, XXIV, 305.

44. *Ibid.*

45. "The Deer Hounding Law," *Ibid.*, June 18, 1885, XXIV, 405.

46. "The Adirondack Deer Law," *Ibid.*, December 31, 1885, XXV, 441.

47. "The Adirondack Deer," *Ibid.*, January 21, 1886, XXV, 501.

48. *Ibid.*, January 28, 1886, XXVI, 7.

49. *Ibid.*, May 20, 1886, XXVI, 325.

50. A leading representative of the New York patrician class, Grant was also a lawyer and a hunter-naturalist. He is best known for his *Passing of the Great Race* (1916), which helped to bring about the anti-immigration legislation of the 1920s. A founder of the New York Zoological Gardens ("Bronx Zoo"), the Save-the-Redwoods League and other organizations, he was one of the Boone and Crockett Club's most active members. After being proposed by Grinnell, he joined in 1893. Grant and Roosevelt soon became close friends and co-workers in conservation. The latter wrote Grinnell in early 1894: "I am inclined to think that Madison Grant is a genuine acquisition; he strikes me as a good fellow"; Roosevelt to Grinnell, January 13, 1894, Boone and Crockett Club File.

51. *Ibid.*

52. Roosevelt to Grinnell, January 30, 1894, *Ibid.*

53. *Forest and Stream*, May 15, 1897, XLVIII, 381. Also, see William Cary Sanger, "The Adirondack Deer Law," in George Bird Grinnell and Theodore Roosevelt, eds., *Trail and Camp-Fire* (New York, 1897), 264–78.

54. Grinnell to T. E. Hofer, December 20, 1886, Letter Book, 51–52; *Forest and Stream,* January 12, 1888, XXVIII, 481; Grinnell to Archibald Rogers, August 8, 1888, Letter Book, 444; *Forest and Stream*, September 12, 1889, XXXIII, 141; Grinnell to William Hallett Phillips, November 7, 1889, Letter Book, 454; Grinnell to William M. Springer, May 9, 1890, *Ibid.*, 309.

55. "The Hon. S. S. Cox on Angling and Fish Protection," *American Angler,* June 21, 1884, V, 385–89.

56. Nash, *Wilderness and the American Mind,* 114.

57. For example, Roosevelt, *Hunting Trips of a Ranchman: Sketches of Sport on the Northern Cattle Plains* (Upper Saddle River, New Jersey, 1970), 149; this is a reprint (Literature House) of a work first published in 1885. Also see Roosevelt, *Ranch Life and the Hunting-Trail* (New York, 1969), 134–35; this is a reprint (Winchester Press) of a work first published in 1888.

58. Grinnell, "Introduction," *The Works of Theodore Roosevelt* (National Edition), I, xxiii.

59. As a sample: "A Territorial Dogberry," September 3, 1885, XXV, 101; "Another Syndicate," November 12, 1885, XXV, 301; "A Report on the National Park," December 3, 1885, XXV, 361; "Game in the National Park," December 17, 1885, XXV, 401; "The Yellowstone National Park," December 24, 1885, XXV, 421; "Senator Vest's Park Bill," December 31, 1885, XXV, 441; "No Railroad in Yellowstone Park," February 18, 1886, XXVI, 62; "A Railroad to Cooke City," March 11, 1886, XXVI, 121–22; "Is There an African in the Woodpile?" March 25, 1886, XXVI, 161–62; "Railroad Routes to Cooke,"

April 8, 1886, XXVI, 201–02; "The Railroads and the Park," May 13, 1886, XXVI, 301; "How the Case Stands," May 20, 1886, XXVI, 325; "Waking up at Last," June 3, 1886, XXVI, 365; "The National Park in 1887," September 15, 1887, XXIX, 141; "The National Park in 1887," September 22, 1887, XXIX, 161; "Park Matters in Congress," January 12, 1888, XXIX, 481; "In Behalf of the Park," March 8, 1888, XXX, 121; "The Park Bill in the House," April 5, 1888, XXX, 201; "Mr. Plumb's Ignorance," April 19, 1888, XXX, 241; "Important Measures," July 26, 1888, XXXI, 1; August 2, 1888, XXXI, 21; September 12, 1889, XXXIII, 141; December 5, 1889, XXXIII, 381; "The New Park Bill," January 30, 1890, XXXIV, 21; "Scheming for a Railroad," February 20, 1890, XXXIV, 81; February 27, 1890, XXXIV, 101; "The Yellowstone Park Bill," April 3, 1890, XXXIV, 205 and 207; "To the House of Representatives," April 24, 1890, XXXIV, 265; "A Natural Reservoir," May 1, 1890, XXXIV, 285; "Mr. Carey's Responsibility," May 15, 1890, XXXIV, 325; "Game in the Great West," July 3, 1890, XXXIV, 469; "What About the Park?" December 11, 1890, XXXV, 409; "The National Park Bill," March 12, 1891, XXXVI, 145; "Yellowstone Park Legislation," February 25, 1892, XXXVIII, 169; "The National Park Grab Bill," March 17, 1892, XXXVIII, 245; "Danger to the Park," May 19, 1892, XXXVIII, 469 and 474; "An Individual Appeal," December 15, 1892, XXXIX, 507; "Patriotism in 1893," December 29, 1892, XXXIX 551.

60. Grinnell to Luther H. North, February 17, 1887, Letter Book, 70.

61. Grinnell to George Gould, March 18, 1887, *Ibid.*, 92.

62. "In Behalf of the Park," *Forest and Stream,* March 8, 1888, XXX, 121.

63. *Ibid.,* March 29, 1888, XXX, 186.

64. *Ibid.*

65. Grinnell to Lyman, April 23, 1890, Letter Book, 289.

66. Grinnell to Archibald Rogers, December 19, 1890, *Ibid.*, 129.

67. *Ibid.*; Grinnell to Captain F. A. Boutelle, December 9, 1890, *Ibid.*, 80–81.

68. Rogers was a regular member of the club and, of course, an avid hunter; see his "Big Game in the Rockies," in Roosevelt and Grinnell, eds., *American Big-Game Hunting,* 90–128, an article originally appearing in *Scribner's Magazine.*

69. Grinnell to Arnold Hague, December 1, 1890, Letter Book, 64–65.

70. Grinnell to Archibald Rogers, December 24, 1890, *Ibid.,* 133.

71. Grinnell to Arnold Hague, January 13, 1891, *Ibid.,* 183.

72. Grinnell to Archibald Rogers, January 17, 1891, *Ibid.,* 186–88.

73. Since the summer of 1886, the park had been under the control of the army; Grinnell, ed., *A Brief History of the Boone and Crockett Club,* 16–17.

74. "Boone and Crockett Club Meeting," *Forest and Stream,* January 22, 1891, XXXVI, 3.

75. *Ibid.*; a third resolution endorsed "the efforts now being made to preserve the groves of big trees [giant sequoias] in California" and thanked "the Secretary of the Interior for his interest in this matter."

76. Grinnell to Archibald Rogers, January 17, 1891, Letter Book, 186–87.

77. "Cages in Place of Bullets," *Forest and Stream,* August 21, 1890, XXXV, 85; *Ibid.,* January 8, 1891, XXXV, 489.

78. An important manifestation of the regard Roosevelt had for *Forest and Stream*'s editor is the fact that he very much wanted Grinnell to be his hunting partner, which for Roosevelt was the ultimate compliment. See Grinnell to James Willard Schultz, May 24, 1888, Letter Book, 361; and Grinnell to Archibald Rogers, August 8, 1888, *Ibid., 444.*

Another example of Roosevelt's admiration for Grinnell is an 1894 letter of his to their mutual friend, Madison Grant. In it, he urges Grant to send Grinnell some photographs of Roosevelt, apparently showing the big-game animals the future President had just bagged in the West; Roosevelt to Grant, October 10, 1894, in Morison and Blum, eds., *The Letters of Theodore Roosevelt,* I, 401.

79. Grinnell to Archibald Rogers, January 17, 1891, Letter Book, 187.

80. *Ibid.*

81. "The National Park Bill," *Forest and Stream,* March 12, 1891, XXXVI, 145.

82. See Chapter IV, above; plus Grinnell to "Editor of Scribner's Magazine," April 28, 1887, Letter Book, 109; and Grinnell to Hart Lyman (New York *Tribune*), April 23, 1890, *Ibid.,* 289. For later efforts, see Grinnell to W. H. Phillips, March 28, 1892, *Ibid.,* 865, describing interview with editor of *Garden and Forest Magazine;* and Grinnell to Caspar W. Whitney (*Harper's Weekly*), October 11, 1894, *Ibid.,* 241.

83. Grinnell to R. U. Johnson, May 6, 1891, *Ibid.,* 407–08.

84. Grinnell to Arnold Hague, May 7, 1891, *Ibid.,* 412–13.

85. Grinnell to W. H. Phillips, February 23, 1892, *Ibid.,* 780; Grinnell to W. H. Phillips, March 28, 1892, *Ibid.,* 865; Grinnell to Arnold Hague, May 14, 1892, *Ibid.,* 102; Grinnell to George S. Anderson, December 13, 1892, *Ibid.,* 639; Grinnell to W. H. Phillips, December 23, 1892, *Ibid.,* 692; Grinnell to T. G. Pearson, March 28, 1921, *Ibid.,* 324.

86. Trefethen, *Crusade for Wildlife,* 35–36; Grinnell to George S. Anderson, November 28, 1892, Letter Book, 571; *Forest and Stream,* December 15, 1892, XXXIX, 507. The Louisville *Commercial* (December 20, 1892), the New York *Sun* (December 20, 1892), and the New York *Times* (December 25, 1892) were three of the papers that backed up *Forest and Stream*'s stand in behalf of the park.

87. *Forest and Stream,* March 17, 1892, XXXVIII, 245.

88. Grinnell to George S. Anderson, November 28, 1892, Letter Book, 571; Grinnell states that he is also asking for letters from Phillips, Roosevelt, and Hague.

89. "A Standing Menace," *Forest and Stream,* December 8, 1892, XXXIX, 485; and "A Standing Menace," *Ibid.,* December 15, 1892, XXXIX, 514; the letters were supposedly a spontaneous response to the editorial. (Anderson has already been identified as a sportsman.)

90. Mining interests and real-estate speculators in Cooke City, Montana, just outside the northeastern corner of the park, were the ones pushing for the railroad.

91. *Forest and Stream,* December 15, 1892, XXXIX, 514.

92. Grinnell to W. H. Phillips, December 15, 1892, Letter Book, 648; Grinnell to Charles Sheldon, January 30, 1920, *Ibid.,* 134.

93. Grinnell to W. H. Phillips, December 15, 1892, *Ibid.,* 648.

94. "An Individual Appeal," *Forest and Stream,* December 15, 1892, XXXIX, 507.

95. Grinnell to W. H. Phillips, March 1, 1892, Letter Book, 803.

96. *Forest and Stream,* February 23, 1893, XL, 155; Trefethen, *Crusade for Wildlife,* 36.

97. "The Account of Howell's Capture," *Forest and Stream,* May 5, 1894, XLII, 377–78.

98. See Hough, *Getting a Wrong Start: A Truthful Autobiography* (New York, 1915), 132–42, for a description of George Bird Grinnell and the inner workings of *Forest and Stream.*

99. *Ibid.,* 69 and 141.

100. Grinnell to Horace Albright, February 23, 1922, Letter Book, 169–70; Grinnell to T. E. Hofer, May 3, 1922, *Ibid.,* 378.

101. *Forest and Stream,* XLII, 243.

102. "Dangers of Segregation," *Ibid.,* March 31, 1894, XLII, 265; "Save the Park Buffalo," April 14, 1894, XLII, 309; "The Account of Howell's Capture," May 5, 1894, XLII, 377–78.

103. *Ibid.,* 377.

104. Grinnell, ed., *A Brief History of the Boone and Crockett Club,* 19; Theodore Roosevelt and George Bird Grinnell, eds., *Hunting in Many Lands* (New York, 1895), 9–10.

105. Nash, *Wilderness and the American Mind,* 114; Nash is quoting the *Congressional Record.*

106. Grinnell, ed., *A Brief History of the Boone and Crockett Club,* 19.

107. Chittenden, *The Yellowstone National Park,* 119–20. In 1892 Grinnell estimated the number of bison in the park at 400, but by 1894, this figure had been sharply reduced; a year later, the Superintendent thought there were only about 200 in the reserve; Mark Sullivan, "The Bison Still Lives," Boston *Evening Transcript,* October 10, 1900.

108. Trefethen, *Crusade for Wildlife,* 140.

109. "Protection for the Park," *Forest and Stream,* May 12, 1894, XLII, 327; Ise, *Our National Park Policy,* 45–46.

110. Grinnell to Roosevelt, May 8, 1894, Letter Book, 57–58.

111. *Ibid.;* Grinnell is paraphrasing what Roosevelt had written him.

112. Chittenden, *The Yellowstone National Park,* 119–20; Robert Shankland, *Steve Mather of the National Parks,* 45.

113. Grinnell to Roosevelt, May 8, 1894, Letter Book, 57–58.

114. Trefethen, *Crusade for Wildlife,* 42.

115. Page 21.

116. Page 23.

117. Ernest F. Swift, *The Public's Land: Our Heritage and Opportunity* (Washington, D. C., 1963), 7.

118. "Utilize the Streams," *Forest and Stream,* August 11, 1887, XXIX, 41; "Forests of the Rocky Mountains I," *Ibid.,* October 25, 1888, XXXI, 261–62; "Forests of the Rocky Mountains II," *Ibid.,* November 1, 1888, XXXI, 282–83; "Forests of the Rocky Mountains III," *Ibid.,* November 8, 1888, XXXI, 301–02; "Popular Forestry Instruction," *Ibid.,* December 6, 1888, XXXI, 381; "Practical Forest Restoration I," *Ibid.,* February 28, 1889, XXXII, 105; "Practical Forestry Restoration II," *Ibid.,* March 14, 1889, XXXII, 149; "Practical Forest Restoration III," *Ibid.,* March 21, 1889, XXXII, 169; "Practical Forest Restoration IV," *Ibid.,* March 28, 1889, XXXII, 189.

119. "Forests of the Rocky Mountains I," *Ibid.,* October 25, 1888, XXXI, 261–62.

120. *Ibid.*

121. "Forests of the Rocky Mountains III," *Ibid.,* November 8, 1888, XXXI, 301–02.

122. *Ibid.,* 302.

123. Volume XXXI, 381.

124. *Ibid.*

125. *Ibid.*

126. Grinnell, ed., *A Brief History of the Boone and Crockett Club,* 23.

127. Grinnell went so far as to claim that it was "through the influence of William Hallett Phillips [that] . . . a few lines inserted in an act passed by Congress March 3, 1891, permitted the establishment of forest reserves. . . ." (Grinnell, "Big-Game Refuges," in Grinnell, ed., *American Big Game in Its Haunts,* 443.) While Noble is generally credited with having actually obtained the insertion of those all-important lines, Grinnell was probably correct in believing that the "influence" of Phillips—a friend of the Secretary and an active worker for forest preservation since the mid-'80s—played a key role in the evolution of Noble's commitment to the woodlands.

For an example of Phillips' early dedication to the forests of the Yellowstone, see *Forest and Stream,* February 11, 1886, XXVI, 41. In "Secretary Noble's Monument," *Forest and Stream,* March 9, 1893, XL, 203, Grinnell wrote: "It will be remembered that *beginning* [italics mine] with the Yellowstone National Park, which was brought to the notice of Mr. Noble early in his administration, he has given much attention to the question of our parks and timber reservation[s]"; this statement undoubtedly refers mainly to Phillips.

For examples of the close working relationship between Phillips and Noble, see Grinnell to Phillips, May 25, 1889, Letter Book, 322; Grinnell to Noble, May 25, 1889, *Ibid.,* 321 [letter crossed out and apparently never sent]; Grinnell to Phillips, May 28, 1889, *Ibid.,* 329; Grinnell to Phillips, June 5, 1889, *Ibid.,*

354; Grinnell to Phillips, November 7, 1889, *Ibid.*, 453–55; Grinnell to Phillips, December 4, 1889, *Ibid.*, 16; and Grinnell to Phillips, April 24, 1891, *Ibid.*, 383.

For the fact that Noble is usually credited with obtaining the insertion of the important lines in the 1891 act, see John Ise, *The United States Forest Policy* (New Haven, 1920), 115. Although he admits that the history of this issue is extremely vague, Ise nevertheless accepts Bernhard E. Fernow's later claim that he and Edward A. Bowers, of the American Forestry Association, "had educated Noble up to the point" of demanding the insertion of the forest-reserve clause. While Fernow and Bowers deserve credit for exerting some influence, Phillips was probably easily as important—despite the fact that, unlike Fernow, he left no readily accessible documentation of his role. Like many other patrician pioneers of conservation, "he . . . labored long and earnestly for the public good [but] . . . preferred that his efforts should not be known, and that others should receive the credit for what he did"; "William Hallett Phillips," *Forest and Stream,* May 15, 1897, XLVIII, 381. This citation refers to an unsigned obituary of Phillips written by Grinnell; the former had drowned near Washington, D.C., on May 9, at about the age of forty-five.

128. From the late 1880s on, *Forest and Stream* and Grinnell's Letter Books are replete with examples of his efforts in behalf of Indians.

129. Grinnell to Phillips, May 25, 1889, Letter Book, 322; Grinnell to Noble, May 25, 1889, *Ibid.*, 321 [letter crossed out and apparently never sent]; Grinnell to Phillips, May 28, 1889, *Ibid.*, 329; "Secretary Noble and the Indians," *Forest and Stream,* May 30, 1889, XXXII, 373; Grinnell to Phillips, June 5, 1889, Letter Book, 354; and Grinnell to Noble, June 19, 1889, *Ibid.*, 380–81.

For some examples of Grinnell's efforts to get the Indian agent removed, see Grinnell to Commissioner of Indian Affairs, November 20, 1888, *Ibid.*, 497–502; Grinnell to Commissioner of Indian Affairs, November 30, 1888, *Ibid.*, 39–66; Grinnell to J. W. Schultz, December 4, 1888, *Ibid.*, 7–9; Grinnell to L. H. North, December 13, 1888, *Ibid.*, 34–35; Grinnell to Joseph Kipp, December 20, 1888, *Ibid.*, 86–87; Grinnell to George Gould, December 26, 1888, *Ibid.*, 96–97; Grinnell to H. H. Garr, January 3, 1889, *Ibid.*, 180; Grinnell to Garr, January 7, 1889, *Ibid.*, 128–29; Grinnell to William Russell, February 13, 1889, *Ibid.*, 212; Grinnell to Gould, April 26, 1889, *Ibid.*, 267–68; Grinnell to Garr, May 11, 1889, *Ibid.*, 282; and Grinnell to J. B. Monroe, April 29, 1913, *Ibid.*, 27–28.

130. Patrician angler George Edmunds, Senator from Vermont, who has been cited above for his efforts in behalf of fish culture and Yellowstone National Park, had already obtained, on two different occasions, Senate approval of a bill to establish a forest reserve "at the headwaters of the Missouri River." In both cases, however, the "democratic" House spurned the bill. See Ise, *The United States Forest Policy,* 113–14.

131. Arnold Hague to Grinnell, April 11, 1910, Grinnell File.

132. Bernard E. Fernow to Grinnell, April 12, 1910, Grinnell File.

133. Grinnell to John W. Noble, February 28, 1910, Letter Book, 910.

134. Arnold Hague to Grinnell, April 11, 1910, Grinnell File.

135. *Forest and Stream,* April 9, 1891, XXXVI, 225.

136. Arnold Hague to Grinnell, April 11, 1910, Grinnell File.

137. A copy of this resolution, dated April 8, 1891, is in the Boone and Crockett Club File.

138. *Forest and Stream,* April 9, 1891, XXXVI, 225; *Ibid.,* October 22, 1891, XXXVII, 265; *Ibid.,* December 3, 1891, XXXVII, 385.

139. John W. Noble to Grinnell, March 11, 1910, Boone and Crockett Club File; Noble to Grinnell, March 15, 1910, Grinnell File.

140. Roosevelt is attributed with saying: "The conservation movement was a direct outgrowth of the forest movement. . . . Without the basis of public sentiment which had been built up for the protection of the forests, and without the example of public foresight in the protection of this, one of the great natural resources, the conservation movement would have been impossible"; *Theodore Roosevelt: An Autobiography,* in *The Works of Theodore Roosevelt* (Memorial Edition, New York, 1923–26), XXII, 463. Samuel P. Hays is probably correct in assuming that the conservation chapters of the "autobiography" were written by Pinchot and James R. Garfield, Roosevelt's last Secretary of the Interior; Hays, *Conservation and the Gospel of Efficiency: The Progressive Conservation Movement, 1890–1920* (Cambridge, 1959), 280–81. Also see Pinchot's memoirs, *Breaking New Ground,* and his article, "How Conservation Began," *Agricultural History,* XI (October, 1937), 255–65.

141. Henry Clepper, "The Conservation Movement: Birth and Infancy," in Clepper, ed., *Origins of American Conservation* (New York, 1966), 9; Arthur B. Meyer, "Forests and Forestry," *Ibid.,* 43; and Pinkett, *Gifford Pinchot,* 8. In its conclusions, the last work is an uncritical rehashing of *Breaking New Ground,* Pinchot's autobiography.

142. An example of Roosevelt's selective "memory" is the fact that in his autobiographical sketch for *Who's Who,* he neglected to mention that he had unsuccessfully run for the Presidency in 1912! [Jacques Barzun and Henry F. Graff, *The Modern Researcher* (New York, 1970), 84–85; this is a revised edition of work originally published in 1957.]

As to Pinchot's concern for what occurred in conservation before *he* arrived on the scene, we have the following comments from the beginning of his published memoirs: "This is not a formal history, decorated and delayed by references to authorities. As to nearly every statement it contains, you will have to take it or leave it on my say-so. About many parts of the story of forestry in America from 1885 to 1910, I am the only living witness. That is another reason why you must take my word or leave it"; Pinchot, "On Writing History," in *Breaking New Ground,* xvii.

143. See Olson, *The Depletion Myth,* for the thesis that there was really no approaching "timber famine," despite the warnings of Roosevelt and others.

144. Harold T. Pinkett's assertion that "the ruthless exploitation of natural

resources was first most obvious and alarming in the continuing devastation of the nation's forests" is simply inaccurate; Pinkett, *Gifford Pinchot*, 8.

145. I am speaking here, of course, only of renewable resources like wildlife and forests.

CHAPTER SIX: *Establishment of a National Conservation Policy*

1. "The Smirch of Politics," *Forest and Stream*, August 30, 1888, XXXI, 101; *Ibid.*, November 17, 1894, XLIII, 419; *Ibid.*, December 15, 1894, XLIII, 507; "Fish, Forests and Politics," *Ibid.*, February 2, 1895, XLIV, 81.

2. *Ibid.*, May 6, 1899, LII, 341.

3. "New York Game Protectors," *Ibid.*, December 9, 1899, LIII, 469.

4. *Ibid.*

5. "The New York Fish Commission," *Ibid.*, December 9, 1899, LIII, 461.

6. Pinchot, *Breaking New Ground*, 145.

7. "The New York Fish Commission," *Forest and Stream*, December 9, 1899, LIII, 461.

8. "The New York Fish Commission," *Ibid.*, February 24, 1900, LIV, 141.

9. For a different interpretation of this issue, see G. Wallace Chessman, *Governor Theodore Roosevelt . . .* (Cambridge, Massachusetts, 1965), 251–52.

10. "The New York Commission," *Forest and Stream*, March 10, 1900, LIV, 181.

11. Roosevelt to Grinnell, March 14, 1900, Roosevelt Papers, Library of Congress, Series 2.

12. Letter of James B. Trefethen to the author, October 23, 1967.

13. Grinnell to Roosevelt, March 17, 1900, Letter Book, 799–800.

14. "The New York Commission," *Forest and Stream*, March 24, 1900, LIV, 221.

15. Roosevelt to Grinnell, March 24, 1900, Roosevelt Papers, Library of Congress, Series 2.

16. Grinnell to Roosevelt, March 26, 1900, Letter Book, 817; Grinnell to Roosevelt, April 26, 1900, *Ibid.*, 862; "The New York Commission," *Forest and Stream*, May 5, 1900, LIV, 341.

17. Grinnell to Roosevelt, April 26, 1900, Letter Book, 862.

18. Undated clipping, sometime in early 1901, Boone and Crockett Club File.

19. "The Pollution of Waters," *Forest and Stream*, January 27, 1900, LIV, 61. Early sportsmen's efforts against water pollution are discussed in Chapter II, above.

20. *The Gun*, undated clipping, Boone and Crockett Club File.

21. Grinnell to Roosevelt, August 29, 1900, Letter Book, 14.

22. Presidents Harrison, Cleveland, and McKinley had all established forest

reserves, which by 1901 covered about 50,000,000 acres. But Roosevelt did much more. By the end of his tenure, "the number of national forests had been increased to 159, with a total area of over 150,000,000 acres—three times the area at the beginning of Roosevelt's administration"; Ise, *The United States Forest Policy*, 161.

23. What can be considered the first national wildlife refuge was the "Afognak Forest and Fish-Culture Reserve" (north of Alaska's Kodiak Island) proclaimed by President Harrison in 1892. Besides Harrison, those instrumental in its creation were angler-fish culturist Livingston Stone, George Bird Grinnell, and John W. Noble. See Grinnell to Noble, April 14, 1891, Letter Book, 370; "A Marine Reservation," *Forest and Stream*, April 23, 1891, XXXVI, 265; Grinnell to Noble, April 24, 1891, Letter Book, 385; "Destruction of Seal Life," *Forest and Stream*, April 30, 1891, XXXVI, 285; "Marine Reservations," *Ibid.*, 287; "Marine Reservations," *Ibid.*, May 21, 1891, XXXVI, 347; "The Reservation of Afognak," *Ibid.*, January 12, 1893, XL, 23; Trefethen, *Crusade for Wildlife*, 64–66; and Cart, "The Struggle for Wildlife Protection in the United States, 1870–1900," 4 and 111–12. The Letter Book citations and *Forest and Stream* editorials reveal that Noble and Grinnell worked closely together to "prepare" the public for the announcement of the reserve.

Cart is quite right in perceiving that "the language of Harrison's proclamation indicated that the Afognak Reserve was not only the first federal wildlife refuge, but also the first federal 'wilderness area,' anticipating the spirit of the Wilderness Act of 1964 by seventy two years"; Cart, "The Struggle for Wildlife Protection in the United States, 1870–1900," 111.

24. Roosevelt to Grinnell, May 5, 1897, Roosevelt Papers, Library of Congress, Series 2.

25. Roosevelt to Grinnell, June 7, 1897, *Ibid.*

26. Roosevelt to Grinnell, August 3, 1897, *Ibid.*

27. Roosevelt to Grinnell, December 27, 1897, *Ibid.* For other evidence of the closeness of this literary partnership and Roosevelt's tendency to follow Grinnell's lead, see Roosevelt to Grinnell, January 30, 1894, Boone and Crockett Club File; Roosevelt to Grinnell, August 2, 1897, Roosevelt Papers, Library of Congress, Series 2; Roosevelt to Grinnell, August 24, 1897, *Ibid.*; Roosevelt to Grinnell, August 30, 1897, *Ibid.*; Roosevelt to Grinnell, January 8, 1898, *Ibid.*; Roosevelt to Grinnell, February 18, 1899, *Ibid.*, XV; Roosevelt to Grinnell, February 23, 1900, *Ibid.*, Series 2; Grinnell to C. Grant LaFarge, March 19, 1900, Letter Book, 801; Grinnell to Gifford Pinchot, March 13, 1901, *Ibid.*, 463; Grinnell to Madison Grant, June 19, 1901, *Ibid.*, 737.

28. *Forest and Stream*, April 15, 1899, LII, 290.

29. As we have seen, this concept was the heart of Grinnell's plan for the country's forests. Roosevelt is attributed with saying, "the conservation movement was . . . nothing more than the application to our natural resources of the principles which had been worked out in connection with the forests"; *The Works of Theodore Roosevelt* (Memorial Edition), XXII, 463.

30. Pinkett, *Gifford Pinchot;* M. Nelson McGeary, *Gifford Pinchot: Forester-Politician* (Princeton, 1960); Martin L. Fausold, *Gifford Pinchot, Bull Moose Progressive* (Syracuse, 1961).

31. Pinchot, *Breaking New Ground,* particularly 319–26.

32. After leaving the Presidency, Roosevelt stated that the men most responsible for the success of the conservation movement were Pinchot and James R. Garfield, his Secretary of the Interior: "I saw them work while I was President, and I can speak with the fullest knowledge of what they did. They took the policy of conservation when it was still nebulous and they applied it and made it work. They actually did the job that I and the others talked about"; speech at Harvard University, December 14, 1910, *The Works of Theodore Roosevelt* (Memorial Edition), XV, 558. Here, as elsewhere, Roosevelt pays tribute to the public officials who administered his conservation program, but at no time does he acknowledge those who influenced him *before* he came to the Presidency.

33. See Chapter Three, above. There is much evidence to indicate that Grinnell played a crucial role in bringing Pinchot and Roosevelt together. In his autobiography the forester states that it was through C. Grant LaFarge, son of the famous artist and Secretary of the Boone and Crockett Club, that he met Roosevelt in 1897, although they did not become intimately acquainted until early 1899. Actually, Harold T. Pinkett in *Gifford Pinchot* (page 34) shows that Pinchot had met Roosevelt on May 21, 1894, but the encounter seems to have been forgotten by the forester. While LaFarge may have actually arranged the 1897 meeting, Grinnell, and probably Arnold Hague, induced it. Since 1894, Grinnell had been publicizing Pinchot's forestry work, emphasizing that he was one of the first to apply to American conditions the theoretical principles of the European science. By 1896, he and Pinchot were well acquainted, and the latter thought enough of Grinnell, as an expert in his own right, to ask him to be one of the contributors to a special issue on the forest reserves that Pinchot was compiling for *The Forester,* a publication of the American Forestry Association; Pinchot, *Breaking New Ground,* 144–45; "The Biltmore Forest," *Forest and Stream,* January 6, 1894, XLII, 1; J. B. Monroe to Grinnell, July 12, 1896, letter in possession of Mrs. John P. Holman, Fairfield, Connecticut; Monroe to Grinnell, December 2, 1896, *Ibid.;* Grinnell to Pinchot, November 19, 1897, Letter Book, 164; Grinnell to Pinchot, December 31, 1897, *Ibid.,* 301–02; Grinnell to Pinchot, January 15, 1898, *Ibid.,* 347; Grinnell, "Opening up Forest Reserves," *The Forester,* IV (February, 1898), 42–44. Grinnell's admiration for Pinchot is revealed in a letter to his Montana hunting guide, who, on Grinnell's recommendation, was employed by Pinchot several times. Grinnell told his Western friend that he was sorry he could not guide the forester on his next trip, for "I should think [he] would be a charming man to travel with and . . . is certainly one from whom you can learn a great deal"; Grinnell to J. B. Monroe, May 3, 1897, Letter Book, 395.

34. Pinkett, *Gifford Pinchot,* 53–54.

35. New York *Times,* May 16, 1925; Washington [D.C.] *Star,* May 16, 1925. A third medal went to Martha Berry, the educator.

36. For examples of Roosevelt's veneration of Grinnell—besides those already given—see the comments of two famous naturalists: C. Hart Merriam to Grinnell, April 29, 1902, Grinnell File; Merriam, "Roosevelt, the Naturalist," *Science,* LXXV (February 12, 1932), 183; and George Shiras, 3d, to Grinnell, May 2, 1925, Grinnell File.

Probably the very best demonstration of Roosevelt's deep respect for Grinnell was his effort to save *Forest and Stream.* Two years after Roosevelt left the Presidency, in April, 1911, Grinnell parted with the weekly after an association of thirty-five years. When Grinnell left, the quality of the periodical, particularly the natural history section, rapidly declined. Roosevelt was so alarmed by this development that he arranged a luncheon at Oyster Bay to which he invited Grinnell, *Forest and Stream*'s new editor, and several of the nation's leading naturalists to talk over what might be done to rectify the situation. It was decided to establish a "Governing Board" picked by Roosevelt to advise the journal's new owners. But the editor put the names of famous naturalists like Grinnell, Merriam, Shiras, Carl E. Akeley, Edmund Heller, and Wilfred H. Osgood in the periodical's masthead simply as a gimmick for selling papers; the "governing" board was never allowed to govern. With much sadness, Grinnell and Roosevelt watched *Forest and Stream*'s standing continue to deteriorate; it went from a weekly to a monthly in 1915, and finally ceased publication in August, 1930, after first selling its subscription lists to the present *Field and Stream;* Grinnell to Charles Otis, September 25, 1911, Letter Book, 452; Grinnell to C. H. Merriam, January 22, 1920, *Ibid.,* 100–01; Grinnell to John P. Holman, April 28, 1919, *Ibid.,* 609–10; Grinnell to Arthur L. Clark, December 19, 1923, *Ibid.,* 277; interview with the late John P. Holman, March 1, 1969, Fairfield, Connecticut; Grinnell to Charles Sheldon, May 8, 1919, Letter Book, 651.

37. Trefethen to the author, October 23, 1967.

Because Roosevelt was already committed to Grinnell's conservation ideas, Grinnell used his influence with the President mainly in an effort to improve the government's treatment of the Indian. Publicly, in *Forest and Stream,* Grinnell described and endorsed each step of Roosevelt's conservation program, but in private discussions with the President, he limited himself to matters pertaining to the aborigine. Once Roosevelt's chief conservation adviser, Grinnell now became his most trusted consultant on Indian affairs. Among the services he performed for Roosevelt was the settlement in 1902 of a national scandal involving a proposal to lease to cattlemen large sections of the Standing Rock Sioux Reservation in North Dakota; the writing of parts of his 1902 and 1904 annual messages to Congress that dealt with Indians; and the suggestion of Francis E. Leupp for Commissioner of Indian Affairs, the man who filled that office with distinction during Roosevelt's second administration.

For examples of *Forest and Stream*'s support of the Roosevelt-Pinchot conservation program, see "Forest Reserves as Game Refuges," February 8, 1902, LVIII, 101; "Sportsmen in the White House," May 10, 1902, LVIII, 361; "President Roosevelt as a Sportsman," December 5, 1903, LXI, 437; January 30, 1904, LXII, 81; "The President's Message," December 17, 1904, LXIII, 505; "Transfer of Forest Reserves," February 11, 1905, LXIV, 109; "More National Parks," September 9, 1905, LXV, 205; "The Forest Reserves," December 16, 1905, LXV, 485; "The Forest Service," January 26, 1907, LXVIII, 127; and May 23, 1908, LXX, 807.

For the fact that Grinnell limited himself to Indian affairs when talking with the President, see Grinnell to Mrs. G. W. H. Stouch, February 8, 1907, Letter Book, 869. Of course, this does not mean that Grinnell's interest in conservation had lessened. For a sketch of his later activities in this area, see Madison Grant, *Early History of Glacier National Park Montana* (Washington, D.C., 1919); and Trefethen, *Crusade for Wildlife,* 97–109, 150–78, 206–84, and 325–28.

For documentation of the "services" mentioned above, which Grinnell performed for Roosevelt in the area of Indian affairs, see C. H. Merriam to Grinnell, February 8, 1902, Grinnell Collection, item no. 206; Grinnell to Merriam, February 19, 1902, Letter Book, 151; Roosevelt to Grinnell, April 28, 1902, Roosevelt Papers, Library of Congress, Series 2; George Kennan to Grinnell, April 28, 1902, Grinnell Collection, item no. 170; Merriam to Grinnell, April 29, 1902, Grinnell File; Grinnell to Merriam, April 30, 1902, Letter Book, 351; Grinnell to S. M. Brosius, April 30, 1902, *Ibid.,* 352; Grinnell to Roosevelt, May 1, 1902, *Ibid.,* 374; Grinnell to Emerson Hough, May 2, 1902, *Ibid.,* 377; Grinnell to Hamlin Garland, May 7, 1902, *Ibid.,* 395; "STANDING ROCK AGENCY, FORT YATES, N. DAK. MAY 23, 1902. MEMORANDUM AGREEMENT. Negotiated by GEORGE BIRD GRINNELL . . . ," Grinnell Collection, item no. 549; Grinnell [as Special Confidential Indian Agent] to Secretary of the Interior, May 29, 1902 [Grinnell's report], Grinnell File; Roosevelt to Grinnell, June 13, 1902, Roosevelt Papers, Library of Congress, Series 2; "THE STANDING ROCK INDIANS AND THE GRAZING LEASES" (June, 1902), Grinnell Collection, item no. 206; Grinnell to George B. Cortelyou, October 24, 1902, Letter Book, 575; Willis Fletcher Johnson, ed., *Addresses and Papers of Theodore Roosevelt* (New York, 1909), 97–98; Grinnell to John Pitcher, December 8, 1904, Letter Book, 244; "The President's Message," *Forest and Stream,* December 17, 1904, LXIII, 505; Grinnell to Roosevelt, November 17, 1904, Letter Book, 191–92; Grinnell to F. E. Leupp, November 21, 1904, *Ibid.,* 208; Grinnell to Pitcher, December 8, 1904, *Ibid.,* 244; and Grinnell to "The President," October 31, 1912, *Ibid.,* 467.

For further documentation of Grinnell's role as Roosevelt's chief adviser on Indian matters, see Roosevelt to Grinnell, July 2, 1902, Roosevelt Papers, Library of Congress, Series 2; Grinnell to Roosevelt, July 18, 1902, Letter Book, 422–23; Grinnell to James McLaughlin, July 21, 1902, *Ibid.,* 430; Grinnell to Hamlin Garland, November 13, 1902, *Ibid.,* 605; Grinnell to J. B. Monroe, January 27, 1903, *Ibid.,* 789; Grinnell to Roosevelt, February 5, 1903, *Ibid.,*

822; Grinnell to E. Hofer, February 6, 1903, *Ibid.*, 828; Roosevelt to Grinnell, February 9, 1903, Roosevelt Papers, Library of Congress, Series 2; Grinnell to Roosevelt, February 14, 1903, Letter Book, 849; Grinnell to William Loeb, Jr., March 2, 1903, *Ibid.*, 887; Grinnell to Roosevelt, March 12, 1903, *Ibid.*, 909; Grinnell to Roosevelt, March 24, 1903, *Ibid.*, 938; Grinnell to Roosevelt, June 3, 1903, *Ibid.*, 99; Roosevelt to Grinnell, July 22, 1903, Roosevelt Papers, Library of Congress, Series 2; Roosevelt to Ethan Allen Hitchcock, July 22, 1903, *Ibid.*; Grinnell to Roosevelt, August 22, 1903, Letter Book, 175–76; Grinnell to W. A. Jones, August 29, 1903, *Ibid.*, 191; Grinnell to Roosevelt, September 14, 1903, *Ibid.*, 225–26; Roosevelt to Henry Cabot Lodge, September 30, 1903, Morison and Blum, eds., *Letters of Theodore Roosevelt,* III, 606; Grinnell to Joseph Kipp, October 3, 1903, Letter Book, 285; Grinnell to C. H. Merriam, November 30, 1903, *Ibid.*, 406–07; Grinnell to Charles Aubrey [no date: *circa* January 22, 1904], *Ibid.*, 494; Grinnell to Monroe, January 29, 1904, *Ibid.*, 522; Grinnell to Roosevelt, March 10, 1904, *Ibid.*, 675; Grinnell to Merriam, March 12, 1904, *Ibid.*, 680; Grinnell to Roosevelt, March 16, 1904, *Ibid.*, 687; Grinnell to Roosevelt, March 23, 1904, *Ibid.*, 723–24; Grinnell to Roosevelt, July 14, 1904, *Ibid.*, 16; Grinnell to Roosevelt, July 19, 1904, *Ibid.*, 29; Roosevelt to Hitchcock, July 23, 1904, Morison and Blum, eds., *Letters of Theodore Roosevelt,* IV, 864; Grinnell to Frank Mead, July 25, 1904, Letter Book, 37–38; Grinnell to Roosevelt, July 25, 1904, *Ibid.*, 35; Grinnell to Mead, July 28, 1904, *Ibid.*, 39–40; Grinnell to F. E. Leupp, August 27, 1904, *Ibid.*, 99; Grinnell to Loeb, September 6, 1904, *Ibid.*, 109; Grinnell to Lapsley A. McAfee, November 7, 1904, *Ibid.*, 142; Grinnell to Roosevelt, November 11, 1904, *Ibid.*, 152; Grinnell to Pitcher, November 18, 1904, *Ibid.*, 201; Grinnell to Loeb, November 22, 1904, *Ibid.*, 212–13; Grinnell to Merriam, May 25, 1905, *Ibid.*, 622; Grinnell to Mrs. F. N. Doubleday, June 10, 1905, *Ibid.*, 670; Grinnell to Mead, June 23, 1905, *Ibid.*, 697; Grinnell to Roosevelt, November 29, 1905, *Ibid.*, 965; Grinnell to Joseph M. Dixon, June 21, 1906, *Ibid.*, 451; Grinnell to James A. Perrine, June 22, 1906, *Ibid.*, 469–70; Grinnell to Monroe, July 2, 1906, *Ibid.*, 492; Grinnell to Perrine, July 2, 1906, *Ibid.*, 489; and Grinnell to Hofer, July 7, 1906, *Ibid.*, 499.

SELECTED
BIBLIOGRAPHY

Note: Because many naturalists and a few conservation historians have been sportsmen, their writings reflect at least some appreciation of the sportsman's role in conserving wildlife and wilderness. However, the following listing also includes many works that ignore or castigate sportsmen, and, for reasons already discussed, most of the secondary works cited below put an interpretation of the origins of conservation that is very different from the interpretation presented in the preceding pages. Where titles do not fully describe a work's contents—or where I wish to draw attention to some important finding—I have provided annotations.

Aside from manuscript collections pertaining to individual hunters and fishermen, the best libraries for primary, published sources on sport are Harvard (fishing), Yale (hunting), Princeton (fishing), and the New York Public Library (both hunting and fishing). By "published sources," I also mean privately printed works, a number of which are included below. Harvard has complete, or nearly complete, files of all of the "big four" sporting newspapers of the 1870s and '80s.

ADAMS, JOHN QUINCY. *Life in a New England Town: 1787, 1788. Diary of John Quincy Adams, While a Student in the Office of Theophilus Parsons at Newburyport.* Boston, 1903. Diary published by his grandson, Charles Francis Adams.

ADAMS, JR., ROBERT. "The Oldest Club in America." *Century Magazine,* XXVI (August, 1883), 544–50. On the Schuylkill Fishing Company, founded in Pennsylvania in 1732.

AKEHURST, RICHARD. *Sporting Guns.* New York, 1968. A history—from the sixteenth century to the present.

ALLARD, JR., DEAN C. "Spencer Fullerton Baird and the U.S. Fish Commission: A Study in the History of American Science." Ph.D. dissertation, George Washington University, 1967.

ALLEN, DURWARD L. *The Life of Prairies and Plains.* New York, 1969. First published in 1967. Much on the life history of the bison.

ALLEN, JOEL A. *The American Bisons, Living and Extinct. Memoirs of the Museum of Comparative Zoology.* IV (1876). Cambridge, Massachusetts, 1876.

———. *Autobiographical Notes and a Bibliography of the Scientific Publications of Joel Asaph Allen.* New York, 1916.

———. "On the Decrease of Birds in the United States." *Penn Monthly* (December, 1876), 931–44. Bound copy in the library of Harvard's Museum of Comparative Zoology. Recommends the formation of societies to protect nongame birds and points out the fallacy of trying to discriminate between "beneficial" and "injurious" birds.

ALTSHELER, BRENT, [comp.] *Natural History Index-Guide: An Index to 3,365 Books and Periodicals in Libraries . . . in All Countries. . . .* New York, 1940. Revised edition of book first published in 1936. Sporting and "scientific" works juxtaposed throughout.

American Angler. 30 vols. New York, 1881–1900.

American Naturalist. 35 vols. Salem, Massachusetts, 1867–1901.

American Sportsman [later *Rod and Gun*]. 10 vols. West Meriden, Connecticut, 1871–1874; and New York, 1874–1877. Merged with *Forest and Stream* in 1877.

AMERY, C. F. *Notes on Forestry.* London, 1875. A treatise that influenced Grinnell and others.

ANONYMOUS. "Conservationists Clash with Preservationists." *American Rifleman,* CXXI (September, 1973), 12. On which "conservation" organizations support, accept, or oppose hunting.

———. "Game Protectors at Dinner." New York *Times,* May 22, 1894, 4. Describes meeting of New York Association for the Protection of Game, founded in 1844.

———. "Sportsman Take Notice." New York *Evening Post,* March 24, 1806. Early statement of what I have called the code of the sportsman, plus the fact that a "New York Sporting Club" had just been formed to make sure the game laws were enforced and the game preserved.

———. *The Sportsman's Companion or, An Essay on Shooting: Illustriously Shewing [sic] in what Manner to Fire at Birds of Game, in Various Directions and Situations; And, Directions to Gentlemen for the Treatment and Breaking [of] their Own Pointers and Spaniels, and the Necessary Precautions to Guard against many Accidents that Attend this Pleasant Diversion.* . . . Harrisburg, Pennsylvania, 1948. Originally published in New York in 1783, "By a Gentleman," this reprint contains a Preface, copious Notes, and a Bibliography of important sporting books, all by editor Jan Thornton. It is generally regarded as the first book on sport hunting published in America, and the code of the sportsman is already apparent in its pages.

———. "Too Much Hunting?" *National Wildlife,* VI (April–May, 1968), 22–23. Readers' letters to the editor attacking or supporting hunting. The editors invited the letters, and this represents only a sample of the "ensuing blizzard of mail" they received.

ATHEARN, ROBERT G. *Westward the Briton: The Far West, 1865–1900, as Seen by British Sportsmen and Capitalists, Ranchers and Homesteaders, Lords and Ladies.* Lincoln, Nebraska, 1971. First published in 1953. Has a bibliography containing English sporting works on America.

AUDUBON, JOHN JAMES. *Delineations of American Scenery and Character.* New York, 1970. Reprint of book first published in 1926. Contains a bibliography of Audubon's works and an Introduction by his biographer, Francis Hobart Herrick.

AUSTIN, ELIZABETH S., ed. *Frank M. Chapman in Florida: His Journals and Letters.* Gainesville, 1967.

BACHELDER, JOHN B. *Popular Resorts, and How to Reach Them. Combining a Brief Description of the Principal Summer Retreats in the United States, and the Routes of Travel Leading to Them.* Boston, 1874.

BALDWIN, DONALD N. *The Quiet Revolution: The Grass Roots of Today's Wilderness Preservation Movement.* Boulder, Colorado, 1972. Seeks to prove that sportsman Arthur H. Carhart, and not that other sportsman, Aldo Leopold, was the "Father of the Wilderness Concept." Actually, the concept goes back *at least* to 1892—with the establishment of the Afognak Forest and Fish-Culture Reserve in Alaska.

BALTZELL, E. DIGBY. *The Protestant Establishment: Aristocracy and Caste in America.* New York, 1966. First published in 1964.

BANCROFT, HUBERT HOWE. *The Book of the Fair: An Historical and Descriptive Presentation of the World's Science, Art, and Industry, as Viewed through the Columbian Exposition at Chicago in 1893.* This is a recent reprint, by Bounty Books, of a book apparently published in 1894. Place of publication of original work, or the reprint, is not given. Contains an interesting description of the Boone and Crockett Club exhibit at the fair.

BARBER, JOEL. *Wild Fowl Decoys.* New York, 1954. First published in 1934. Much on the history of their use.

BARNETT, LEROY. "The Buffalo Bone Commerce on the Northern Plains."

North Dakota History, XXXIX (Winter, 1972), 23–42. Incredible photographs.

BARTLETT, RICHARD A. *Great Surveys of the American West.* Norman, Oklahoma, 1962.

BATCHELDER, CHARLES F. *An Account of the Nuttall Ornithological Club, 1873 to 1919. Memoirs of the Nuttall Ornithological Club.* No. VIII. Cambridge, Massachusetts 1937.

BATES, J. LEONARD. "Fulfilling American Democracy: The Conservation Movement, 1907 to 1921." *Mississippi Valley Historical Review,* XLIV (June, 1957), 29–57.

BEACH, WILLIAM. *In the Shadow of Mount McKinley.* New York, 1931. Travel and big-game hunting. Introduction by Robert Sterling Yard and Foreword by John Burnham, both important conservationists of a later period.

BEECHER, HENRY WARD. *Star Papers; or, Experiences of Art and Nature.* New York, 1855. Has chapters called "Trouting," "The Morals of Fishing," etc.

BENT, ARTHUR CLEVELAND. *Life Histories of North American Shore Birds.* 2 vols. New York, 1962. Originally published in 1927 and 1929.

———. *Life Histories of North American Wild Fowl.* 2 vols. New York, 1962. Originally published in 1923 and 1925.

BERKELEY, GEORGE C. G. F. *The English Sportsman in the Western Prairies.* London, 1861. Travel and hunting.

[BETHUNE, GEORGE W., ed.] *The Complete Angler; or, the Contemplative Man's Recreation* [*1653*]. *By Isaac Walton and Charles Cotton. With Notes, a Bibliographical Preface, and a Notice of Cotton and his Writings, by the American Editor.* New York, 1847.

BETTS, JOHN RICKARDS. *America's Sporting Heritage: 1850–1950.* Reading, Massachusetts, 1974.

———. "Sporting Journalism in Nineteenth-Century America." *American Quarterly,* V (Spring, 1953), 39–56. On all sports, but much on hunting and fishing.

BILL, LEDYARD. *A Winter in Florida; or, Observations on the Soil, Climate, and Products of Our Semi-Tropical State; With Sketches of the Principal Towns and Cities in Eastern Florida. To which is Added A Brief Historical Summary; Together with Hints to the Tourist, Invalid, and Sportsman.* New York, 1870. First published in 1869.

BILLINGTON, RAY ALLEN. *Frederick Jackson Turner: Historian, Scholar, Teacher.* New York, 1973. Has information on Turner as a sportsman.

BLACK, JOHN D. *Biological Conservation; With Particular Emphasis on Wildlife.* New York, 1954. Much on history of wildlife conservation, as well as an excellent annotated bibliography.

BLACKORBY, E. C. "Theodore Roosevelt's Conservation Policies and their Impact Upon America and the American West." *North Dakota History,* XXV (October, 1958), 107–17.

BLUM, JOHN MORTON. *The Republican Roosevelt.* New York, 1964. First published in 1954. An interpretation of Theodore Roosevelt.

BONGARTZ, ROY. "The Man Who Loved Birds But Shot Them." *New York Times,* February 25, 1973, Sect. XI, 1 and 8. On Audubon.

"Boone and Crockett Club File." Theodore Roosevelt Birthplace National Historic Site, New York City. See my "Notes" for description of this source, never before used by a professional historian.

BOURJAILY, VANCE. *The Unnatural Enemy.* New York, 1963. Contains a number of profound insights into the meaning of hunting.

———. "You Can Tell a Hunter by What He Hunts." *National Wildlife,* V (October-November, 1967), 14–17. Contains a number of insights into the deeper meaning of hunting.

BOYLE, ROBERT H. *The Hudson River: A Natural and Unnatural History.* New York, 1969. An important environmental history by a dedicated hunter and angler. Contains much on recent efforts by fishermen to preserve the river, plus an annotated bibliography.

BRANCH, E. DOUGLAS. *The Hunting of the Buffalo.* Lincoln, Nebraska, 1962. First published in 1929. Much on hide hunting.

BRANDER, MICHAEL. *Hunting and Shooting: From Earliest Times to the Present Day.* New York, 1971. Deals with subject on a worldwide basis.

BREWSTER, WILLIAM. *The Birds of the Cambridge Region of Massachusetts. Memoirs of the Nuttall Ornithological Club.* No. IV. Cambridge, Massachusetts, 1906.

BRINLEY, FRANCIS. *Life of William T. Porter.* New York, 1860. On an early and important sporting figure.

BRODHEAD, MICHAEL J. "Elliott Coues and the Sparrow War." *New England Quarterly,* XLIV (September, 1971), 420–32. His efforts to eradicate the English sparrow.

BROWN, JOHN J. *The American Angler's Guide; or, Complete Fisher's Manual, For the United States: Containing the Opinions and Practices of Experienced Anglers of Both Hemispheres. . . .* New York, 1857. First published in 1845.

BRUETTE, WILLIAM. *American Duck, Goose, and Brant Shooting.* New York, 1945. First published in 1929. By a later editor of *Forest and Stream.*

BRUSEWITZ, GUNNAR. *Hunting: Hunters, Game, Weapons and Hunting Methods from the Remote Past to the Present Day.* New York, 1969. Translation of work first published in Sweden in 1967. Deals only with Europe. Apparently without seeing its importance to American readers, the author cites the use of wooden duck decoys in Scandinavia in the 1830s as already being a "traditional" method of waterfowl hunting. American writers have always assumed that their use was unique to North America.

BRYDON, NORMAN. "New Jersey Wildlife Conservation and the Law." *New Jersey History,* LXXXVI (Winter, 1968), 215–35. An overview from colonial times to 1968.

BUCHHEISTER, CARL W., AND GRAHAM, JR., FRANK. "From the Swamps and Back: A Concise and Candid History of the Audubon Movement." *Audubon,* LXXV (January, 1973), 4–45.

BURDICK, JR., WALTER E. "Elite in Transition: From Alienation to Manipula-

tion." Ph.D. dissertation, Northern Illinois University, 1969. A study of
the elite "mentality," including that of Theodore Roosevelt.

BURNHAM, JOHN B. "Conservation's Debt to Sportsmen." *North American Review,* CCXXVI (September, 1928), 296–302. An attempt to set the record
straight—an excellent historical overview.

———. "The Old Era—and the New." *Bulletin of the American Game Protective [and Propagation] Association,* XIV (January, 1925), 13. On central
role of sportsmen in early wildlife conservation.

BURROUGHS, JOHN. *Camping and Tramping with Roosevelt.* New York, 1970.
Reprint of work first published in 1907.

———. *Locusts and Wild Honey.* Boston, 1879. Much on angling and its
meaning.

———. "One Duck—A Potomac Sketch." *Scribner's Monthly,* XXI (December,
1880), 245–48. Combines hunting and nature study.

BUTLER, OVID M., ed. *American Conservation in Picture and in Story.* Washington, D.C., 1935.

CAMERON, JENKS. *The Bureau of Biological Survey: Its History, Activities and
Organization.* Baltimore, 1929. Has a wealth of information on early wildlife conservation.

CAMP, RAYMOND R., ed. *The Hunter's Encyclopedia.* Harrisburg, Pennsylvania,
1948.

CANTWELL, ROBERT. *Alexander Wilson: Naturalist and Pioneer, A Biography.*
Philadelphia and New York, 1961.

CARAS, ROGER A. *Last Chance on Earth: A Requiem For Wildlife.* New York,
1972. First published in 1966. A discussion of endangered wildlife, but with
the erroneous implication that sport hunting is a causative factor. Ironically,
he ends the book with the "conservation creed" of waterfowl-painter Peter
Scott, who was an avid waterfowl hunter for many years.

CARHART, ARTHUR H. "Fly and Spinner." *American Forestry,* XXIX (July,
1923), 401–05. A later wilderness proponent, Carhart was also an enthusiastic angler, as this article proves.

———. "Live Game and Forest Recreation." *American Forestry,* XXVI
(December, 1920), 723–27. Partly an ode to the joys and benefits of sport
hunting.

CART, THEODORE W. "The Federal Fisheries Service, 1871–1940." M.A. thesis,
University of North Carolina, 1968.

———. "The Lacey Act: America's First Nationwide Wildlife Statute." *Forest
History,* XVII (October, 1973), 4–13.

———. "The Struggle for Wildlife Protection in the United States, 1870–1900:
Attitudes and Events Leading to the Lacey Act." Ph.D. dissertation, University of North Carolina, 1971.

CARTER, PAUL A. *The Spiritual Crisis of the Gilded Age.* DeKalb, Illinois, 1971.
Good background material for the changes in social values in the late nineteenth century.

"Castlemon, Harry" [Charles A. Fosdick]. *Frank on the Prairie*. Cincinnati, 1870. One of the "Gun-Boat Series" for boys, this work was apparently first published in 1868. Typical of the juvenile literature that influenced countless boys to take up the adventurous sport of hunting.

Catlin, George. *North American Indians: Being Letters and Nòtes on their Manners, Customs, and Conditions, Written During Eight Years' Travel Amongst the Wildest Tribes of Indians in North America. 1832–1839*. Philadelphia, 1913. 2 vols. Originally published in London in 1841, as a collection of articles which Catlin had written in the previous decade.

Caton, John Dean. *The Antelope and Deer of America: A Comprehensive Scientific Treatise Upon the Natural History, Including the Characteristics, Habits, Affinities, and Capacity for Domestication of the Antilocapra, and Cervidae of North America*. New York, 1877.

Century Association. *Clarence King Memoirs: The Helmet of Mambrino*. New York, 1904. Mainly reminiscences of King by various people. Includes his hunting exploits.

Chapman, Frank M. *Autobiography of a Bird-Lover*. New York, 1935. First published in 1933.

———. *Camps and Cruises of an Ornithologist*. New York, 1908.

Chessman, G. Wallace. *Governor Theodore Roosevelt: The Albany Apprenticeship, 1898–1900*. Cambridge, Massachusetts, 1965.

Chittenden, Hiram Martin. *The Yellowstone National Park*. Cincinnati, 1905. First published in 1895.

Clark, Galen. *Indians of the Yosemite Valley and Vicinity: Their History, Customs and Traditions*. Yosemite Valley, California, 1904. In Introduction W. W. Foote cites Clark's hunting interests.

Clark, Michael D. "American Patricians as Social Critics, 1865–1914." Ph.D. dissertation, University of North Carolina, 1965.

Clarke, C. H. D. "Autumn Thoughts of a Hunter." *Journal of Wildlife Management*. XXII (October, 1958), 420–27. A biologist analyzes the virulent anti-hunting mentality and shows how hunting has always been an important human activity—and one that meshes perfectly with ecology.

Clawson, Marion, and Knetsch, Jack L. *Economics of Outdoor Recreation*. Baltimore, 1966.

Clepper, Henry, ed. *Leaders of American Conservation*. New York, 1971. Biographical sketches, including their major publications, of well-known conservationists, but *many* of the nineteenth-century pioneers have been left out.

———, ed. *Origins of American Conservation*. New York, 1966. Articles by various authorities. In "The Conservation Movement: Birth and Infancy," Clepper makes the following, astounding statement: "The rank and file of these [early, private] organizations were ordinary citizens, public-spirited to be sure, but nevertheless not otherwise distinguished." The two organizations he had just been discussing were the Boone and Crockett Club and the American Game Protective [and Propagation] Association, both of which were founded by patrician sportsmen and which contained few, if any, "ordinary citizens."

———. *Professional Forestry in the United States.* Baltimore, 1971. Has much on the beginning of forestry.

CLEVELAND, GROVER. *Fishing and Shooting Sketches.* New York, 1906. Contains "The Mission of Sport and Outdoor Life," "The Serene Duck Hunter," and other essays revealing the former President's deep commitment to what I have called the "code of the sportsman."

COCHRAN, THOMAS C. *Railroad Leaders, 1845–1890: The Business Mind in Action.* Cambridge, Massachusetts, 1953.

COLE, NATHAN. *The Royal Parks and Gardens of London, Their History and Mode of Embellishment. . . .* London, 1877.

COMMAGER, HENRY STEELE. *The American Mind: An Interpretation of American Thought and Character Since the 1880's.* New York, 1970. Originally published in 1950.

CONNETT, EUGENE V., ed. *Duck Shooting Along the Atlantic Tidewater.* New York, no date. Reprint, by Bonanza Books, of work first published in 1947. Has material on history of sport and commercial hunting extending back into the last century. The names of some of the contributors are very well known to historians of hunting.

———, ed. *Wildfowling in the Mississippi Flyway.* New York, 1949. Articles by various authorities—has some history.

COON, CARLETON S. *The Story of Man: From the First Human to Primitive Culture and Beyond.* New York, 1962. Revised edition of work first published in 1954. Has some material on meaning of hunting in human history.

CORY, CHARLES B. *How to Know the Ducks, Geese and Swans of North America.* Boston, 1897.

———. *Hunting and Fishing in Florida, Including a Key to the Water Birds Known to Occur in the State.* New York, 1970. Reprint of book originally published in 1896.

COUES, ELLIOTT. *Handbook of Field and General Ornithology; A Manual of the Structure and Classification of Birds with Instructions for Collecting and Preserving Specimens.* London, 1890. This is a new edition, for a British audience, of certain portions of Coues' *Key to North American Birds* which first appeared in 1872.

———. "Sketch of North American Ornithology in 1879." *American Naturalist,* XIV (January, 1880), 20–25. Shows difficulty of separating "sport" and "science."

COYLE, DAVID CUSHMAN. *Conservation: An American Story of Conflict and Accomplishment.* New Brunswick, New Jersey, 1957.

CROSBY, JR., ALFRED W. *The Columbian Exchange: Biological and Cultural Consequences of 1492.* Westport, Connecticut, 1972. A model environmental history of early European man's impact on the land and aborigines of North America.

CROSS, WHITNEY R. "Ideas in Politics: The Conservation Policies of the Two Roosevelts." *Journal of the History of Ideas,* XIV (June, 1953), 421–38.

CUTRIGHT, PAUL RUSSELL. *Theodore Roosevelt the Naturalist.* New York, 1956. Foreword by Fairfield Osborn.

DALL, WILLIAM HEALEY. *Spencer Fullerton Baird: A Biography, Including Selections from his Correspondence with Audubon, Agassiz, Dana, and Others.* Philadelphia, 1915.

DANA, EDWARD SALISBURY, et al. *A Century of Science in America with Special Reference to the American Journal of Science, 1818–1918.* New Haven, 1918.

DANA, SAMUEL T. *Forest and Range Policy: Its Development in the United States.* New York, 1956.

DANIELS, GEORGE H. *Science in American Society: A Social History.* New York, 1971.

DANKER, DONALD F., ed. *Man of the Plains: Recollections of Luther North, 1856–1882.* Lincoln, Nebraska, 1961.

DARY, DAVID A. *The Buffalo Book: The Full Saga of the American Animal.* Chicago, 1974.

DASMANN, RAYMOND F. *The Destruction of California.* New York, 1971. First published in 1965.

———. *The Last Horizon.* New York, 1963. Much on environmental change in the nineteenth century.

DAY, ALBERT M. *North American Waterfowl.* Harrisburg, Pennsylvania, 1949. Much on history of waterfowl conservation and contains a brief Introduction by duck-hunter J. N. "Ding" Darling.

DEGLER, CARL N. *The Age of the Economic Revolution: 1876–1900.* Glenview, Illinois, 1967.

DEKAY, JAMES E. *Anniversary Address on the Progress of the Natural Sciences in the United States: Delivered Before the Lyceum of Natural History, of New-York, Feb. 1826.* New York, 1970. Reprint of work originally published in 1826.

Derrydale Press. *A Decade of American Sporting Books and Prints By the Derrydale Press, 1927–1937.* New York, 1937. A bibliography, with an Introduction by the press's founder and president, Eugene V. Connett, III. Among the contributors to Derrydale books are noted conservationists John Burnham and Robert Sterling Yard.

DETWEILER, ROBERT; SUTHERLAND, JON N.; AND WERTHMAN, MICHAEL S., eds. *Environmental Decay in Its Historical Context.* Glenview, Illinois, 1973.

DIBNER, BERN. *Darwin of the Beagle.* New York, 1960. Implies that Darwin's youthful zest for hunting was an important factor in the development of his scientific interests. The same could be said for most American naturalists.

DIMOCK, A. W. *The Book of the Tarpon.* New York, 1911.

DIX, JOHN ADAMS. *Sketch of the Resources of the City of New-York.* New York, 1970. Reprint of work originally published in 1827.

DODDS, GORDON B., ed. "Conservation and Reclamation in the Trans-Mississippi West: A Critical Bibliography." *Arizona and the West,* XIII (Summer, 1971), 143–71.

———. "The Historiography of American Conservation: Past and Prospects." *Pacific Northwest Quarterly,* LVI (April, 1965), 75–81.

DODGE, RICHARD I. *The Hunting Grounds of the Great West: A Description of the Plains, Game and Indians of the Great North American Desert.* London, 1877. Important account of the slaughter of the southern buffalo herds.

DUDLEY, SUSAN, AND GODDARD, DAVID R. "Joseph T. Rothrock and Forest Conservation." *Proceedings of the American Philosophical Society,* CXVII (February 16, 1973), 37–50.

DULLES, FOSTER RHEA. *America Learns to Play: A History of Popular Recreation, 1607–1940.* New York, 1940. Much on hunting and fishing.

DUNRAVEN, EARL OF. *Hunting in the Yellowstone: On the Trail of the Wapiti with Texas Jack in the Land of Geysers.* Ed. by Horace Kephart. New York, 1917. Originally published in London in 1876. Good description of Yellowstone Park in its early years.

DUPREE, A. HUNTER. *Science in the Federal Government: A History of Policies and Activities to 1940.* Cambridge, Massachusetts, 1957.

EARNEST, ADELE. *The Art of the Decoy: American Bird Carvings.* New York, 1965. Illustrations and history.

EHRENFELD, DAVID W. *Biological Conservation.* New York, 1970. Excellent summary of recent environmental destruction, plus an analysis of how hunting and ecology go together.

EKIRCH, JR., ARTHUR A. *Man and Nature in America.* Lincoln, Nebraska, 1973. First published in 1963. Mainly a discussion of the various ways in which Americans have perceived the natural environment.

ELLIOT, DANIEL G. *North American Shore Birds: A History of the Snipes, Sandpipers, Plovers and their Allies . . . A Reference Book for the Naturalist, Sportsman and Lover of Birds.* New York, 1895.

———. *The Wild Fowl of the United States and British Possessions; or, the Swan, Geese, Ducks, and Mergansers of North America with Accounts of their Habits, Nesting, Migrations and Dispersions, Together with Descriptions of the Adults and Young, and Keys for the Ready Identification of the Species. A Book for the Sportsman, and for Those Desirous of Knowing How to Distinguish These Web-footed Birds and to Learn Their Ways in Their Native Wilds.* New York, 1898.

ELLIOTT, WILLIAM. *Carolina Sports, By Land and Water; Including Incidents of Devil-Fishing. . . .* Charleston, 1846. The "devil" in the title was a common name for the manta ray.

ELMAN, ROBERT. *The Atlantic Flyway.* New York, 1972. With photographs by Walter Osborne, this beautiful book has much on the early history of waterfowl hunting.

———. *The Great American Shooting Prints.* New York, 1972. Hunting in America as portrayed by a selection of paintings and lithographs from the 1820s to the present. Elman's accompanying text amounts to a history of sport.

EMMONS, DAVID M. *Garden in the Grasslands: Boomer Literature of the Central Great Plains.* Lincoln, Nebraska, 1971. Discussion of one aspect of the propaganda of "progress."

———. "Theories of Increased Rainfall and the Timber Culture Act of 1873." *Forest History,* XV (October, 1971), 6–14.

EVENDEN, FRED G. "Wildlife Exploitation—Is Preservation the Answer?" Presentation before the National Science Teachers Association, North Central Regional Conference, Pfister Hotel, Milwaukee, Wisconsin, October 1, 1971. The Executive Director of the Wildlife Society argues that man has always been a hunter and that sportsmen have been by far the most important contributors to wildlife conservation. Ends with a plea for unity among all conservationists.

EWAN, JOSEPH. *Rocky Mountain Naturalists.* Denver, 1950.

FARQUHAR, FRANCIS P., ed. *Up and Down California in 1860–1864: The Journal of William H. Brewer.* New Haven, 1930.

FAUSOLD, MARTIN L. *Gifford Pinchot, Bull Moose Progressive.* Syracuse, New York, 1961.

FEIN, ALBERT. *Frederick Law Olmsted and the American Environmental Tradition.* New York, 1972.

FERNOW, BERNHARD E. *A Brief History of Forestry in Europe, the United States and Other Countries.* Toronto, 1907.

Field and Stream [later *The Field, Chicago Field,* and finally *American Field*]. 54 vols. Chicago, 1874–1900. Published in both Chicago and New York after 1881.

FILENE, PETER G. "An Obituary for 'The Progressive Movement.'" *American Quarterly,* XXII (Spring, 1970), 20–34.

"FIN, OLD." "Seth Green as an Angler." *American Angler,* XXVII (July–August, 1897), 178–81.

FISHER, ALBERT K. "In Memoriam: George Bird Grinnell." *The Auk,* LVI (January, 1939), 1–12. Summary of his achievements.

FLADER, SUSAN L. "Aldo Leopold and the Evolution of an Ecological Attitude." Ph.D. dissertation, Stanford University, 1971.

———. "A Biographical Study of Aldo Leopold: Thinking Like a Mountain." *Forest History,* XVII (April, 1973), 15–28.

FORBES, JAMES E. "Environmental Deterioration and Declining Species." *Conservationist,* XXV (August–September, 1970), 21–26. This review of eighty-nine endangered species of mammals, birds, and fish shows that sport hunting and fishing have had little or nothing to do with their precarious positions.

FORBUSH, EDWARD H. *A History of the Game Birds, Wild-Fowl and Shore Birds of Massachusetts and Adjacent States.* Boston, 1916. Second edition of work originally published in 1912. Much on history of both sport and commercial hunting, plus a section called "The Viewpoint of the [Sport] Hunter," in which Forbush criticizes the anti-hunting position.

————, AND MAY, JOHN B. *A Natural History of American Birds of Eastern and Central North America.* Boston, 1939. Originally in three volumes, the first of which appeared in 1925.

Forest and Stream. 77 vols. New York, 1873–1911.

"FORESTER, FRANK" [HENRY WILLIAM HERBERT]. *American Game in Its Seasons . . . Illustrated from Nature, and on Wood, by the Author.* New York, 1853.

————. *The Complete Manual for Young Sportsmen: With Directions for Handling the Gun, the Rifle, and the Rod; the Art of Shooting on the Wing; the Breaking, Management, and Hunting of the Dog; the Varieties and Habits of Game; River, Lake, and Sea Fishing . . . Prepared for the Instruction and Use of the Youth of America.* New York, 1856.

————. *Frank Forester's Fish and Fishing of the United States, and British Provinces of North America.* London, 1849.

FREDERICK, DUKE; HOWENSTINE, WILLIAM L.; AND SOCHEN, JUNE, eds. *Destroy to Create: Interaction with the Natural Environment in the Building of America.* Hinsdale, Illinois, 1972. A book of readings.

FREDRICKSON, GEORGE M. *The Inner Civil War: Northern Intellectuals and the Crisis of the Union.* New York, 1968. Contains insights that can be applied to the development of conservation.

FROME, MICHAEL. *The Forest Service.* New York, 1971. Some history.

————. "George Bird Grinnell: Grandfather of Conservation." *Field & Stream,* LXXV (June, 1970), 52, and 170–72. A sketch of Grinnell's achievements.

————. *Whose Woods These Are: The Story of the National Forests.* Garden City, New York, 1962.

FULLER, WAYNE E. "The Rural Roots of the Progressive Leaders." *Agricultural History,* XLII (January, 1968), 1–13.

GARD, WAYNE. *The Great Buffalo Hunt.* Lincoln, Nebraska, 1971. First published in 1959. Focusing on the years 1871 to 1883, this work describes the hide hunting that wiped out the bison.

GARLICK, THEODATUS. *A Treatise on the Artificial Propagation of Fish; Also, Directions for the Most Successful Modes of Angling.* Cleveland, 1857.

GATES, PAUL W. "Public Land Issues in the United States." *Western Historical Quarterly,* II (October, 1971), 363–76.

GATES, PAUL W., AND SWENSON, ROBERT W. *History of Public Land Law Development.* Washington, D.C., 1968.

GATEWOOD, WILLARD B. "Theodore Roosevelt: Champion of 'Governmental Aesthetics'." *Georgia Review,* XXI (1967), 172–83.

GEDDES, JR., JAMES. *Memories of a College Professor.* Ed. by Samuel M. Waxman. Boston, 1945. Includes memories of Theodore Roosevelt at Harvard.

GEE, ERNEST R. *Early American Sporting Books, 1734–1844: A Few Brief Notes.* New York, 1928.

———. *The Sportsman's Library: Being a Descriptive List of the Most Important Books on Sport.* New York, 1940.

GEISER, SAMUEL WOOD. *Naturalists of the Frontier.* Dallas, 1937.

GERRARE, WIRT. "Evolution of Sport with the Gun." *Outing,* XXXVII (September, 1901), 701–06. On European origins of hunting as sport.

GINGRICH, ARNOLD. *The Fishing in Print, A Guided Tour Through Five Centuries of Angling Literature.* New York, 1974. Much on American angling in fresh water.

GIRAUD, JR., J. P. *The Birds of Long Island.* New York, 1844.

Glacier National Park. Papers. Glacier National Park Library, West Glacier. Miscellaneous items relating to the reserve's early history, including many papers of George Bird Grinnell, the park's "father."

GLACKEN, CLARENCE J. "The Origins of the Conservation Philosophy." *Journal of Soil and Water Conservation,* II (1956), 63–66.

GODWIN, PARKE. *A Biography of William Cullen Bryant, with Extracts from his Private Correspondence.* 2 vols. New York, 1883.

GOETZMANN, WILLIAM H. *Exploration and Empire: The Explorer and the Scientist in the Winning of the West.* New York, 1966.

GOHDES, CLARENCE, ed. *Hunting in the Old South: Original Narratives of the Hunters.* Baton Rouge, Louisiana, 1967. In addition to his selections, the editor has provided valuable background material.

GOODE, GEORGE BROWN. *American Fishes: A Popular Treatise upon the Game and Food Fishes of North America, with Especial Reference to Habits and Methods of Capture.* New York, 1888. First published in 1887.

———, ed. *The Smithsonian Institution, 1846–1896: The History of its First Half Century.* Washington, D.C., 1897.

GOODSPEED, CHARLES ELIOT. *Angling in America: Its Early History and Literature.* Boston, 1939. This standard work on history of fresh-water fishing contains an important, annotated bibliography covering the years 1660–1900.

GRAHAM, EDWARD H. *The Land and Wildlife.* New York, 1947. Much on the history of wildlife conservation and the techniques of game management.

GRAHAM, JR., FRANK. *Man's Dominion: The Story of Conservation in America.* New York, 1971.

GRANT, MADISON. *Early History of Glacier National Park Montana.* Washington, D.C., 1919.

GRANTHAM, JR., DEWEY W. "Theodore Roosevelt in American Historical Writing, 1945–1960." *Mid-America,* XLIII (January, 1961), 3–35.

GRAY, PRENTISS N., ed. *Records of North American Big Game.* New York, 1932. Contains a list of trophy heads shot by well-known naturalists—published under the auspices of the National Collection of Heads and Horns of the New York Zoological Society.

GREEN, SETH. *Home Fishing and Home Waters: A Practical Treatise on Fish Culture.* New York, 1888.

————. "Letter from Seth Green: The Trials and Tribulations and Early Experiences of a Practical Fish-Culturist." *Forest and Stream,* II (March 12, 1874), 68.

————, AND COLLINS, A. S. *Trout Culture.* Rochester, New York, 1870.

GREENER, WILLIAM W. *The Gun and its Development; With Notes on Shooting.* London and New York, 1881.

GRINNELL, GEORGE BIRD, ed. *American Big Game in Its Haunts.* New York, 1904. Articles on the history and objectives of conservation, including "Theodore Roosevelt," by Grinnell, and "Wilderness Reserves," by Roosevelt.

————. *American Duck Shooting.* New York, 1901.

————. *American Game-Bird Shooting.* New York, 1910. Deals only with upland game.

————, ed. *Audubon Magazine,* I (February, 1887–January, 1888).

[————.] "The Biltmore Forest." *Forest and Stream,* XLII (January 6, 1894), 1. Explanation of the forestry work on George W. Vanderbilt's estate in western North Carolina.

————, ed. *A Brief History of the Boone and Crockett Club With Officers, Constitution and List of Members for the Year 1910.* New York, 1910.

[————.] "Charles Hallock." *Forest and Stream,* LXXXVIII (February, 1918), 92.

————. Collection of Journals, Field Notes and other Materials on the Plains Indians, 1870–1930. Southwest Museum Library, Los Angeles. Also contains some natural-history material.

————. "The Crown of the Continent." *Century Magazine,* LXII (September, 1901), 660–72. On the area that later became Glacier National Park.

[————.] "Dr. J. A. Allen." *Forest and Stream,* XCI (October, 1921), 449.

————. "Foreword." *Roosevelt Wild Life Bulletin,* I (1922), 9–10. Comments on Theodore Roosevelt as a naturalist.

————. "Grinnell File." Birdcraft Museum of the Connecticut Audubon Society, Fairfield. See my "Notes" for description of this source, never before used by a professional historian.

————, AND SHELDON, CHARLES, eds. *Hunting and Conservation.* New Haven, 1925. Key work for documenting the role of sportsmen in wildlife conservation, saving the redwoods, and the establishment of Glacier and Mt. McKinley National Parks.

————, ed. *Hunting At High Altitudes.* New York, 1913. Incorporates Grinnell's *Brief History of the Boone and Crockett Club,* published in book form in 1910.

————; ROOSEVELT, KERMIT; CROSS, W. REDMOND; AND GRAY, PRENTISS N., eds. *Hunting Trails on Three Continents.* New York, 1933. A Boone and Crockett Club book that contains some history of conservation.

————. *Jack the Young Ranchman; or, A Boy's Adventures in the Rockies. . . .* New York, 1899. The first of seven volumes in the "Jack" series for boys. As Grinnell's Letter Books prove, these works were based on his own experiences or on the carefully authenticated experiences of friends.

———. "The Last of the Buffalo." *Scribner's Magazine,* XII (September, 1892), 267–86. Perhaps no one has ever surpassed this poetic tribute to the vanished multitudes. The two bison skulls, a bull and cow, that he describes picking up on the prairie "to keep as mementoes of the past" are on exhibit in the Birdcraft Museum of the Connecticut Audubon Society, Fairfield.

———. Letter Books, August 2, 1886, to October 17, 1929. Birdcraft Museum of the Connecticut Audubon Society, Fairfield. See my "Notes" for description of this source, never before used by a professional historian.

———. Letters and other papers in the possession of Mrs. John P. Holman, Fairfield, Connecticut. This material has never been used before by a professional historian.

———. "Opening Up Forest Reserves." *The Forester,* IV (February, 1898), 42–44.

———. "Othniel Charles Marsh, Paleontologist." *Leading American Men of Science,* ed. by David Starr Jordan, 283–312. New York, 1910.

[———.] "President Roosevelt as a Sportsman." *Forest and Stream,* LXI (December 5, 1903), 437.

[———.] "The Reservation of Afognak." *Forest and Stream,* XL (January 12, 1893), 23. Brief history of the creation of what was, in fact, the first federal wildlife refuge and first federal "wilderness area."

[———.] "Secretary Noble's Monument." *Forest and Stream,* XL (March 9, 1893), 203. On Noble's conservation achievements.

———. "Sketch of Professor O. C. Marsh." *The Popular Science Monthly,* XIII (1878), 612–17.

[———.] "Sportsmen in the White House." *Forest and Stream,* LVIII (May 10, 1902), 361.

———. "Tenure of Land Among the Indians." *American Anthropologist,* IX (January–March, 1907), 1–11. Contains an early statement of the Indian's communal notion of land "ownership" and their reverence for the land and its wild creatures, plus the idea that these temporary "possessions" must be passed on in good order to future generations. But like the sportsman, the aborigine found no inconsistency in loving to hunt the animals he revered.

———, AND ROOSEVELT, THEODORE, eds. *Trail and Camp-Fire.* New York, 1897. Includes a Preface dealing with conservation written by the editors, and an article by Madison Grant on the origins of the New York Zoological Society.

———. *Two Great Scouts and Their Pawnee Battalion.* Cleveland, 1928. On Luther and Frank North.

[———.] "William Hallett Phillips." *Forest and Stream,* XLVIII (May 15, 1897), 381.

————, ed. *The Wolf Hunters: A Story of the Buffalo Plains; Edited and Arranged from the Manuscript Account of Robert M. Peck.* New York, 1914. An account of men who made their living poisoning wolves for their pelts.

GRISCOM, JOHN H. *The Uses and Abuses of Air: Showing its Influence in Sustaining Life, and Producing Disease; With Remarks on the Ventilation of Houses, and the Best Methods of Securing a Pure and Wholesome Atmosphere Inside of Dwellings, Churches, Court-Rooms, Workshops, and Buildings of all Kinds.* New York, 1970. Reprint of 1850 second edition of work evidently published first in 1849. An old book on a supposedly new problem: air pollution.

GUTERMUTH, C. R., AND MAUNDER, ELWOOD R. "Origins of the Natural Resources Council of America: A Personal View." *Forest History,* XVII (January, 1974), 4–17. On later, leading role of sportsmen in conservation and the unfortunate consequences of the "pulling apart of [conservation] organizations" since the 1960s.

GWYNNE, PETER. "Hunting Under Fire: Amid the Uproar, a Search for Common Ground." *National Wildlife,* XII (October–November, 1974), 38–41. An explanation of how regulated hunting meshes perfectly with ecology, plus a plea for unity among hunting and nonhunting conservationists by Thomas L. Kimball, sportsman and Executive Vice-President of the National Wildlife Federation.

HADLEY, EDITH JANE. "John Muir's Views of Nature and their Consequences." Ph.D. dissertation, University of Wisconsin, 1956.

HAGEDORN, HERMANN. *Roosevelt in the Bad Lands.* Boston, 1921. On his ranching experiences.

HALLOCK, CHARLES. *An Angler's Reminiscences: A Record of Sport, Travel and Adventure; With [an] Autobiography of the Author.* Ed. by Fred E. Pond ["Will Wildwood"]. Cincinnati, 1913. Important book in the history of angling and conservation; contains a key essay on the literature of sport fishing.

———— [comp.]. *Camp Life in Florida: A Handbook for Sportsmen and Settlers.* New York, 1876. Compilation of articles appearing in *Forest and Stream* and describes the expeditions sent by Hallock to explore the still-wild Lake Okeechobee-Everglades region.

————. *The Fishing Tourist: Angler's Guide and Reference Book.* New York, 1873.

————. *Hallock's American Club List and Sportsman's Glossary.* New York, 1878.

————. *The International Association for Protecting Game and Fish.* New York, 1876. Report of Hallock, the organization's Secretary. This sportsmen's association was initiated by Hallock at a meeting of the American Fish Culturists' Association in 1874, and it included members from British Canada and American "scientists" like Elliott Coues, E. D. Cope, Theodore Gill, and G. B. Goode. Hallock's aim was the establishment of a uniform code of game laws for North America, to be based on isothermal determinants.

————. *The Sportsman's Gazetteer and General Guide. The Game Animals, Birds and Fishes of North America: Their Habits and Various Methods of Capture. Copious Instructions in Shooting, Fishing, Taxidermy, Woodcraft, Etc. Together with a Glossary, and a Directory to the Principal Game Resorts of the Country; Illustrated with Maps.* New York, 1879. This standard work of the day first appeared in 1877, and even though George Bird Grinnell and others wrote most of it, Hallock took the credit. Contains a "Bibliography for Sportsmen."

HAMMOND, SAMUEL H. *Hunting Adventures in the Northern Wilds; or, A Tramp in the Chateaugay Woods, Over Hills, Lakes, and Forest Streams.* New York, 1856. First published in 1854 under a different title.

————. *Wild Northern Scenes; or, Sporting Adventures with the Rifle and the Rod.* New York, 1857.

HAMPTON, H. DUANE. *How the U.S. Cavalry Saved Our National Parks.* Bloomington, Indiana, 1971.

————, ed. "With [George Bird] Grinnell in North Park." *Colorado Magazine,* XLVIII (Fall, 1971), 273–98. A hunting account published in *Forest and Stream.*

HANSON, HERBERT C. *Dictionary of Ecology.* New York, 1962.

Harriman Alaska Expedition [1899]. *Alaska. . . .* Vols. 1 and 2 [14 vols. in all.] New York, 1901. Contributions by George Bird Grinnell, C. Hart Merriam, John Muir, John Burroughs, etc. This important expedition was initiated because of E. H. Harriman's desire to shoot a trophy Kodiak bear.

HARRIS, HARRY. "Robert Ridgway with a Bibliography of his Published Writings and Fifty Illustrations." *The Condor,* XXX (January, 1928), 5–118.

HARRIS, WILLIAM C. *The Angler's Guide-Book and Tourist's Gazetteer.* New York, 1884.

[————.] "The Fisheries Buildings at the World's Columbian Exposition." *American Angler,* XXII (September, 1893), 407–12. Part I of a series. Contains a description of the contributions of *American Angler* and *Forest and Stream* to the exhibits.

HASKELL, WILLIAM S. *The American Game Protective and Propagation Association: A History.* New York, 1937.

HAWKER, PETER. *Instructions to Young Sportsmen, in All that Relates to Guns and Shooting . . . To Which is Added the Hunting and Shooting of North America, with Descriptions of the Animals and Birds . . . Collated . . . by W. T. Porter.* Philadelphia, 1846.

HAYS, SAMUEL P. *Conservation and the Gospel of Efficiency: The Progressive Conservation Movement, 1890–1920.* New York, 1969. First published in 1959. In Preface to new edition Hays tells the reader that his book has been misinterpreted by many—it is primarily about "political structure" and *not* conservation.

————. "The Politics of Reform in Municipal Government in the Progressive Era." *Pacific Northwest Quarterly,* LV (October, 1964), 157–69. In this important article Hays seems to have changed his earlier view that "progressivism" was middle class in origin, at least that aspect of the so-called "movement" that dealt with municipal reform. He now believes that despite the reformers' democratic rhetoric, "the source of support for reform in municipal government did not come from the lower or middle classes, but from the upper class." Of course, the same was true of conservation.

HEADLEY, JOEL T. *The Adirondack; or, Life in the Woods.* New York, 1849.

———. *Letters from the Backwoods and the Adirondac.* New York, 1850.

HEDGES, CORNELIUS. "Journal of Judge Cornelius Hedges [Kept on the 1870 Washburn-Doane Expedition]." *Contributions to the Historical Society of Montana . . . ,* V (1904), 370–94.

HEILNER, VAN CAMPEN. *A Book on Duck Shooting.* New York, 1946. Originally published in 1939. Much on the methods of waterfowl hunting around the world, with a Foreword by Robert Cushman Murphy of the American Museum of Natural History.

HENDERSON, ROBERT W. [comp.]. *Early American Sport: A Check-List of Books by American and Foreign Authors Published in America Prior to 1860, Including Sporting Songs.* New York, 1953. Revised and enlarged edition of work first published in 1937. Listed chronologically and with brief annotations, this compilation includes all sports, not just hunting and fishing.

HENSHALL, JAMES A. *Book of the Black Bass, Comprising Its Complete Scientific and Life History, Together with a Practical Treatise on Angling and Fly Fishing and a Full Description of Tools, Tackle and Implements.* Cincinnati, 1881.

HERRICK, FRANCIS HOBART. *Audubon the Naturalist: A History of His Life and Times.* 2 vols. New York, 1917.

HIGGINSON, A. HENRY. *British and American Sporting Authors: Their Writings and Biographies.* Berryville, Virginia, 1949. Most of those cited are British; fox hunting is Higginson's main interest.

HIGHSMITH, JR., RICHARD M.; JENSEN, J. GRANVILLE; AND RUDD, ROBERT D. *Conservation in the United States.* Chicago, 1962. On theories and practices of resource management.

HINMAN, BOB. *The Golden Age of Shotgunning.* New York, 1971. Concentrating on last thirty years of nineteenth century, the book discusses both sport and market hunting, as well as the development of shotguns and shotgunning.

HOFSTADTER, RICHARD. *The Age of Reform: From Bryan to F.D.R.* New York, 1955. Despite the title, the author ignores a major reform movement—conservation.

———. "Theodore Roosevelt: The Conservative as Progressive." *The American Political Tradition and the Men Who Made It* by Richard Hofstadter, 206–37. New York, 1948.

HOLDER, CHARLES FREDERICK, AND JORDAN, DAVID STARR. *Fish Stories, Alleged and Experienced, with a Little History, Natural and Unnatural.* New York, 1909.

HOLDER, CHARLES FREDERICK. *Louis Agassiz: His Life and Work.* New York, 1893. Cites Agassiz's boyhood fishing interests.

HOLLANDER, RON. "On Safari: 'It is a Tribute to the Animal.'" New York *Times,* June 9, 1974, 7 and 29. Analysis of an African big-game hunt by a nonhunting wildlife photographer. At one point he says: "There was a troubling sense of having been closer to the animals in this one afternoon of killing than I had been in four months of photographing them. The voyeur's slack between us had vanished."

HOLLIDAY, J. S. "The Politics of John Muir." *Sierra Club Bulletin,* LVII (October–November, 1972), 10–13. By a director of the California Historical Society, this article is typical of the never-ending adulation heaped upon Muir by historians—even if history must be distorted to do so. Holliday goes so far as to suggest that President Harrison set aside the first forest reserve because of Muir's influence.

HOLLIMAN, JENNIE. *American Sports, 1785–1835.* Durham, North Carolina, 1931. Much on hunting and fishing.

HORNADAY, WILLIAM T. *Camp-Fires in the Canadian Rockies. . . .* New York, 1906. Shows Hornaday is an enthusiastic hunter.

———. *The Extermination of the American Bison; With a Sketch of Its Discovery and Life History.* Smithsonian Report (1887), Part II, 367–548. Washington, D.C., 1889.

———. *Our Vanishing Wild Life: Its Extermination and Preservation.* New York, 1913.

———. *Thirty Years War for Wild Life: Gains and Losses in the Thankless Task.* New York, 1970. Reprint of work originally published in 1931. It reveals that Hornaday—like Gifford Pinchot in forest conservation—believed that little had occurred before *he* arrived on the scene. Unfortunately, many historians have accepted their claims.

———. *Two Years in the Jungle: The Experiences of a Hunter and Naturalist in India, Ceylon, The Malay Peninsula and Borneo.* New York, 1886. Though he later attacked hunters because he believed they failed to live up to his own interpretation of the code of the sportsman, Hornaday here describes the utter joy of hunting.

———. *Wild Life Conservation in Theory and Practice.* New York, 1972. Reprint of work originally published in 1914.

HOUGH, EMERSON. *Getting a Wrong Start: A Truthful Autobiography.* New York, 1915. Particularly good for a picture of the inner workings of *Forest and Stream.*

HOUGH, FRANKLIN B. Papers. Manuscripts and History Division, New York State Library (Albany).

HUNT, WILLIAM S. *Frank Forester [Henry William Herbert]; A Tragedy in Exile.* Newark, New Jersey, 1933. A good biography, based on extensive research, and containing a "Chronology of [Herbert's] Writings."

HUNTINGTON, DWIGHT W. *Our Big Game: A Book for Sportsmen and Nature*

Lovers. New York, 1904. Much on sportsmen's clubs and private game parks and preserves.

———. *Our Feathered Game: A Handbook of the North American Game Birds.* New York, 1903. By a sportsman-naturalist, this work contains a recommendation for a "state park" in the Everglades to save that region's bird life. This suggestion antedates by forty-four years the establishment of Everglades National Park and is the earliest such proposal this writer has found.

HUTH, HANS. *Nature and The American: Three Centuries of Changing Attitudes.* Lincoln, Nebraska, 1972. Originally published in 1957.

———. "Yosemite: The Story of an Idea." *Sierra Club Bulletin,* XXXIII (1948), 46–78. Limited to earliest history of what became Yosemite National Park. Contains introduction by David R. Brower of the Sierra Club claiming—erroneously—that Yosemite, and not Yellowstone, was the first national park.

IDDINGS, JOSEPH P. "Memorial of Arnold Hague." *Bulletin of the Geological Society of America,* XXIX (1918), 35–48.

INGERSOLL, ERNEST. "A History of the Audubon Movement." *Forest and Stream,* LXXXII (March 14, 1914, and March 28, 1914), 339–40 and 406–407.

INMAN, HENRY. *The Old Santa Fé Trail; The Story of a Great Highway.* New York, 1897. Contains information on the commercial buffalo slaughter, including a controversial figure on the total number killed.

IRVING, WASHINGTON. *The Sketch Book of Geoffrey Crayon, Gent.* No. VII. New York, 1820. Contains "The Angler," 29–49.

———. *A Tour on the Prairies.* Ed. by John F. McDermott. Norman, Oklahoma, 1956. First published in 1835. Lots of hunting.

ISE, JOHN. *Our National Park Policy: A Critical History.* Baltimore, 1961.

———. *The United States Forest Policy.* New York, 1972. Reprint of work originally published in 1920. A history of federal activities in forest conservation.

JACKSON, CLARENCE S. *Picture Maker of the Old West: William H. Jackson.* New York, 1947.

JACKSON, JOHN B. *American Space—the Centennial Years: 1865–1876.* New York, 1972. Describes and analyzes the environmental changes taking place in those years.

JACKSON, W. TURRENTINE. "The Creation of Yellowstone National Park." *Mississippi Valley Historical Review,* XXIX (September, 1942), 187–206.

JACKSON, WILLIAM H., AND DRIGGS, HOWARD R. *The Pioneer Photographer: Rocky Mountain Adventures with a Camera.* Yonkers-on-Hudson, New York, 1929.

JACKSON, WILLIAM H. *Time Exposure: The Autobiography of William Henry Jackson.* New York, 1940.

JACOBS, WILBUR R. "The Indian and the Frontier in American History—A Need for Revision." *Western Historical Quarterly,* IV (January, 1973), 43–56. Presents the "dark side" of frontier expansion.

JAHER, FREDERIC COPLE, ed. *The Rich, the Well-Born, and the Powerful: Elites and Upper Classes in History.* Urbana, Illinois, 1974. Contains an article on New York high society in late nineteenth century.

JAQUES, FLORENCE PAGE. *Francis Lee Jaques: Artist of the Wilderness World.* Garden City, New York, 1973.

JOB, HERBERT K. *Among the Water-Fowl—Observation, Adventure, Photography. A Popular Narrative Account of the Water-Fowl as Found in the Northern and Middle States and Lower Canada, East of the Rocky Mountains.* New York, 1903. First published in 1902. Contains many photographs by this pioneer photographer and avid duck hunter.

JOHNSON, ROBERT UNDERWOOD. *Remembered Yesterdays.* Boston, 1923.

JOHNSON, WILLIS FLETCHER, ed. *Addresses and Papers of Theodore Roosevelt.* New York, 1909.

JONES, HOLWAY R. *John Muir and the Sierra Club: The Battle for Yosemite.* San Francisco, 1965.

JONES, HOWARD MUMFORD. *The Age of Energy: Varieties of American Experience, 1865–1915.* New York, 1973. First published in 1970.

JORDAN, DAVID STARR, AND EVERMANN, BARTON WARREN. *American Food and Game Fishes. A Popular Account of All the Species Found in America North of the Equator, with Keys for Ready Identification, Life Histories and Methods of Capture.* New York, 1902.

JORDAN, DAVID STARR. *Science Sketches.* Chicago, 1888. Includes his reminiscences of boyhood fishing experiences.

JUDD, DAVID W., ed. *The Life and Writings of Frank Forester (Henry William Herbert).* 2 vols. New York, 1882.

KAPLAN, MOISE N. *Big Game Anglers' Paradise: A Complete, Non-Technical Narrative-Treatise on Salt Water Gamefishes and Angling in Florida and Elsewhere.* New York, 1937. Contains "Philosophy of Angling," a section tracing the appeal, and benefits, of angling from ancient times to the modern period.

KELLAM, AMINE. "The Cobb's Island Story." *Virginia Cavalcade,* XXIII (Spring, 1974), 18–27. History of famous Eastern Shore waterfowl and shore-bird shooting resort of last century.

KELLINGER, CESI. "How to Understand Hunting." *Field & Stream,* LXXVIII (October, 1973), 47, 183, and 185.

KELLY, LUTHER S. *"Yellowstone Kelly": The Memoirs of Luther S. Kelly.* Ed. by M. M. Quaife. New Haven, 1926. This reliable account of a well-known frontiersman has important material on commercial "wolfing"—the poisoning of wolves (with strychnine) for their pelts.

KEYSER, CHARLES S. *Fairmount Park: Sketches of Its Scenery, Waters, and History.* Philadelphia, 1872. Evidently first published in 1871. By a pioneer in the city-park movement, this work contains a section on "The State in Schuylkill" which reflects the author's tremendous affection for angling, although he never says he is a fisherman.

KIMBALL, DAVID AND JIM. *The Market Hunter*. Minneapolis, Minnesota, 1969. History of this infamous breed, with some important insights into the meaning of hunting in contemporary society and its relationship to ecology and conservation.

KING, JUDSON. *The Conservation Fight from T.R. to T.V.A.* Washington, D.C., 1959.

KINNEY, J. P. *The Development of Forest Law in America: A Historical Presentation of the Successive Enactments, by the Legislatures of the Forty-eight States of the American Union and by the Federal Congress, Directed to the Conservation and Administration of Forest Resources.* New York, 1972. Reprint of book originally published in 1917.

KIRKLAND, EDWARD C. *Dream and Thought in the Business Community, 1860–1900.* Ithaca, New York, 1956.

KIRKWOOD, JAMES P. *A Special Report on the Pollution of River Waters.* New York, 1970. Reprint, with different title, of work published in 1876. Shows that water pollution was already a serious problem in Massachusetts.

KOHLSAAT, H. H. "The Greatest Game Market in the World." *Saturday Evening Post,* CXCVI (April 26, 1924), 72. On Chicago market of last century.

KORTRIGHT, FRANCIS H. *The Ducks, Geese and Swans of North America: A vade mecum for the Naturalist and the Sportsman.* Harrisburg, Pennsylvania, 1960. First published in 1942. Long the leading work of its kind, it was compiled by an amateur naturalist and duck hunter from Toronto, Canada. Includes an Introduction by Aldo Leopold.

KRAMER, HOWARD D. "The Scientist in the West, 1870–1880." *Pacific Historical Review,* XII (September, 1943), 239–51.

KRANZ, MARVIN W. "Pioneering in Conservation: A History of the Conservation Movement in New York State, 1865–1903." Ph.D. dissertation, Syracuse University, 1961.

KRIDER, JOHN. *Krider's Sporting Anecdotes, Illustrative of the Habits of Certain Varieties of American Game.* New York, 1966. Reprint of book originally published in 1853. One of the more notable items in this work is the fact that many sportsmen were already aware that the ingestion by waterfowl of spent lead pellets (on shooting grounds) caused lead poisoning and paralysis.

KUTZLEB, CHARLES R. "Can Forests Bring Rain to the Plains?" *Forest History,* XV (October, 1971), 14–21.

LACEY, JOHN F. "Let Us Save the Birds: Speech of Hon. John F. Lacey, in the House of Representatives." *Recreation,* XIII (July, 1900), 33–35.

LANGFORD, NATHANIEL PITT. *The Discovery of Yellowstone Park: Journal of the Washburn Expedition to the Yellowstone and Firehole Rivers in the Year 1870.* Lincoln, Nebraska, 1972. Reprint, with Foreword by Aubrey L. Haines, of book originally published in 1905.

LANMAN, CHARLES. *Adventures of an Angler in Canada, Nova Scotia and the United States.* London, 1848.

[————]. *Letters From a Landscape Painter.* Boston, 1845. Contains angling.

LAPHAM, INCREASE A. *Wisconsin: Its Geography and Topography, History, Geology, and Mineralogy: Together with Brief Sketches of Its Antiquities, Natural History, Soil, Productions, Population, and Government.* Milwaukee, 1846; first published in 1844. At one point, Lapham states: "For the scientific naturalist, the sportsman and the angler, Wisconsin affords a very interesting and highly attractive field."

LASCH, CHRISTOPHER. *The New Radicalism in America, 1889–1963; The Intellectual as a Social Type.* New York, 1967. First published in 1965.

LAYCOCK, GEORGE. *The Alien Animals: The Story of Imported Wildlife.* Garden City, New York, 1966. History of successes, such as the ringneck pheasant, and disasters, such as the carp. The latter, of course, far outnumber the former.

————. *The Sign of the Flying Goose: The Story of Our National Wildlife Refuges.* Garden City, New York, 1973. Originally published in 1965. Much history.

LEFFINGWELL, WILLIAM BRUCE. *The Art of Wing Shooting: A Practical Treatise on the Use of the Shot-Gun, Illustrating, By Sketches and Easy Reading, How to Become an Expert Shot. . . Also Treating of the Habits and Resorts of Game Birds and Water Fowl. . . .* New York, 1967. Reprint of work first published in 1894.

————. *Wild Fowl Shooting. Containing Scientific and Practical Descriptions of Wild Fowl: Their Resorts, Habits, Flights and the Most Successful Method of Hunting Them.* Chicago, 1888.

LEISZ, DOUGLAS R. "Clearcut: In Reply." *American West,* IX (January, 1972), 48 and 64. A good answer, by a professional forester, to those environmental historians who use the term "clearcut" as a synonym for "forest rape," without understanding that clearcutting is, in fact, one valid technique of scientific forestry.

LEONARD, JUSTIN W. "Protectionism Versus the 'Wise Use' Concept in Conservation." Presentation before the 18th Annual Conservation Conference, held at the headquarters of the National Wildlife Federation, Washington, D.C., December 9, 1971. After surveying the literature on conservation, this University of Michigan wildlife expert concluded: "I was disappointed that so many writers missed a wonderful opportunity to say a few truly perceptive words about the hunter, instead of ignoring or castigating him."

LEOPOLD, A. STARKER. "The Essence of Hunting." *National Wildlife,* X (October–November, 1972), 38–40. By an eminent ecologist, Aldo Leopold's son, this article probes the deeper meaning of hunting. It also points out that the bulk of the wildlife-conservation bill is paid by sportsmen.

LEOPOLD, ALDO. *Game Management.* New York, 1933. Much on history and meaning of hunting and wildlife conservation.

————. *A Sand County Almanac; With other Essays on Conservation from*

Round River. New York, 1966. *A Sand County Almanac* first appeared in 1949 and *Round River* in 1953. In many ways, these two works together represent the highest expression ever achieved of the ethic contained in the code of the sportsman.

Lewes, Elisha J. *The American Sportsman: Containing Hints to Sportsmen, Notes on Shooting, and the Habits of the Game Birds and Wild Fowl of America.* Philadelphia, 1863. Originally published, under a different title, in 1851.

Lillard, Richard G. *The Great Forest.* New York, 1947. Good on the history of man's impact on the environment.

Long, Joseph W. *American Wild-Fowl Shooting. Describing the Haunts, Habits, and Methods of Shooting Wild Fowl, Particularly Those of the Western States of America. With Instructions Concerning Guns, Blinds, Boats, and Decoys; The Training of Water-Retrievers, etc.* New York, 1874.

Long, William J. *Northern Trails: Some Studies of Animal Life in the Far North.* Boston, 1905. By the leading "nature faker"—as Roosevelt called those whose works reeked with anthropomorphism.

Lowenthal, David. *George Perkins Marsh: Versatile Vermonter.* New York, 1958.

Ludlow, William. *Report of a Reconnaissance from Carroll, Montana Territory, on the Upper Missouri, to the Yellowstone National Park, and Return, Made in the Summer of 1875.* Washington, D.C., 1876.

———. *Report of a Reconnaissance of the Black Hills of Dakota, Made in the Summer of 1874.* Washington, D.C., 1875.

Lynes, Russell. "Countryman-poet, Let Some Fresh Air into Old New York." *Smithsonian,* IV (March, 1974), 81–86. William Cullen Bryant and the origins of Central Park in New York City.

McCarthy, G. Michael. "White River Forest Reserve: The Conservation Conflict." *Colorado Magazine,* XLIX (Winter, 1972), 55–67.

McClane, A. J., ed. *McClane's New Standard Fishing Encyclopedia and International Angling Guide.* New York, 1974. Revised edition of book first published in 1965. Has an excellent section entitled "Literature of Angling."

McConnell, Grant. "The Conservation Movement—Past and Present." *Western Political Quarterly,* VII (September, 1954), 463–78.

McCreight, M. I. *Buffalo Bone Days.* Dubois, Pennsylvania, 1939. Much on commercial exploitation of buffalo.

McDermott, John F., ed. *The Western Journals of Washington Irving.* Norman, Oklahoma, 1944.

McDonald, John. *The Origins of Angling.* Garden City, New York, 1963. Combined with a new printing of *The Treatise of Fishing with an Angle* (1496)—the first published essay on sport fishing—this work concludes that angling owes a large debt to hunting. Important early literature on both hunting and fishing is cited.

McGeary, M. Nelson. *Gifford Pinchot: Forester-Politician.* Princeton, 1960.

McHenry, Robert, ed. *A Documentary History of Conservation in America.* New York, 1972.

McHugh, Tom. *The Time of the Buffalo.* New York, 1972. Much on the commercial slaughter of the last century.

McIlhenny, Edward Avery. *The Wild Turkey and Its Hunting.* Garden City, New York, 1914. Compiled by a sportsman-naturalist who did much to save the snowy egret from extinction.

MacKey, Jr., William J. *American Bird Decoys.* New York, no date. Reprint, by Bonanza Books, of work first published in 1965. Contains a chapter on American decoys as folk art by Quintina Colio.

McLaughlin, Charles C. "Selected Letters of Frederick Law Olmsted." Ph.D. dissertation, Harvard University, 1960.

Maclay, Alfred B. [comp.]. *Five Centuries of Sport: Hunting, Racing, Shooting, Falconry, Riding, Cock-Fighting, Fox-Hunting, Coursing, Angling and Coaching—Rare American Sporting Periodicals. First Editions in Original Parts. The Distinguished Collection Formed by the Late Alfred B. Maclay. Sold by Order of Mrs. Alfred B. Maclay. . . .* [Parke-Bernet Galleries, Inc.] New York, 1945.

Main, Jackson T. "History of the Conservation of Wild Life in Wisconsin." M.A. thesis, University of Wisconsin, 1940.

Manchester, Herbert. *Four Centuries of Sport in America, 1490–1890.* New York, 1968. First published in 1931. All sports, but stresses hunting and fishing. Contains important "List of Sources."

Mann, William M. *Wild Animals In and Out of the Zoo.* New York, 1930. Vol. VI of Smithsonian Scientific Series. New York, 1930 and 1934. Contains information on the establishment of the National Zoological Park, particularly the roles of Senator George F. Edmunds and William T. Hornaday, both sportsmen.

Marcham, Frederick G., ed. *Louis Agassiz Fuertes and the Singular Beauty of Birds.* New York, 1971.

Marsh, George Perkins. *Man and Nature; or, Physical Geography as Modified by Human Action.* New York, 1864.

———. *Report, Made Under Authority of the Legislature of Vermont, on the Artificial Propagation of Fish.* Burlington, 1857.

Marvinney, Sandy. "Theodore Roosevelt, Conservationist." *Conservationist,* XXVI (June–July, 1972), 18–21 and 46.

Mather, Fred. *Men I Have Fished With: Sketches of Character and Incident with Rod and Gun, From Childhood to Manhood; From the Killing of Little Fishes and Birds to a Buffalo Hunt.* New York, 1897. By a leading fish culturist.

———. *Modern Fishculture in Fresh and Salt Water.* New York, 1900. Has some history of the subject.

———. *My Angling Friends: Being a Second Series of Sketches of Men I Have*

Fished With. New York, 1901. Includes Chester A. Arthur, Charles Hallock, and Thaddeus Norris.

————. "Progress in Fish-Culture." *Century Magazine,* XXVII (April, 1884), 900–13. A history.

MATTHIESSEN, PETER. *Wildlife in America.* New York, 1964. First published in 1959.

MAYER, ALFRED M., ed. *Sport with Gun and Rod in American Woods and Waters.* 2 vols. Edinburgh, Scotland, 1884. First published in New York in 1883. With a few exceptions, this is a collection of articles originally appearing in *Century Magazine.* Among the contributors are George Bird Grinnell, Thaddeus Norris, John Burroughs, and Charles E. Whitehead.

MELOSI, MARTIN V. " 'Out of Sight, Out of Mind': The Environment and Disposal of Municipal Refuge, 1860–1920." *Historian,* XXXV (August, 1973), 621–40.

MERRIAM, C. HART. *A Review of the Birds of Connecticut.* New Haven, 1877.

————. "Roosevelt, the Naturalist." *Science,* LXXV (February 12, 1932), 181–83.

MERRILL, HORACE S. *Bourbon Leader: Grover Cleveland and the Democratic Party.* Boston, 1957.

MERRITT, H. CLAY. *The Shadow of a Gun.* Chicago, 1904. The classic, book-length account of nineteenth-century market hunting by one of the most successful commercial gunners and game merchants of the Middle West. Contains many examples of hatred between sportsmen and market hunters.

MERSHON, WILLIAM B. [comp.]. *The Passenger Pigeon.* New York, 1907.

————. *Recollections of My Fifty Years Hunting and Fishing.* Boston, 1923.

MESSITER, CHARLES A. *Sport and Adventures Among the North American Indians.* New York, 1966. Reprint of work originally published in 1890. Hunting in the 1860s and '70s, mainly in the West.

MIGEL, J. MICHAEL, ed. *The Stream Conservation Handbook.* New York, 1974. Contributions by various authorities revealing the continuing efforts of sportsmen-naturalists to preserve both their sport and the environment that produces it.

MILBERT, JACQUES G. *Picturesque Itinerary of the Hudson River and the Peripheral Parts of North America.* Ridgewood, New Jersey, 1968. Reprint of work originally published in French in 1828–29. A wonderful description by a French hunter-naturalist that includes an eloquent plea for forest conservation.

MILLER, HOWARD S. *Dollars for Research: Science and Its Patrons in Nineteenth-Century America.* Seattle, 1970.

MILNE, LORUS J. AND MARGERY. *The Balance of Nature.* New York, 1960. Excellent study of the ecology of native wildlife and the impact of alien species.

MONEY, ALBERT W., et al. *Guns, Ammunition, and Tackle.* New York, 1904.

MORGAN, H. WAYNE. "America's First Environmental Challenge, 1865–1920." *Essays on the Gilded Age,* ed. by Margaret F. Morris, 87–108. Austin, Texas,

1973. Despite the title of his essay, Morgan has almost nothing to say on the years before 1890.

————, ed. *Victorian Culture in America: 1865–1914*. Itasca, Illinois, 1973.

MORISON, ELTING E., AND BLUM, JOHN M., eds. *The Letters of Theodore Roosevelt*. 8 vols. Cambridge, Massachusetts, 1951–54.

MOWRY, GEORGE E. *The Progressive Era, 1900–20: The Reform Persuasion*. Washington, D.C., 1972. Earlier versions of this pamphlet were published in 1958 and 1964. An interpretation of "progressivism," as well as a survey of the literature.

MURPHY, JOHN MORTIMER. *American Game Bird Shooting*. New York, 1882.

MURPHY, ROBERT CUSHMAN. *Fish-Shape Paumanok: Nature and Man on Long Island [New York]*. Philadelphia, 1964. An environmental history.

MURPHY, ROBERT W. *Wild Sanctuaries: Our National Wildlife Refuges—A Heritage Restored*. New York, 1968. Has material on market hunting of various species.

MURRAY, WILLIAM H. H. *Adventures in the Wilderness; or, Camp-Life in the Adirondacks*. Syracuse, New York, 1970. New edition—edited by William K. Verner and with Introduction and Notes by Warder H. Cadbury—of work originally published in 1869.

NASH, RODERICK, ed. *The American Environment: Readings in the History of Conservation*. Reading, Massachusetts, 1968. Includes Nash's thesis on "Conservation as Anxiety," plus a comprehensive "Selected Bibliography," with annotations, that concentrates on the history of the conservation movement.

————. "The American Invention of National Parks." *American Quarterly*, XXII (Fall, 1970), 726–35.

————. "The State of Environmental History." *The State of American History*, ed. by Herbert J. Bass, 249–60. Chicago, 1970.

————. *Wilderness and the American Mind*. New Haven, 1973. Revised edition, with updated "Note on the Sources," of book first published in 1967.

New York Association for the Protection of Game. Papers. Manuscripts and History Division, New York State Library (Albany). Miscellaneous items pertaining to a conservation organization founded in 1844.

New York Public Library. *List of Works in the New York Public Library on Sport in General, and on Shooting in Particular*. Reprint from library *Bulletin*, VII (May and June, 1903).

New York Zoological Society. *First Annual Report of the New York Zoological Society*. New York, 1897. Has some history of the organization, and lists its leaders. The organization grew out of the efforts of big-game hunters in the Boone and Crockett Club, their main purpose being the preservation of big-game animals.

————. *New York Zoological Society—New York Zoological Park, New York Aquarium, [and] Department of Tropical Research—A Presentation of the Aims and Achievements of a Great Institution*. New York, 1937. Copy in New York Public Library. Contains some history.

NOBLE, DONALD R. "James Fenimore Cooper and the Environment." *Conservationist,* XXVI (October–November, 1971), 3–7.

NORRIS, THADDEUS. *The American Angler's Book: Embracing the Natural History of Sporting Fish, and the Art of Taking Them. With Instructions in Fly-Fishing, Fly-Making, and Rod-Making; And Directions for Fish-Breeding. . . .* Philadelphia, 1865 [?]. First published in 1864.

———. *American Fish-Culture, Embracing all the Details of Artificial Breeding and Rearing of Trout, the Culture of Salmon, Shad and other Fishes.* Philadelphia, 1868. Cites the practice of marking salmon to trace their migrations, a fact that should not be surprising since Izaak Walton also mentions it in his *Compleat Angler,* first published in 1653!

———. "The Michigan Grayling." *Scribner's Monthly,* XIX (November, 1879), 17–23.

NORTHRUP, ANSEL J. *Camps and Tramps in the Adirondacks, and Grayling Fishing in Northern Michigan.* Syracuse, New York, 1880.

OLMSTED, FREDERICK LAW. *A Journey Through Texas; or, a Saddle-Trip on the Southwestern Frontier.* New York, 1857. Contains hunting.

OLSON, SHERRY H. *The Depletion Myth: A History of Railroad Use of Timber.* Cambridge, Massachusetts, 1971.

O'NEILL, EUGENE J. "Parks and Forest Conservation in New York, 1850–1920." Ed.D. dissertation, Columbia University, 1963.

ORTEGA Y GASSET, JOSÉ. *Meditations on Hunting.* New York, 1972. Originally published in Madrid in 1943. By Spain's leading twentieth-century philosopher, this brilliant work contains a wealth of insights into anthropology and ecology. Ortega is particularly good on how hunting attunes one to the natural environment and the reasons why photographing game is not a substitute for hunting.

ORVIS, CHARLES F., AND CHENEY, A. NELSON [comps.]. *Fishing with the Fly: Sketches by Lovers of the Art, with Illustrations of Standard Flies Collected by Charles F. Orvis and A. Nelson Cheney.* Manchester, Vermont, 1883. Contributions by Charles Hallock, Seth Green, Robert Barnwell Roosevelt, and other well-known anglers.

OSBORN, HENRY FAIRCHILD. *The American Museum of Natural History: Its Origin, Its History, [and] the Growth of Its Departments to December 31, 1909.* New York, 1911.

———. *Impressions of Great Naturalists: Reminiscences of Darwin, Huxley, Balfour, Cope and Others.* New York, 1924. The "others" include Theodore Roosevelt and John Burroughs.

PALMER, THEODORE S. *Chronology and Index of the More Important Events in American Game Protection, 1776–1911.* U.S. Biological Survey Bulletin No. 41. Washington, D.C., 1912.

———. *Digest of Game Laws for 1901.* U.S. Biological Survey Bulletin No. 16. Washington, D.C., 1901.

———. *Hunting Licenses: Their History, Objects, and Limitations.* U.S. Biological Survey Bulletin No. 19. Washington, D.C., 1904.

————. *Legislation for the Protection of Birds other than Game Birds.* U.S. Biological Survey Bulletin No. 12. Washington, D.C., 1900.

————. "Lest We Forget." *Bulletin of the American Game Protective [and Propagation] Association,* XIV (January, 1925), 11–12 and 19. Greatest expert on history of wildlife legislation gives brief biographies of five key figures in history of wildlife conservation: "Frank Forester"; Royal Phelps (who with Charles E. Whitehead, another member of the N.Y. Association for the Protection of Game, achieved a crucial legal precedent when they won a case against a New York City game dealer, Joseph H. Racey, for illegal possession of quail); Charles Hallock; George Bird Grinnell; and Theodore Roosevelt. All five men were sportsmen.

————. *National Reservations for the Protection of Wildlife.* U.S. Biological Survey Circular No. 87. Washington, D.C., 1912.

————. *Private Game Preserves and their Future in the United States.* U.S. Biological Survey Circular No. 72. Washington, D.C., 1910.

————. *A Review of Economic Ornithology in the United States.* Reprint of a publication [1899?] of the Bureau of Biological Survey, U.S. Department of Agriculture, in the New York Public Library.

PARKMAN, FRANCIS. "The Forests of the White Mountains." *Garden and Forest,* I (February 29, 1888), 2.

————. *The Oregon Trail: Sketches of Prairie and Rocky-Mountain Life.* Boston, 1872. First appeared in 1847.

PARMALEE, PAUL W., AND LOOMIS, FORREST D. *Decoys and Decoy Carvers of Illinois.* DeKalb, Illinois, 1969.

PAXSON, FREDERIC L. "The Rise of Sport." *Mississippi Valley Historical Review,* IV (September, 1917), 143–68. Has information on George Bird Grinnell, the history of the Boone and Crockett Club, changing attitudes toward hunting, etc.

PEARSON, T GILBERT. *Adventures in Bird Protection: An Autobiography . . . with an Introduction by Frank M. Chapman.* New York, 1937.

————, ed. *Birds of America.* Garden City, New York, 1936. First published in 1917. Some material on history of bird conservation.

————. *Fifty Years of Bird Protection in the United States.* New York, 1933.

PENICK, JR., JAMES. "The Progressives and the Environment: Three Themes from the First Conservation Movement." *The Progressive Era,* ed. by Lewis L. Gould, 115–31. Syracuse, New York, 1974. Suggests the central role of patricians in conservation during the "progressive" period and has some interesting comments concerning John Muir.

————. Review of Harold T. Pinkett's *Gifford Pinchot* (1970). *Pacific Northwest Quarterly,* LXII (October, 1971), 141. Criticizes Pinkett because "the functional relationship between Pinchot's social class and his profession is not explored, although forestry in the Progressive era is an example of patrician reform, and the profession is peculiarly dependent on the support of the upper class. But other historians have also avoided this problem."

————. Review of Robert V. Hine's *American West—An Interpretative History* (1973). *Journal of the West,* XIII (April, 1974), 113–14. Contains a good criticism of the "fashion" of splitting environmental groups into "conservationists" and "preservationists," with the latter seen as pure and everyone else as tainted.

PERSONS, STOW. *The Decline of American Gentility.* New York, 1973. Contains important insights regarding the social and intellectual milieu from which many conservationists came.

PETERSEN, EUGENE T. *Conservation of Michigan's Natural Resources.* Lansing, 1960.

————. "The History of Wild Life Conservation in Michigan, 1859–1921." Ph.D. dissertation, University of Michigan, 1953.

PETERSON, JON A. "The Origins of the Comprehensive City Planning Ideal in the United States, 1840–1911." Ph.D. dissertation, Harvard University, 1967.

PHILLIPS, JOHN C. [comp.]. *American Game Mammals and Birds: A Catalogue of Books, 1582 to 1925.* Boston, 1930. Over 600 pages long, this annotated bibliography of works on hunting, natural history, and conservation is a must for all students of these subjects.

————. *The American Wild Fowlers: A Brief History of the Association, 1927–1931.* A pamphlet, with no date or place or publication, in the possession of the late John P. Holman, Fairfield, Connecticut. Good for later waterfowl-conservation efforts of sportsmen like Phillips, Charles Sheldon, and George Bird Grinnell.

————. *Boy Journals, 1887–1892.* Cambridge, Massachusetts, 1915. Has a chapter on early recollections of hunting.

————. *Migratory Bird Protection in North America: The History of Control by the United States Federal Government and a Sketch of the Treaty with Great Britain.* Cambridge, Massachusetts, 1934.

————. *A Natural History of the Ducks.* 4 vols. Boston, 1922–26. A massive work by the noted sportsman-naturalist.

————. "Naturalists, Nature Lovers, and Sportsmen." *The Auk,* XLVIII (January, 1931), 40–46. Among the more notable items in this article is an attack on "the appalling threat of oil" which is "killing countless thousands of our finest . . . marine ducks, loons, auks, grebes and gulls."

————, ed. *Shooting Journal of George Henry Mackay, 1865–1922.* Cambridge, Massachusetts, 1929. Cites William Dutcher, founder of what became the National Audubon Society, as a sportsman, and includes a bibliography of Mackay's contributions to *The Auk.*

————. *Shooting-Stands of Eastern Massachusetts.* Cambridge, Massachusetts, 1929. On waterfowling.

PINCHOT, GIFFORD. *Biltmore Forest, the Property of Mr. George W. Vanderbilt: An Account of its Treatment, and the Results of the First Year's Work.* New York, 1970. Reprint of work originally published in 1893.

———. *Breaking New Ground.* New York, 1947.

———. *The Fight for Conservation.* New York, 1910.

———. "How Conservation Began in the United States." *Agricultural History,* XI (October, 1937), 255–65. The opening line is "Conservation grew out of forestry, as many of you know."

———. "How the National Forests Were Won." *American Forests and Forest Life, XXXVI* (1930), 615–19, and 674.

———. *Just Fishing Talk.* New York, 1936. Reminiscences of angling, including that boyhood fishing trip to the Adirondacks that "not improbably . . . had much to do with making me a forester."

———. Papers. Manuscript Division, U.S. Library of Congress.

———. "Roosevelt's Part in Forestry." *Journal of Forestry,* XVIII (February, 1919), 122–24.

PINKETT, HAROLD T. *Gifford Pinchot: Private and Public Forester.* Urbana, Illinois, 1970.

POTTER, DAVID M. *People of Plenty: Economic Abundance and the American Character.* Chicago, 1965. First published in 1954. Helps explain why Americans historically have been reluctant to accept the tenets of conservation.

PROUTY, LORENZO. *Fish: Their Habits and Haunts and the Methods of Catching Them, Together with Fishing as a Recreation.* Boston, 1883.

PULLING, PIERRE. *Game and the Gunner: Observations on Game Management and Sport Hunting.* New York, 1973. Written by a biologist-hunter.

PUTER, S. A. D., AND STEVENS, HORACE. *Looters of the Public Domain: Embracing a Complete Exposure of the Fraudulent System of Acquiring Titles to the Public Lands of the United States.* Portland, Oregon, 1908.

PUTNAM, CARLETON. *Theodore Roosevelt: The Formative Years, 1858–1886.* New York, 1958.

RACQUET AND TENNIS CLUB [New York City]. *A Dictionary Catalogue of the Library of Sports in the Racquet and Tennis Club, with Special Collections on Tennis, Lawn Tennis and Early American Sports.* 2 vols. Boston, 1971. All sports, but much on hunting and fishing.

RADFORD, HARRY V. *Adirondack Murray: A Biographical Appreciation.* New York, 1905. Includes a list of Murray's published works.

RAKESTRAW, LAWRENCE. "Conservation Historiography: An Assessment." *Pacific Historical Review,* XLI (August, 1972), 271–88. Traces the "trends" in the historiography of conservation and offers his own important reinterpretation of the supposed "preservation" versus "conservation" split.

———. Review of Henry Clepper's *Professional Forestry in the United States* (1971), in *Pacific Historical Review,* XLII (February, 1973), 118. Asserts that Gifford Pinchot had an interest in aesthetic conservation.

———. Review of *Man's Dominion* (1971), by Frank Graham, Jr., in *Forest History,* XVI (April, 1972), 31–32. Reinterpretation of the supposed "preservation" versus "conservation" clash, particularly as it has been applied to Gifford Pinchot. Rakestraw observes that Pinchot has been judged "by his rhetoric, rather than by his actions."

RAYMOND, GEORGE B. [comp.]. *Catalogue of Books on Angling, Shooting, Field Sports, Natural History, the Dog, Gun, Horse, Racing, and Kindred Subjects.* New York, 1904.

Recreation. 15 vols. New York, 1894–1901.

REED, HENRY HOPE, AND DUCKWORTH, SOPHIA. *Central Park: A History and a Guide.* New York, 1967.

REEVES, JR., JOHN H. "The History and Development of Wildlife Conservation in Virginia: A Critical Review." Ph.D. dissertation, Virginia Polytechnic Institute, 1960.

REEVES, THOMAS C. "President Arthur in Yellowstone National Park." *Montana the Magazine of Western History,* XIX (July, 1969), 18–29. Mentions Arthur's angling, as well as that of Senator George G. Vest, who was in the President's party.

REID, [THOMAS] MAYNE. *The Hunter's Feast; or, Conversations Around the Campfire.* New York, 1856. Reid inspired countless boys—George Bird Grinnell and Theodore Roosevelt among them—to seek the same adventures described in his many books. The one cited here is noteworthy, as it contains an account of a hunting trip Reid took with Audubon.

REIGER, GEORGE W. "The Conservation Movement: A Natural Habitat for Hunters." Washington [D.C.] *Post,* November 15, 1973. An effective answer to an earlier attack on hunting printed in the *Post* (October 23).

————. *Profiles in Saltwater Angling: A History of the Sport—Its People and Places, Tackle and Techniques.* Englewood Cliffs, New Jersey, 1973. The only comprehensive history of saltwater sport fishing. Includes a bibliography.

REIGER, JOHN F. "George Bird Grinnell." *National Wildlife,* XI (February–March, 1973), 12–13.

————. "George Bird Grinnell and the Development of American Conservation, 1870–1901." Ph.D. dissertation, Northwestern University, 1970. Contains some details of Grinnell's life not included in the present work.

————, ed. *The Passing of the Great West: Selected Papers of George Bird Grinnell.* New York, 1972. Based on Grinnell's previously unpublished "Memoirs," which trace his life from 1849–83, this work blends his words with the editor's commentary to paint a picture of the virgin West's last years.

————, ed. "Sailing in South Florida Waters in the Early 1880s." Parts I and II. *Tequesta,* XXXI (1971), 43–66 and XXXII (1972), 58–78. Description of extended hunting-fishing trip taken by sportsman-naturalist James A. Henshall. The account originally appeared in *Forest and Stream.*

REMSBURG, JOHN E. AND GEORGE J. *Charley Reynolds: Soldier, Hunter, Scout and Guide.* Kansas City, Missouri, 1931.

REYNOLDS, CHARLES B. *The Game Laws in Brief. Laws of the United States and Canada, Relating to Game and Fish Seasons. For the Guidance of Sportsmen and Anglers.* New York, 1895. Published by *Forest and Stream.*

RICHARDSON, ELMO R. *The Politics of Conservation: Crusades and Controversies, 1897–1913.* Berkeley, California, 1962.

RILING, RAY [comp.]. *Guns and Shooting: A Selected Chronological Bibliography.* . . . New York and Toronto, 1951. The chronology is from 1420 to 1950 and includes European, English, and American works.

ROBBINS, ROY M. *Our Landed Heritage: The Public Domain, 1776–1936.* Lincoln, Nebraska, 1962. First published in 1942.

ROBINSON, DONALD H. *Through the Years in Glacier National Park: An Administrative History.* West Glacier, Montana, 1967. First published in 1960. Contains material on Grinnell's efforts to establish the park.

RODGERS III, ANDREW DENNY. *Bernhard E. Fernow: A Story of North American Forestry.* New York, 1968. Reprint of work first published in 1951.

ROE, FRANK GILBERT. *The North American Buffalo: A Critical Study of the Species in Its Wild State.* Toronto, 1951.

ROOSEVELT, ROBERT BARNWELL, AND GREEN, SETH [order of authors' names on title page—in reverse order on spine]. *Fish Hatching, and Fish Catching.* Rochester, New York, 1879.

ROOSEVELT, ROBERT BARNWELL. *Florida and the Game Water-Birds of the Atlantic Coast and the Lakes of the United States. With a Full Account of the Sporting Along Our Seashores and Inland Waters, and Remarks on Breech-Loaders and Hammerless Guns.* New York, 1884.

———. *Game Fish of the Northern States of America, and British Provinces.* New York, 1862.

———. *Superior Fishing; or, the Striped Bass, Trout, and Black Bass of the Northern States.* . . . New York, 1865.

ROOSEVELT, THEODORE, AND GRINNELL, GEORGE BIRD, eds. *American Big-Game Hunting.* New York, 1901. First published in 1893. Includes articles on the conservation needs of the nation, written by the editors.

ROOSEVELT, THEODORE. "Big Game Disappearing in the West." *The Forum,* XV (August, 1893), 767–74. Includes hunting experiences of Clarence King.

———. VAN DYKE, T. S.; ELLIOT, D. G.; AND STONE, A. J. *The Deer Family.* New York, 1902.

———. AND GRINNELL, GEORGE BIRD, eds. *Hunting in Many Lands.* New York, 1895. Includes material on conservation written by the editors.

———. *Hunting Trips of a Ranchman: Sketches of Sport on the Northern Cattle Plains.* Upper Saddle River, New Jersey, 1970. Reprint of work first published in 1885.

———. "My Life as a Naturalist: With a Presentation of Various First-Hand Data on the Life Histories and Habits of the Big Game Animals of Africa." *American Museum Journal* (later *Natural History*), XVIII (May, 1918), 320–50.

————. *Notes on Some of the Birds of Oyster Bay, Long Island.* Salem, Massachusetts [?], 1879. Copy in Houghton Library, Harvard University.

————. *Papers.* Houghton Library, Harvard University.

————. *Papers.* Manuscript Division, U.S. Library of Congress.

————. *Ranch Life and the Hunting-Trail.* New York, 1969. Reprint of work first published in 1888.

————, AND MINOT, H. D. *The Summer Birds of the Adirondacks in Franklin County, N.Y.* Salem, Massachusetts [?], 1877. Copy in the Houghton Library, Harvard University.

————. *Theodore Roosevelt: An Autobiography.* New York, 1913.

————. *Theodore Roosevelt's Diaries of Boyhood and Youth.* New York, 1928. No editor cited.

————. *Works.* Memorial Edition. 24 vols. New York, 1923–26.

————. *Works.* National Edition. 20 vols. New York, 1926.

ROSENKRANTZ, BARBARA GUTMANN, AND KOELSCH, WILLIAM A., eds. *American Habitat: A Historical Perspective.* New York, 1973.

ROTHROCK, JOSEPH T. *Vacation Cruising in Chesapeake and Delaware Bays.* Philadelphia, 1884.

RUNTE, ALFRED. "Beyond the Spectacular: The Niagara Falls Preservation Campaign." *New-York Historical Society Quarterly,* LVII (January, 1973), 30–50.

————. " 'Worthless' Lands—Our National Parks." *American West,* X (May, 1973), 5–11.

SANDOZ, MARI. *The Buffalo Hunters—The Story of the Hide Men.* New York, 1954.

SARGENT, D. A., et al. *Athletic Sports.* New York, 1897. Has section entitled "Country Clubs and Hunt Clubs in America," showing that the former grew out of the latter.

SARGENT, SHIRLEY. "Galen Clark—Mr. Yosemite." *Yosemite: Saga of a Century, 1864–1964,* published by the Yosemite Natural History Association, 19–20. Oakhurst, California, 1964.

————. *Galen Clark, Yosemite Guardian.* San Francisco, 1964.

SAVETH, EDWARD N. "The American Patrician Class: A Field for Research." *American Quarterly,* XV (Summer, 1963), 235–52.

SCHENCK, CARL A. *The Biltmore Story: Recollections of the Beginnings of Forestry in the United States.* St. Paul, Minnesota, 1955. Ed. by Ovid Butler. Contains reference to his establishing a "deer park" at Biltmore "to get acquainted with the feeding and breeding habits of the native Virginia [white-tailed] deer."

SCHMITT, PETER J. *Back to Nature: The Arcadian Myth in Urban America.* New York, 1969. Schmitt dates the "back to nature" craze from around the turn of the century to shortly after World War I, when in fact it was already in high gear by the 1870s—at least among thousands of sportsmen.

SCHORGER, A. W. *The Passenger Pigeon: Its Natural History and Extinction.* Norman, Oklahoma, 1973. First published in 1955.

SCHUCHERT, CHARLES, AND LeVENE, CLARA MAE. *O. C. Marsh, Pioneer in Paleontology.* New Haven, 1940.

SCHURZ, CARL. "Reminiscences of a Long Life." *McClure's Magazine,* XXVI (November and December, 1905), 6, 14, and 170–71. Cites his youthful interest in hunting and shooting. The pages given here refer to only *part* of a much longer article.

SCHWERDT, C. F. G. R. [comp.]. *The Schwerdt Collection: Catalogue of the Renowned Collection of Books, Manuscripts, Prints, and Drawings Relating to Hunting, Hawking and Shooting Formed by the Late C. F. G. R. Schwerdt. . . .* London, 1939 and 1946. Published in six (6) "Portions": 1–4 published in 1939 and 5–6 in 1946. Bound in one volume in New York Public Library. Some American items, but useful mainly for Old World antecedents of sport.

SCOTT, GENIO C. *Fishing in American Waters.* New York, 1875. First published in 1869.

SECCOMBE, JOSEPH. *A Discourse Utter'd in Part at Ammauskeeg-Falls in the Fishing-Season, 1739.* Barre, Massachusetts, 1971. Reprint—with an Introduction by C. K. Shipton and illustrations by Michael McCurdy—of a work originally published in Boston in 1743. This sermon on the benefits of angling is generally regarded as the first work on sport fishing to be published in America.

SELMEIER, LEWIS W. "First Camera on the Yellowstone—A Century Ago. . . ." *Montana the Magazine of Western History,* XXII (Summer, 1972), 42–53. On William H. Jackson.

SETON, GRACE GALLATIN. *Nimrod's Wife.* New York, 1907. "Nimrod" is Ernest Thompson Seton.

SHANKLAND, ROBERT. *Steve Mather of the National Parks.* New York, 1951.

SHAW, DALE L. "The Hunting Controversy: Attitudes and Arguments." *Big Sky,* II (Spring, 1974), 1–5. Summary of the findings of his Ph.D. dissertation (Colorado State University, 1973) of the same name.

SHAW, S. M., ed. *A Centennial Offering, Being a Brief History of Cooperstown with a Biographical Sketch of J. F. Cooper, by Hon. Isaac N. Arnold, Together with other Interesting Local Facts and Data.* Cooperstown, New York, 1886. Cites fact that Cooper was very fond of fishing and hunting in his youth.

SHELDON, CHARLES. *The Wilderness of Denali: Explorations of a Hunter-Naturalist in Northern Alaska.* New York, 1960. First published in 1930, it contains an Introduction by C. Hart Merriam and deals with the Mt. McKinley region, which was set aside as a national park largely through Sheldon's efforts.

SHEPARD, PAUL. *The Tender Carnivore and the Sacred Game.* New York, 1973.

Argues that modern man's most cherished qualities and abilities are the result of his hunter-gatherer past.

SHERWOOD, MORGAN B. *Exploration of Alaska, 1865–1900.* New Haven, 1965.

SHIELDS, GEORGE OLIVER, ed. *American Game Fishes: Their Habits, Habitat, and Peculiarities; How, When, and Where to Angle for Them.* Chicago and New York, 1892. Papers by a number of authorities.

———, ed. *The Big Game of North America: Its Habits, Habitat, Haunts, and Characteristics; How, When, and Where to Hunt It. . . .* Chicago and New York, 1890. Papers by a number of authorities.

———. *Hunting in the Great West: Hunting and Fishing by Mountain and Stream.* Chicago, 1883. Contains an Introduction by Nicholas Rowe, editor of *American Field* (later name of *Field and Stream*), emphasizing the code of the sportsman. Later, Shields edited *Recreation,* a very popular sportsman's periodical.

SHIRAS, GEORGE, 3d. *Hunting Wild Life with Camera and Flashlight: A Record of Sixty-Five Years' Visits to the Woods and Waters of North America.* 2 vols. Washington, D.C., 1936. First published in 1935. By a leading sportsman-conservationist and pioneer wildlife photographer.

SHOEMAKER, CARL D. *The Stories Behind the Organization of the National Wildlife Federation and Its Early Struggles for Survival.* Washington, D.C., 1960.

SMALLWOOD, WILLIAM M. *Natural History and the American Mind.* New York, 1967. First published in 1941.

SMITH, CHARLES D. "The Appalachian National Park Movement, 1885–1901." *North Carolina Historical Review,* XXXVII (January, 1960), 38–65.

SMITH, DARRELL H. *The Forest Service: Its History, Activities and Organization.* Washington, D.C., 1930. Much on nineteenth-century background.

SMITH, FRANK E. *The Politics of Conservation.* New York, 1971. First published in 1966. Has material relating to the nineteenth century but is largely undocumented.

SMITH, HENRY NASH. *Virgin Land: The American West as Symbol and Myth.* New York, 1957. First published in 1950.

SMITH, HERBERT A. "The Early Forestry Movement in the United States." *Agricultural History,* XII (October, 1938), 326–46.

SMITH, JEROME V. C. *Natural History of the Fishes of Massachusetts, Embracing a Practical Essay on Angling.* Boston, 1833.

SPRAGUE, MARSHALL. *A Gallery of Dudes.* Boston, 1966. On English, European, and east-coast "dudes" who went west and what they found.

STARR, JR., GEORGE ROSS. *Decoys of the Atlantic Flyway.* New York, 1974. Some history of waterfowl hunting.

STEGNER, WALLACE. *Beyond the Hundredth Meridian: John Wesley Powell and the Second Opening of the West.* Boston, 1962. First published in 1953.

STERLING, KEIR BROOKS. *Last of the Naturalists: The Career of C. Hart Merriam.* New York, 1974.

[STILLMAN, WILLIAM JAMES.] "The Adirondacks To-Day." *The Nation,* XXXIX (August 14, 1884), 130–31.

STIMSON, HENRY L. *My Vacations.* New York [?], 1949. Privately printed copy in possession of the late John P. Holman, Fairfield, Connecticut. Describes travel and hunting in area that became Glacier National Park. Also cites the hunting activities of Gifford Pinchot.

STODDARD, S. R. *The Adirondacks.* Glen Falls, New York, 1893 [?]. 1894 (24th edition) of guidebook first published in 1874. Copyright year of this edition is 1893.

STONE, LIVINGSTON. *Domesticated Trout. How to Breed and Grow Them.* Charlestown, New Hampshire, 1877. First published in 1872. Includes "Books on Fish Culture" and an account from an earlier work describing tagging of salmon to learn about their life histories.

———. "The Early Days of Fish Culture in the United States." *American Angler,* XXVIII (November, 1898), 217–24.

STRONG, DOUGLAS H. *The Conservationists.* Reading, Massachusetts, 1971.

———. "The Rise of American Esthetic Conservation: Muir, Mather and Udall." *National Parks Magazine,* XLIV (February, 1970), 5–9.

STROUT, CUSHING. *The American Image of the Old World.* New York, 1963. Has much on the Anglophilia of the upper class in the last nineteenth century.

SWIFT, ERNEST F. *A Conservation Saga.* Washington, D.C., 1967. Some material on former wildlife abundance, plus an analysis of the conservation philosophy.

———. *The Public's Land: Our Heritage and Opportunity.* Washington, D.C., 1963.

TEBEAU, CHARLTON W. *Man in the Everglades: 2000 Years of Human History in the Everglades National Park.* Miami, 1968. First published in 1964 under different title.

THELEN, DAVID P. *The New Citizenship: Origins of Progressivism in Wisconsin, 1885–1900.* Columbia, Missouri, 1972.

THOREAU, HENRY DAVID. *Cape Cod.* New York, 1951. Dudley C. Lunt's edition of book first published in 1865.

———. *The Concord and the Merrimack.* New York, 1954. Dudley C. Lunt's edition of *A Week on the Concord and Merrimack Rivers,* published by Thoreau in 1849.

———. *The Maine Woods.* New York, 1950. Dudley C. Lunt's edition of book first published in 1864.

TOMSICH, JOHN. *A Genteel Endeavor: American Culture and Politics in the Gilded Age.* Palo Alto, California, 1971.

TOWNSEND, CHARLES H. *Guide to the New York Aquarium.* New York, 1929. Contains an outline history of this institution, founded by sportsmen-naturalists.

TREFETHEN, JAMES B. *Crusade for Wildlife: Highlights in Conservation Prog-*

ress. Harrisburg, Pennsylvania, 1961. Mainly a history of the Boone and Crockett Club, this work traces the development of wildlife conservation—conceived in its broadest sense—through the 1950s. Almost every individual cited was a sportsman.

TRUE, WEBSTER P. *The Smithsonian Institution.* Vol. I of the Smithsonian Scientific Series. New York, 1929 and 1934. On origins of National Zoo, U.S. Fish Commission, etc.

UDALL, STEWART L. *The Quiet Crisis.* New York, 1967. First published in 1963. General history of Americans' impact on the natural environment and the rise of the conservation movement.

UNDERHILL, LONNIE E., AND LITTLEFIELD, JR., DANIEL F. "Quail Hunting: Big Business in Early Oklahoma." *Chronicles of Oklahoma,* XLIX (Autumn, 1971), 315–33. On market hunting.

U.S. Bureau of Outdoor Recreation. *The 1970 Survey of Outdoor Recreation Activities—Preliminary Report.* Washington, D.C., 1972.

U.S. Bureau of Sport Fisheries and Wildlife. *Sport Fishing U.S.A.* Washington, D.C., 1971 [?]. On present status of recreational angling, with contributions from many authorities, and it includes an essay on angling literature by Carl Otto von Kienbusch.

———. *Threatened Wildlife of the United States.* Washington, D.C., 1973. Includes section on extinct species.

U.S. Cartridge Company. *Where to Hunt American Game.* Lowell, Massachusetts, 1898. State-by-state survey.

U.S. Commission of Fish and Fisheries. *Report on the Condition of the Sea Fisheries of the South Coast of New England in 1871 and 1872.* Washington, D.C., 1873.

U.S. Department of the Interior. *Waterfowl Tomorrow.* Washington, D.C., 1964. Contains articles by many authorities on the management of ducks and geese, including "Waterfowl and the Hunter," which is partly an analysis of why men hunt.

U.S. Forest Service. *Highlights in the History of Forest Conservation.* Agriculture Information Bulletin No. 83. Washington, D.C., 1968.

VAN BROCKLIN, RALPH M. "The Movement for the Conservation of Natural Resources in the United States Before 1901." Ph.D. dissertation, University of Michigan, 1952.

VAN DYKE, HENRY. *Fisherman's Luck, and Some Other Uncertain Things.* New York, 1905. First published in 1899. Van Dyke's work is notable for portraying the aesthetic quality of angling.

———. *Little Rivers.* New York, 1900. First published in 1895.

VAN DYKE, THEODORE S. *Flirtation Camp; or, the Rifle, Rod, and Gun in California. . . .* New York, 1881. One of the chapters is entitled "The Great American Trout-Swine."

———. *Southern California: Its Valleys, Hills, and Streams; Its Animals, Birds, and Fishes; Its Gardens, Farms, and Climate.* New York, 1886. Mainly a compilation of his previous articles in *American Field* (later name of

Field and Stream), *Forest and Stream,* and other periodicals. Has much on natural history, hunting, and fishing.

———. *The Still Hunter: A Practical Treatise on Deer-Stalking.* New York, 1883.

VAN WINKLE, WILLIAM MITCHELL [comp.] *Henry William Herbert ["Frank Forester"]: A Bibliography of His Writings, 1832–1858; Compiled by William Mitchell Van Winkle, with the Bibliographical Assistance of David A. Randall.* Portland, Maine, 1936.

——— [comp.]. *Hunting, Shooting, Angling, Ornithology, Racing; Including the Sporting Works of "Frank Forester." The Renowned Library on American Sport Collected by . . . Van Winkle . . . Sold by his Order.* [Parke-Bernet Galleries, Inc.] New York, 1940.

VERNER, WILLIAM K. "Wilderness and the Adirondacks: An Historical View." *Living Wilderness,* XXXIII (Winter, 1969), 27–46.

WALLACE, E. R. *Descriptive Guide to the Adirondacks. . . .* New York, 1878. Apparently first published in 1872. Emphasizes that the region is a paradise for sportsmen and calls for the creation of a great state park in its mountains.

WALLIHAN, ALLEN G. *Camera Shots at Big Game.* New York, 1901. Introduction by Theodore Roosevelt.

WALSH, HARRY M. *The Outlaw Gunner.* Cambridge, Maryland, 1971. The history of commercial waterfowl hunting in the Chesapeake Bay region.

WARD, ROWLAND. *The English Angler in Florida, with some Descriptive Notes of the Game Animals and Birds.* London, 1898.

———. *The Sportsman's Handbook to Collecting, Preserving, and Setting-up Trophies and Specimens, Together with a Guide to the Hunting Grounds of the World.* London, 1911. First published in 1880.

WATERMAN, CHARLES F. *Hunting in America.* New York, 1973. A general history, from pre-Columbian times to the present.

WEBB, WALTER PRESCOTT. *The Great Plains.* Boston, 1931. A classic environmental history.

WEBB, WILLIAM E. *Buffalo Land: An Authentic Account of the Discoveries, Adventures, and Mishaps of a Scientific and Sporting Party in the Wild West.* Philadelphia, 1872.

WELKER, ROBERT HENRY. *Birds and Men: American Birds in Science, Art, Literature, and Conservation, 1800–1900.* New York, 1966. First published in 1955.

WELLS, HENRY P. *Fly–Rods and Fly-Tackle: Suggestions as to their Manufacture and Use.* New York, 1885.

WESTWOOD, THOMAS T., AND SATCHELL, THOMAS [comps.]. *Bibliotheca Piscatoria: A Catalogue of Books on Angling, The Fisheries and Fish-Culture, with Bibliographical Notes and an Appendix of Citations Touching on Angling and Fishing from Old English Authors.* London, 1883. First appeared in 1861. Works in all languages and includes some American items.

WETZEL, CHARLES M. [comp.]. *American Fishing Books; A Bibliography from the Earliest Times Up to 1948, Together with a History of Angling and*

Angling Literature in America. Newark, Delaware, 1950. Particularly good for the history of *Forest and Stream.*

WHIPPLE, GURTH. *Fifty Years of Conservation in New York State, 1885–1935.* Syracuse, 1935.

WHITE, G. EDWARD. *The Eastern Establishment and the Western Experience: The West of Frederic Remington, Theodore Roosevelt, and Owen Wister.* New Haven, 1968.

WHITE, JR., LYNN. "The Historical Roots of Our Ecological Crisis." *Science,* CLV (March 10, 1967), 1203–07. On the negative impact of the Judeo-Christian tradition.

WHITE, WILLIAM CHAPMAN. *Adirondack Country.* New York, 1970. Originally published in 1954. Region's history and natural history.

WHITEHEAD, CHARLES E. *Wild Sports in the South; or, The Camp-Fires of the Everglades.* New York, 1860.

WHITNEY, CASPAR; GRINNELL, GEORGE BIRD; AND WISTER, OWEN. *Musk-Ox, Bison, Sheep and Goat.* New York, 1904. Hunting and natural history.

WIEBE, ROBERT H. "The Progressive Years, 1900–1917." *The Re-interpretation of American History and Culture,* ed. by William H. Cartwright and Richard L. Watson, Jr., 425–42. Washington, D.C., 1973. Discussion of the historiography of the so-called "progressive" period.

————. *The Search for Order, 1877–1920.* New York, 1967. Both a synthesis and a new thought-provoking interpretation.

"WILDWOOD, WILL" [Frederick E. Pond], ed. *Frank Forester's Sporting Scenes and Characters.* 2 vols. Philadelphia, 1881.

WILEY, FARIDA A., ed. *Theodore Roosevelt's America: Selections from the Writings of the Oyster Bay Naturalist.* Garden City, New York, 1962. First published in 1955.

WILLIAMS, BURTON J. "Trees But No Timber: The Nebraska Prelude to the Timber Culture Act." *Nebraska History,* LIII (Spring, 1972), 77–86.

WILLISTON, S. W. "The American Antelope." *American Naturalist,* II (October, 1877), 599–603. Typical of many articles in this journal that assume hunting is an integral part of natural-history study.

WILSON, ALEXANDER, *Wilson's American Ornithology, with Notes by Jardine: To which is Added A Synopsis of American Birds, Including Those Described By Bonaparte, Audubon, Nuttall, and Richardson; By T. M. Brewer.* New York, 1970. Reprint of the one-volume 1840 edition. This work originally appeared in nine volumes, beginning in 1808.

WILSON, RAYMOND J. *In Quest of Community: Social Philosophy in the United States, 1860–1920.* New York, 1968.

WILSON, R. L. *Theodore Roosevelt: Outdoorsman.* New York, 1971.

WOLFE, LINNIE MARSH. *Son of the Wilderness: The Life of John Muir.* New York, 1945.

WOODBURY, ROBERT. "William Kent: Progressive Gadfly, 1864–1928." Ph.D. dissertation, Yale University, 1967. Kent was a noted conservationist and enthusiastic hunter.

WOODWARD, C. VANN. *American Attitudes Toward History*. Oxford, England, 1955. A lecture, published in pamphlet form, given at Oxford University on February 22, 1955.

WORSTER, DONALD, ed. *American Environmentalism: The Formative Period, 1860–1915*. New York, 1973. A book of readings.

WRIGHT, LYLE H. [comp.]. *Sporting Books in the Huntington Library*. San Marino, California, 1937.

YATES, NORRIS W. *William T. Porter and the Spirit of the Times. . . .* Baton Rouge, Louisiana, 1957. Information on well-known sportsman and periodical of an earlier day; *Spirit* frequently included articles pertaining to hunting, as well as its usual fare of horse racing.

YELLOWSTONE NATIONAL PARK. Papers. Yellowstone National Park Library, Mammoth Hot Springs. Miscellaneous items relating to the reserve's early history, including some correspondence of Grinnell, Hague, and Superintendent Anderson.

YORKE, F. HENRY. *Our Ducks*. Chicago, 1899. Has good description of the waning of Illinois waterfowling—mainly because of the inroads of "progress."

ZISWILER, VINZENZ. *Extinct and Vanishing Animals: A Biology of Extinction and Survival*. New York, 1967. Originally published in German in 1965.

INDEX